"Unlikely" Entrepreneurs

A Complete Guide to
Business Start-Ups for
People with Disabilities and
Chronic Health Conditions

RoseAnne Herzog

Foreword by Don Anderson

"Unlikely" Entrepreneurs

A Complete Guide to
Business Start-Ups for
People with Disabilities and
Chronic Health Conditions

North Peak Publishing

This publication is designed to provide authoritative information in regard to the subject matter covered. It is sold with the understanding that the publisher is not engaged in rendering legal, accounting, or other professional services. If legal or other expert assistance is required, the services of a competent professional should be sought.

Unlikely Entrepreneurs: A Complete Guide to Business Start-ups for People with Disabilities and Chronic Health Conditions

RoseAnne Herzog

North Peak Publishing
P.O. Box 6832
Traverse City, MI 49696-6832
1-800-733-9712

Library of Congress Cataloging In Publication Data

Herzog, RoseAnne
    Unlikely Entrepreneurs: A Complete Guide to Business Start-up for People with Disabilities and Chronic Health Conditions.
        p.   cm.
    Includes index
    ISBN 0-9664862-0-X
    1. Small Business 2.Self-Employment 3. Disability 4. Success in Business
I. Title   II. Herzog, RoseAnne
1998   98-091687

Book and cover design by Barbara Schiefer

Printed and bound in the United States of America by Bookcrafters, Chelsea, MI

This book is dedicated to my dear friends,
Maureen Dyar and Lisa Gigliotti…

And to the memory of my brother, Tom
and my mother, Betty…

For their courage.

Acknowledgements:

I would like to thank all of the people whose valuable input and contributions made this book possible, including Catherine Gase, Don Anderson, Michelle-Rose Anderson, Dennis Figiel, Heidi Van Arnem, Carol Backus, Jessica Poisson, Robert Collinge, Albert Vickery, John Herzog, Ellen Eagon, Laura Serruto, Mary Herzog, Jim Duby, Barbara Goodman, Lena Ricks, Nancy Arnold, Alice Doyal, Dennis Rizzo, Sue Soderburg, Bob Stevens, Randy Brown, Laurie Pozner, Phyllis Lee, my father Bert Herzog Sr., and to:

Peggy Kelley, for editing, and
Barbara Schiefer, for the cover design and copy layout.

And especially to my husband, Jim Foley, for his love and support.

Foreword

People with disabilities occupy a unique place in American history. Alternately seen as the embodiment of our deepest fears, or vessels of angelic hope and courage, people with disabilities have always struggled, and continue to struggle to be seen, known, and accepted for what they really are: people.

Excluded by a clause in the colonial charter that stated that one needed to be "sound of wind and limb" to emigrate to the New World, people with disabilities were notably absent when the Pilgrims arrived. However, the ban didn't stop people with disabilities from being born, or others from acquiring disabling characteristics. Unfortunately, for those first few colonists with disabilities, the New Testament with its recurring references to people with disabilities as possessed by demons or cursed by God, governed much of daily lives of the original colonists who had also inherited the superstitions of their forefathers. People with disabilities quickly became a repository for the colonists darkest fears and most libidinous impulses, and many were stoned, hanged, or beaten to death.

Shut away in back rooms, attics, and out-buildings for most of American history the roles ascribed to people with disabilities have been largely defined by our popular mythology. For the most part, people with disabilities are perceived to be either the passive, always joyful, dutiful recipients of charity, i.e. Jerry's Kids, or the angry, bitter, overbearing Mr. Potters from the film It's a Wonderful Life. However, fueled by the Civil Rights Movement people with disabilities have begun to dismantle the stereotypes used to justify their imprisonment and exclusion.

Increasingly discontent with the limited roles available to them, people with disabilities have fought for and won the right to assume other roles as well. Taxpayer, home owner, employee, spouse, parent, and employer are among the roles society has begun to recognize for people with disabilities. Not that some people with disabilities weren't these things all along, and more, but to some extent we all internalize, and measure ourselves by the expectations of those around us.

At the leading edge of the change in our society's thinking about people with disabilities are a group of such people who have chosen to adopt for themselves the role of business owner. Owning your own business has always been seen as the way to independence in America, for everyone but people with disabilities that is. Again the popular mythology had excluded people with disabilities from this arena. Owning a business has generally been thought to be either too risky or too demanding for someone with a disability. After all, don't business owners have to toil long hours and endure endless deprivation? Not necessarily is the answer contained in "Unlikely" Entrepreneurs.

Drawing on her ten years of experience assisting people with disabilities create and run successful businesses, the author presents the experiences of seven successful entrepreneurs and draws from her experience working with hundreds of entrepreneurs with disabilities, providing practical lessons for other would-be business owners. Interesting, helpful, motivating and challenging best describe "Unlikely" Entrepreneurs. A 'must have' not just for people with disabilities and chronic health conditions, but for rehabilitation counselors, case managers, employment specialists, and anyone whose job involves helping people with disabilities discover their niche.

Don Anderson
Disability Rights Coordinator, Wayne State University

Table of Contents

Introduction

In 1989, I took a position with a newly created organization called the Handicapper Small Business Association (HSBA). The organization's purpose was to promote entrepreneurship among the disability community. HSBA's creation resulted from the efforts of dozens of business owners with disabilities who saw the need for an association that created and advanced business opportunities for people with disabilities. Over the years HSBA's services have evolved and its name and location have changed, but the vision of the entrepreneurs who founded it remains.

It was a meeting with one of HSBA's founders 10 years ago that intensified my interest in working with entrepreneurs with disabilities and significantly influenced my future. Shortly after starting at HSBA, I was scheduled to meet with Kirby Morgan, HSBA's Board President. All I knew of Kirby Morgan was that his disability was progressive arthritis and that he was an entrepreneur, operating a successful business from his home.

At the arranged meeting time, I arrived at Kirby's home office. I stepped into a living room absent of the furnishings you typically see in people's homes. In their place were computer work stations arranged around a large room. There were several young men working diligently at their stations and a man laying on a large bed in the center of the room. This man was Kirby Morgan.

I observed him, barely able to move, speaking to a worker giving a directive of some kind. I noticed him speak on the telephone and use his computer through an electronic device. The man was running a business, managing five employees, and serving as our Board President from a Striker bed able to move only his head and one arm!

The sight awed and confused me. I had accepted the job because I believed in the organization's mission. Still, it never occurred to me that someone with such a severe disability could succeed in business. I learned later that Kirby's computer programming business held three large contracts and that it had been thriving for over five years. Now, after almost a decade and hundreds of encounters with entrepreneurs like Kirby, I am no longer shocked when I see the achievements of those who are physically challenged.

As a small business consultant, I have had the rare opportunity to work with hundreds of individuals whose entrepreneurial motivations transcend the limits of their disabling conditions. Entrepreneurs with disabilities show us that with a positive mental attitude, persistence and determination, one can accomplish almost anything.

My purpose in writing this book is to share the stories of entrepreneurs like Kirby Morgan with aspiring entrepreneurs with disabilities, and to pass on some helpful information in the process. Part One of this book contains stories of successful entrepreneurs, as well as important lessons on how you too can succeed in business.

In Part One, successful entrepreneurs reveal what personal and professional obstacles they faced, and how they overcame these obstacles to achieve success. They discuss how they utilized technology to work more efficiently, how they solicited the help of family, friends and external resources to reach their goals, and how they stayed focused and confident. These stories are not unlike Kirby's; they are about people who possess discipline, commitment, and persistence. People who believe in themselves first and foremost and who focus not on what they can't do but on what they can do. My hope is that by sharing the experiences of these entrepreneurs, people with disabilities and chronic health conditions can learn effective strategies to succeed in business.

Part Two provides persons with disabilities and chronic health conditions with the tools needed to become self-employed. As a potential business owner, you will learn how to determine if your idea is feasible, how to develop a business plan, how starting a business will impact your Social Security benefits, and how to utilize vocational rehabilitation and other government programs.

A list of resources is included as well as a useful guide on how to utilize these resources most effectively.

This book is intended to be a hands-on, how to guide. My intention is to create a resource book for people with chronic health conditions and disabilities interested in starting a business. In my experience, success in business is often a function of confidence, determination, and the other factors discussed in Part One of this book. Starting a business does have its emotional ups and downs. This is true for all new business owners, but may be especially true for those with disabilities and chronic health conditions. I believe learning how others have succeeded and what characteristics and behaviors contributed to their success is an excellent way to prepare potential entrepreneurs to do the same.

Unlikely Entrepreneurs includes generic information relevant to anyone starting a business, as well as specific resources for people with physical limitations. Its purpose is to offer one guide, inclusive of all the necessary information a person with a disability would need to become successfully self-employed. This book was intended to benefit all persons with special needs, including people with physical or mental disabilities and people with chronic illnesses.

I entitled this book Unlikely Entrepreneurs because many people, disabled or not, view entrepreneurship as a path best taken by those with perfect health and physical stamina. Many of us believe that business owners must be strong and healthy to endure the long hours, hard work, and stress associated with running a small business. However, there is compelling evidence to suggest that this is merely a perception and not a truth.

Actually, the term "unlikely" more aptly describes healthy, abled-bodied entrepreneurs, who according to the U.S. Department of Census are less likely to be self-employed than people with disabilities! The census reveals that people with disabilities become self-employed at almost twice the rate as non-disabled persons.[1]

Why are so many people with disabilities self-employed? Some may be seizing an opportunity to be more creative and to explore uncharted territory through innovation.

---

[1]Arnold, N. and Seekins, T., *Self Employment in Vocational Rehabilitation: Building on Lessons from Rural America,* University of Montana, Rural Institute on Disabilities, 1994.

Others seek autonomy through business ownership by developing opportunities for strategic decision-making, ascending them to a position of control over their destiny. For some, self-employment means creating a job for themselves when job search strategies have failed. For many others, self-employment provides flexibility and often involves the convenience of working from home in an environment designed to meet their personal and business needs.

No matter what the reason for choosing self-employment, the opportunities are boundless. We all possess the potential to succeed if we are willing to work hard and develop the necessary skills and abilities. This is true regardless of the physical limitations you might possess.

The path of business ownership presents many opportunities beyond working for someone else, but it's not for everyone. Self-employment requires a commitment of both time and financial resources. It requires that the owner be prepared to encounter obstacles and take risks, both personal and professional. After reading this book, you should be able to assess your skills and your readiness for starting a business. Defining your goals, and assessing your characteristics and skills will help you decide if being self-employed is right for you.

The road to business ownership is not easy, but with the right idea, a well developed business plan, and ongoing technical support, self-employment can be an ideal option for anyone looking for financial independence and personal freedom. This book is your first step on the road toward business ownership. Good Luck!

For Service Providers

As you well know, finding a job is especially challenging for people with disabilities. Although no employer would readily admit to discriminating based on age or disability, acts which discriminate are widespread and immensely injurious to qualified candidates who are bypassed for younger, more 'able-bodied' individuals. A primary objective of the Americans with Disabilities Act (ADA), passed by Congress in 1990, was to eliminate barriers to competitive employment. The ADA may succeed in some cases, but for most people with disabilities finding employment remains an elusive goal. Currently, the unemployment rate among those with disabilities stands somewhere between 63 and 67 percent. It is unlikely that the ADA by itself will have any significant long-term impact on this disastrously high unemployment rate. In order to reverse the rate of unemployment among persons with disabilities, we must not depend solely on existing employment opportunities. Instead, jobs must be created for people with disabilities. This can be done by supporting the initiatives of entrepreneurs with disabilities.

Most employment studies reveal that the majority of people with disabilities who are unemployed want to work either full-time or part-time. Most individuals assert that it can take years to find a job, and often the job accepted is for less money with less responsibility than what they want. In other words, many of those who are lucky enough to find jobs are under-employed. Self-employment is an alternative for many people with disabilities who are unable to reach their potential in a traditional employment setting.

Self-employment not only creates a job for the owner, but it has the potential to create multiple jobs for people with disabilities. According to the Disabled Businesspersons Association (DBA), a business owner with a disability is four times more likely to have a disabled employee than an able-bodied employer. Furthermore, the DBA reveals that if the business owner obtained assistance from a government agency (most likely through a vocational rehabilitation program), they are seven times more likely to hire another individual with a disability. By supporting programs which promote entrepreneurship, vocational rehabilitation counselors and agencies, and other service providers can impact the economic condition of people with disabilities. If vocational rehabilitation professionals seize the opportunity to support and encourage the efforts of entrepreneurs with disabilities, they will create a pool of potential employers.

This book can be a helpful guide for service providers, vocational counselors, and business consultants who work with people with disabilities or chronic health conditions and who may benefit from understanding the needs of these entrepreneurs. Specifically, this book can be used as a guide for rehabilitation counselors who wish to expand their knowledge of business concepts and resources, and in doing so, can better serve their customers.

PART ONE

THE ENTREPRENEURS

*"Nothing so splendid has ever been achieved except
by those who dared believe that
something inside them was superior to circumstance."*

Bruce Barton

CHAPTER I

Profiles of Success

The following pages include stories of successful entrepreneurs. These are individuals with whom I have had the opportunity to work with over the years. They in no way represent all of the many successful business owners I have encountered. They are just interesting stories of interesting people, who persevered under adverse circumstances and who now operate successful business enterprises.

The definition of "success" is unique to each individual. The Webster's New World Dictionary defines success as "a favorable or satisfactory outcome or result." A person is successful if they have achieved what they intended or set out to achieve. Goals or achievements are different for each person. One individual choosing self-employment may desire wealth, another may seek only enough to sustain themselves, and still another may seek only enough to supplement another source of income. If each has met their objective, they can be thought of as successful.

For the purpose of writing this book, I chose to write about individuals who operate profitable enterprises. The size of the business or the extent of their wealth was not necessarily a primary consideration. What was most important was that they achieved what they had intended to achieve. I also chose people with severe disabilities and chronic illnesses who had tremendous obstacles to overcome. These individuals, through determination, persistence and hard work, persevered to achieve success in business. Finally, I tried to provide some variety. I chose examples of individuals with divergent pasts and circumstances. Their businesses vary in type and size, ranging from one employee to sixteen. The owners have diverse disabilities, as well as different ethnic, social, economic and educational backgrounds.

More important than their differences, however, are their similarities. What makes them successful? What characteristics or circumstances contribute to their success and how can we learn from their experiences? Read on, the answers are provided in the following pages.

Jessica Poisson
Freedom Technologies, Inc.

Jessica Poisson appears an unlikely entrepreneur. Dressed in old blue jeans and a t-shirt, with long, straight hair and bangs that hang in her eyes, she looks more like she belongs at Woodstock than in a business. She seems so unlike the pictures of successful entrepreneurs we see in business magazines, but as the saying goes, looks can be deceiving. Jessica is successful, business savvy, and smart, very smart, especially when it comes to computers.

Jessica used her computer skills and business savvy to start Freedom Technologies, a business that provides home-automation products and services. Home automation – using computers to make people's lives easier – is Jessica's passion. "Anything electric," she says, "can be automated. Lights, heat, air-conditioning, appliances, even a hair dryer can be turned off and on or adjusted using your voice."

To me it seems like Star Trek. I can hear Jean Luc Picard, "Computer, activate..."

With the help of computer software, Jessica works with people with disabilities designing home automation systems that make their lives easier. She credits her business success to her own disability. "If it weren't for my disability, I wouldn't be doing this. I'd never be this successful."

Her story starts while she was working as a computer trainer and technician for Buick, a division of General Motors. After years of working with computer keyboards, she began experiencing extreme pain in her hands and arms. She felt fatigued and ached all over. After numerous visits to several specialists, a battery of tests revealed a condition known as Carpel Tunnel Syndrome. She'll never forget hearing her doctor say, "You won't be able to use a computer. You can't type and you must avoid using your hands." She was devastated. She just couldn't imagine what else she would do.

Jessica continued to experience pain throughout her body and she continued to see specialists for the strange and unexplainable symptoms she was experiencing. After a year of more tests, Jessica was diagnosed with Lupus, a progressive disease which affects nearly every organ in the body. The disease causes severe rashes, fatigue and pain.

Some days Jessica found it difficult to even get out of bed. She was extremely depressed and confused. She felt worthless. Her husband and two sons were very attentive and supportive, but Jessica didn't want to be a burden. It bothered her that she depended upon her husband's salary and she hated asking him for money. "I needed to earn my own money, and I was determined to find a way to do that."

After trying different medications, and undergoing surgeries and physical therapy, Jessica began to see some minor improvement in her condition. She felt ready to re-enter the work force. Her vocational rehabilitation counselor suggested that she go back to school. She kept her mind open and enrolled in the local community college.

Jessica considered pursuing a career as a paralegal, but was soon disappointed to learn that she would earn only $7.50 -$8.00 per hour after graduation. Discouraged, she began to seek out other options. "Just because I had a disability didn't mean I had to make less money. I wanted to earn what I was worth. I knew I could make more money with computers."

That's when she discovered voice-activated computer software that would allow her to operate a computer and design systems without using her hands. This software allowed her to do what she loved to do, and be paid what she felt she was worth.

Finding a solution to her own challenge, Jessica soon developed a vision for a business that could do the same for others. She believed that there was a demand for home automation and voice-activated software. She knew that if she could position herself as an expert there would be more than enough business. Her instincts were right.

Jessica started Freedom Technologies, Inc. knowing that she would succeed. She received assistance from her vocational rehabilitation counselor to purchase the software, but even without this help, she was committed to getting her business off the ground.

Jessica began learning everything she could about voice-activated software and home-automation. Her background and talent with computers made this task relatively easy. She became a software distributor and decided to target the disability market. She promoted her business to vocational rehabilitation programs, and after her first year in business, had more work than she could handle. The subsequent demand for her services created the need to hire two computer technicians. I spoke to her while she was training her two new employees. Impressive, I thought, in business for just over a year and already hiring two employees.

I asked her what contributed to her success. "My business gives me the opportunity to help solve problems for other people. Helping others is very rewarding and helps me get my mind off my problems. If I didn't have my business, I would sit around thinking about how much pain I was in. I am much healthier and happier now that I am busy doing what I love to do."

Running the business is physically challenging. There are days when she has to cancel meetings because of her health. Her family remains supportive and helpful. Jessica is currently training one son to keep her books. Her sons enjoy working with her. "They know that if Mom makes money, they might get some neat things."

Jessica also relies on a Lupus support group she discovered on the Internet. "Lupus is a strange disease. There is always something different happening to your body and it's helpful to talk to others who have had similar experiences with the disease. They may have had the same symptoms and be able to explain what's happening and suggest a remedy. This saves trips to the doctor. If I am prescribed a certain medication, I can ask if anyone has used the drug and what their experience has been. Having the opportunity to share information with people who have the same condition is very comforting. It minimizes the confusion you feel when you don't know what's happening to you."

Prying for information regarding her financial success, she finally offered; "Well I called my bank yesterday to get my balance and I couldn't believe how much I had in there."

Don't we all wish we could say that?

Dennis Figiel

National Millwork, Inc.

When he was 15, Dennis Figiel was hospitalized and diagnosed with Guillain-Barr Syndrome, a rare disease that attacks the sheathing around the nerves, causing paralysis.

There is no known cure for the syndrome and it is extremely baffling because it affects each person differently. Some recover completely. Others, like Dennis, are not so lucky.

Dennis' paralysis started in his legs and moved to his upper body. Within nine months he was using a wheelchair. Dennis began physical therapy and eventually he was able to walk with the use of canes and braces. He returned to school, but not to the high school he had been attending. Instead he was sent to the Oakland School for Crippled Children. "In those days," says Dennis, "children with severe disabilities did not attend regular school." For the majority of his high school education, Dennis received home tutoring. A teacher came to his home twice a week initially and then after she got to know Dennis, offered to come 3 or 4 times per week. "She helped out tremendously. I felt very isolated. My friends didn't have time for me. I had maybe four or five visitors during that time." So Dennis focused on getting a good education. "I made a decision at a young age that if I couldn't do what other people could do, I would have to rely on my brain. I knew education would be very important to my future."

Dennis' educational pursuits included music. "I buried myself in music." He and his brother started a band in which Dennis played saxophone. Eventually he earned enough money to attend college. He graduated Phi Beta Kappa from the University of Michigan with degrees in Ancient Civilizations and History. His real interest was archeology and he was accepted into the graduate school of Archeological Studies at U of M.

Dennis' experience studying archeology proved disappointing when it became clear that the newly hired Dean of the Archeology Department didn't approve of his career choice. "He just didn't see how I could go out on archeological digs. He put up so many barriers, that finally I thought 'what am I doing here.'" Dennis quit school. He became depressed but didn't stay down for long. He says "Sometimes events in life push you. You have control to a certain extent, but to a degree you don't. You come to a fork in the road and you decide what to do." In 1974, Dennis began working at his father's small cabinet-making shop, and thus began his career in business.

His father's business was a two-man shop that made cabinets for homes and stores. In the early 80's the business struggled financially. Dennis remembers, "Those were very lean years - very difficult times." Dennis realized his father, while talented at his craft, was not a business man. He knew that in order for the business to succeed someone needed to learn how to manage it. Dennis began attending night school in business management and accounting. He was committed to avoiding the financial problems that plagued his father. Over the next several years Dennis worked during the week at his father's shop, went to school at night, and then played music on the weekends to make enough money to survive.

Eventually his father left his company and went to work for a competitor. He paid Dennis his accrued payroll in exchange for the company. It took Dennis four years to pay off the business debts. Then in 1984, he started National Millwork with his brother, each investing $15,000. On a shoestring, they moved into a larger facility and began to diversify their customer base. They started with three customers and quickly expanded. Four years later, their father returned as an employee to a very different company with 10 employees and exponential sales growth.

How important was Dennis' business education? "Extremely important." he says. He implemented tight accounting and financial controls. He was able to compare the planned costs and actual costs of each job and this allowed him to track performance in a timely manner. He never finished his degree because the business began to take off and he became too busy. The business continued to expand and now employs 16 people. "We should reach $1.5 million in sales this year," he says "and my goal is $3-4 million within 5 years."

I am sitting in Dennis' home and from the looks of it, he is no longer operating in survival mode. He lives in a beautiful suburban house (which he built himself and has almost completely paid for). He takes vacations every year and takes time out to socialize with family and friends.

Dennis has succeeded in business for many reasons. First, it is obvious from everything he's been through that Dennis is remarkably determined. "When I encounter a problem," he says "I can usually get around it." He tells me a story of a time a few years ago when his tire blew out while he was driving along the expressway. He hauled himself out of the car, pulled the spare tire out of the trunk, and had just started tightening the lug nuts, when a man pulled over to help. When the man noticed Dennis' disability, he said "How in the heck did you do this?"

Dennis also attributes his success to his need for independence. "I hate depending on anybody," he says. "It's the thing about my disability that I hate the most." His parents pushed independence and Dennis pushed himself, almost too hard. Three years ago Dennis built a ramp and began using his wheelchair for the first time in 29 years. "I was struggling and limiting myself because physically I couldn't do things. I kept thinking 'you've got to walk' and I drove myself and ultimately made things harder." He says, "There's a fine line between being determined and being stubborn. I wanted to be independent, but actually I was preventing myself from doing things because I didn't want to do anything, or go anywhere, if it meant that I needed to rely on someone." He pushed himself so hard, his elbow 'blew out' and he finally realized it was time he started using a wheelchair.

If Dennis were to impart just one piece of advice it would be this: "Focus on what you can do, not on what you can't do. Don't set yourself up to fail. People with disabilities have limitations. You must be honest with yourself." He believes one should not try to be a jack of all trades, "If you're not good at something or don't have the answers, ask a consultant or hire someone."

Dennis' success did not come easily, but throughout his life he has managed to keep a positive attitude. "I never felt sorry for myself. I was never bitter." I asked if he ever got depressed. He answered, "Well, not very often, I never really had much time to get depressed, and when I did, I just told myself to get on with things, to move on, and I did." He adds, "I do not have patience for people who stay in the 'victim mode.'"

He never says so, but I believe that Dennis' success is due also to his level of discipline. It took discipline to save money for college and to save in order to start his business. It takes discipline to sacrifice short-term comforts for hopefully long-term gains. Dennis Figiel is not a fool. He endured many lean years not because he enjoys sacrifice, but because he had long-range goals and knew that it would take some sacrifice to achieve them.

National Millwork thrives for many reasons. One reason is that Dennis and his brother treat their employees well. "We're like a family," he says. "We share profits with employees and offer excellent benefits."

His final words of wisdom: "Get a good education and take advantage of technology. Computers present so many business opportunities for people with disabilities. Use computers and technology to stay one step ahead of competitors. With computers, you can access information more quickly and make better decisions."

Albert Vickery
AA Machining

Describing Al Vickery is somewhat of a challenge. He is a man of contradictions. He's sensitive but strong, creative yet realistic, soft-spoken, but also charismatic. Al's varying characteristics reflect a past laden with extreme events and circumstances. A hard core drug user and motorcycle gang member turned introspective business man, he undoubtedly has a few stories to tell. "So you're writing a book," he says, "I have often thought of writing one myself…about my life."

Al describes his childhood as "pretty awful." Left by his father before he was born, Al was raised by his mother and step-father. His mother had severe emotional problems and his step father was an abusive alcoholic. "He busted my piggy bank for beer money and when I asked why, I got a kick for an answer."

Al was born with scoliosis, a curvature of the spine that causes arthritis, chronic pain, and neuropathy, or a loss of sensation. His condition is progressive. He has lost much sensation from the waist down and spent some time in a wheel chair. Seeing him now, his scoliosis doesn't seem very noticeable. His slow movements and his hunched back are the only signs of his disability.

When his disability became so severe that he was forced to use a wheelchair, Al almost gave up. But Al kept going because he says, "I promised myself when I started this business that I would never give up. I had always quit when the going got tough. I was determined that this time would be different."

Al graduated from high school in 1963 and by 1964 he was married. He wed to avoid being drafted for the Vietnam War. "I was young and foolish. I didn't have anyone to tell me what a mistake I was making." He worked as a machinist and a custodian, he demonstrated against the war, and tried hard to support his family. The marriage ended in 1971 when he was just 24 years old.

In that same year he lost his job. He contacted the state-sponsored vocational rehabilitation program where it was discovered that Al also had a learning disability. Al finally understood why learning was not easy for him. Still, he told his counselor he wanted to be an engineer and was eventually enrolled in college level courses for mechanical design and industrial engineering. "For the first time, I felt very optimistic about my future." Then on the day before school was to start Al was arrested for possession of marijuana. He paid a large fine he could barely afford and spent three days in jail. "I tried to explain that I couldn't miss school, but the judge didn't care. I guess he broke my spirit."

The day after he was released, he got on his Harley Davidson and headed for the Rocky Mountains. He essentially "dropped out" for four years, spending time in Canada and California. He joined a motorcycle gang and began using drugs to numb his physical and emotional pain. He remembers those years as very intense. Al wouldn't give many details. Apparently you can get into trouble if you say too much about what happens in a gang, but Al did say that after witnessing the murder of a friend and fellow gang-member, he decided that gang life wasn't for him. "I remember thinking 'I've got to get out of here.'" He packed up his things and never looked back.

He found a job at a Harley Davidson shop, and it was there that he began thinking of starting a business of his own. He soon met the woman who would become his second wife, and who was partly responsible for his transformation from drug abuser to businessman. "She lit a fire under me." He says, "She had faith in me." Al then went to work for a large motor parts store. "I was experienced in machining and automotive, and I began to realize how rare that combination was." During that time Al was like a sponge, absorbing all he could about the business. He learned how to research a job, price services, and work with customers. Two years after he started work, the company went out of business, and Al found himself back at the state vocational rehabilitation office. Only this time he did not want a job; he wanted to work for himself.

"I was very apprehensive when I went to the agency. I knew I had a checkered past and wasn't sure how I'd be received. But my counselor was great, he said 'we've all got bridges to burn Al.'" Al's vocational rehabilitation counselor was impressed by the fact that Al had completed a business plan and had already approached a bank. The counselor referred Al to a marketing consulting firm for a market analysis. The analysis came back positive, and one year after starting his engine machine shop, Al's sales were double what the consultants had predicted.

AA Machining was established in 1992. The state vocational rehabilitation agency invested $6,000 and Al used $10,000 in credit card debt. At one point Al's short-term debt totaled $30,000. "My cash flow was weak and I was experiencing growing pains." But he lived frugally, tried to pay his bills on time, and eventually paid down his debt. Over the last six years the business has grown and last year Al took a big risk and mortgaged his personal property to purchase the building where he runs his business. "Everything I own is on the line. But now I have confidence in myself. I don't fear failure and I never have sleepless nights. I work hard and do the best I can and hope it's enough."

His commitment has not come without sacrifice. Three years ago, he and his second wife divorced. The pain is evident in his eyes when he talks about it. "I was spending so much time building my business and not enough time with her. She just found someone else." It was shortly after the divorce that his condition worsened and he landed in a wheelchair. Al wasn't sure how he could work from a wheelchair, still he never missed a day at the shop. The effort was taking a toll, however, and just when Al was about ready to throw in the towel, he met Tom.

Tom Hall was a loyal customer who, after hearing about Al's predicament, offered to lend a hand. Tom enjoyed working with cars and wanted to learn the business, so he worked for 3 months without pay. Al, in turn, offered him 10% of the business. Tom is now a full-time, paid employee and partner. "I couldn't believe how committed he was to his business." Says Tom, "I figured any guy who was that determined deserved a hand." Tom's goal is to take over the business when Al retires. "It's the best job I've ever had," he says, "Al is more than a boss, he's my best friend."

"I have something to show you," Al says excitedly as he turns on his computer. I wait a few minutes and then look up to see Al's web site. "I designed the web site myself" he adds, "with the help of a friend." I ask how it helps his business. "It gives the impression that I'm on the leading edge. So far, more than two thousand people have visited my site." Al is clearly excited by computer technology. He says it makes doing business more fun.

I ask Al what makes him successful. He looks down, shakes his head and finally says, "People tell me I'm successful – my accountant, my ex-wives – but I don't feel like it. They think I'm successful I guess because I have a viable business, I am honest, I pay my bills, and I love what I do."

Finally, I ask Al what keeps him going. He smiles, his brown eyes twinkle, and he says, "I have no choice but to keep going. When you stop moving forward, you might as well be dead." Then he imparts one of his favorite quotes. "Any bad day living is better than any good day dead."

By the way, Al's web site address is: www.AAEngine.com

Heidi Van Arnem
Travel Headquarters, Inc.

As a sixteen year old, Heidi Van Arnem exuded the self-confidence of a young woman who had just about everything, a loving and affluent family, good looks, excellent health and a vivacious personality. At 16, she was popular, pretty, free-spirited, out-going, active and extremely self-assured. At 16, Heidi Van Arnem's future had no limits.

On March 24, 1983, everything changed. That was the day Heidi was accidentally shot by a friend's brother who was playing with a gun. The bullet invaded Heidi's body severing her spinal chord rendering her paralyzed from the neck down. She remembers the feeling of electricity running through her body, and then nothing. She awoke in the hospital to be told she was paralyzed from the neck down. Since that day, Heidi Van Arnem has tried to feel again like she did when she was 16 – confident and self-assured.

I can only imagine how things must have changed for Heidi once the realities of being a quadriplegic set in. "It was my own private hell," she says, "like a bad dream that wouldn't go away. I would look in the mirror and see nothing. My life was over."

Heidi's story is one of triumph over tragedy. At sixteen, she started her life over and she has lived each day moving forward. Her success in business and in life is not the result of one or two lucky breaks, but a product of the many small and seemingly uneventful accomplishments of her everyday life.

After five long months of rehabilitation, Heidi returned home still grieving her loss, confused about her future, and uncertain what life would be like without the use of her arms and legs. She continued high school but was painfully aware of the pity felt by her classmates. "I felt pathetic and worthless," remembers Heidi. "I was so aware of how different I had become." She continued to struggle through rehabilitation and eventually gained enough movement in her right arm to feed herself. "Gaining some level of independence was very important to me," says Heidi. "It was so hard to rely on others for everything."

Over the next several years, Heidi would continue to strive for greater independence. She graduated from high school and college and eventually went on to law school. She remembers, "When I started college I was just going through the motions. I really didn't know why I was going. But my mother never gave me a choice. She forced me to get up and made me go to school. I continued for her and my family. I didn't want to disappoint anyone." She was plagued with severe pneumonia and bladder infections, and was constantly nauseous and lethargic. Yet she continued to go to school, and eventually began to feel better about herself. "The more I accomplished, the better I felt," remembers Heidi.

After completing her undergraduate degree, Heidi went on to law school, but after one year concluded that the law wasn't for her. So, she decided to look for a job. She sent out resumes and had job interviews. Unfortunately, a year and a half later, Heidi was still unemployed. Angrily she says, "Even after graduating from college with honors and attending law school, I still couldn't find a company that would hire me."

But Heidi kept her resolve to succeed. "I felt that if I could go to law school, I could do almost anything." She says, "I believe that anything is possible if you put your mind to it. I wasn't going to settle for just anything."

It was Heidi's father who suggested that she start her own business. She went to school for real estate but ultimately chose the travel industry. She started Travel Headquarters, Inc. using money she received from her insurance settlement. The business progressed slowly at first, but Heidi was determined to succeed. Bills mounted and money seemed to flow out of the business like water through a sieve. "I thought I would die trying to pay all the bills." She recalls," For three years I never slept. I couldn't believe how expensive everything was. Like payroll taxes. I would say to myself 'where is all this money going?'"

Heidi also had a difficult time supervising people, because she says, "I couldn't walk around to see what they were doing." She was well aware of her limitations and weaknesses and responded by taking the initiative to learn. She went to the library and read about small business management. She learned how to manage people and finances and over time her skills improved and so did her bottom line.

She recalls working 14 hours a day. "Almost everything I did had to do with the business. When I socialized, it was to get more business." She set goals for the business and became driven to meet them. She decided to target her services to the disability community, offering travel services for people with physical disabilities.

"The real test," she says, "came in 1992 when we switched computer systems. The industry was changing and we had to keep up with the trends. This was very difficult and stressful. As important as change is to most businesses, employees don't like it. But our future existence was based on our productivity. So we set goals for ourselves, and after our year review, we realized we had met them. We knew then we were a profitable, viable business."

Heidi believes that to be successful in business you have to be a 'doer.' She says, "You can't think too much, you just have to do it. Everyday I wrote a 'to do' list and then I did it." She also attributes her success to her optimism and perseverance. "Somewhere in the back of my mind I knew I could succeed, so I just kept going. Too many people just give up. The people who succeed in life are those who follow through, those who say they're going to do something and then do it."

Heidi has learned the importance of effectively marketing her business. "At first, we didn't have any clients," Heidi says. "When we finally did get them, we had to be sure the very best service was provided." Heidi began prospecting by calling friends, and friends of friends. She sent information to non-profit and disability-related organizations explaining her special services, and then followed up with a phone call. Finally the business came in.

Heidi adeptly uses the media. "The press is interested in stories of people overcoming tragedy," she says. And it helps busines. According to Heidi, "People associate my business with something positive."

Heidi's studying, learning, and hard work has paid big dividends. With six employees and sales close to $2 million, Travel Headquarters, Inc. is now a flourishing enterprise. But Heidi's accomplishments don't stop at being a successful entrepreneur. She also founded the Heidi Van Arnem Foundation to Cure Paralysis, which since 1992, has raised $150,000 towards spinal chord research. The foundation also sponsors an educational program for teens to educate them about spinal chord injuries and to hopefully prevent what happened to Heidi from happening to others. She is as committed to these causes as she is to her business.

As Heidi sits in her office the signs of her disability and the accommodations she's made are obvious; with her computer keyboard on her lap, she punches the keys using a pencil tied to her hand. She uses a headset connected to a telephone to speak to her staff and customers. The office is buzzing. People are coming in and out, asking her questions. She is a very busy woman and I can tell I won't have much more of her time.

From earlier in our conversation, I remember Heidi describing how she used to feel before her injury. I ask how she feels now, if she feels confident again, like she did when she was sixteen. She smiles and says, "Yes. I think so." She adds, "It took me a long time not to feel disabled. It damned near killed me. I was so active. I wanted to ski, run, or just take a walk. I used to look in the mirror and say, 'God, I can't walk.' But now I look in the mirror and say 'God, my hair doesn't look good.' I am comfortable with myself."

Robert Collinge
R & C Grinding, Inc.

The sound of a baby crying, waves hitting the shore, laughter, or music – these sounds do not exist for Robert Collinge.

I have tried to imagine life as a deaf person. No sound. Nothing. I would not hear. It's hard to imagine yourself without something you've always had. But what's even more difficult to fathom is how someone without the ability to hear or speak can succeed in business. Yet that is what Robert Collinge has done. As owner of R & C Grinding, Inc., Robert has operated his successful roll grinding business for 24 years. His business provides precision grinding services to form steel, which is used in everything from construction to machinery.

How does one get ahead in this world without the ability to speak and to hear? How can someone possibly succeed in business without hearing the tone of a customers voice? I hoped to find the answers to my questions by interviewing Robert. His daughter, Darlene, interpreted our conversation.

It was not surprising to learn that Robert Collinge's experiences as a business man (and before that, as a student and an employee), left him skeptical, frustrated, and angry. His inability to communicate freely in a hearing world has made him somewhat distrustful of many hearing people. "Some hearing people are okay, I guess. Some you can trust, but most you can't." This trepidation was probably why it took some convincing to get him to talk to me about his life and business experiences.

Robert Collinge lost his hearing before his first year of life was over. He is completely deaf, and does not use speech to communicate. He is able to hear only extremely loud sounds, but even then he cannot ascertain their source or meaning. He mutters sounds, but only those who know him well can understand him. He communicates through sign language and by reading people's lips.

As a child Robert attended special schools for the deaf. His memories of his educational experience are not pleasant. He witnessed several acts of abuse and quickly learned how to behave in order to ward off potential violence. He was street smart and established the reputation of a tough guy. He dropped out of school in the 7th grade, at age 15, and went to work.

He remembers his education as being inadequate. "I needed an education, but I wasn't being taught," he says, adding, "Learning through the schools was one of the few opportunities we had to pick up information. It's better now with closed captioned television."

Robert's mother encouraged him to learn a trade and he showed mechanical aptitude right from the start. At 10, he built an airplane with a washing machine engine, he laughs as he recalls the incident, "the thing flew until it came unplugged."

At 15, Robert started working in a tool and die shop. He recalls having a terrible time with his boss. "I was blamed for every mistake made. I was an easy target. I couldn't defend myself." He had the same difficulty with a series of other employers, and ended up moving from job to job.

After years of frustration, Robert finally decided to start his own business. He recognized a need in the marketplace. "Some companies were competitive," he explains, "but they didn't offer fast service." That was how Robert intended to compete. He started his business with just one customer. He approached a former co-worker who agreed to send him work. Robert gave him fast service, and his sole customer promoted his business to others.

Twenty-five years later and Robert Collinge is still in business. He has supported himself, his wife (who is also deaf) and three daughters (all of whom are hearing). He lives in a beautiful home, takes regular vacations, and has a number of expensive hobbies. Currently, he's taking flying lessons. This may all sound quite blissful, but at 52, Robert Collinge looks rugged, like a man who has lived a difficult life. For Robert, success in business has meant long, hard hours spent working in his shop. He explains, "People say, 'your employees are at home and you're working, why?'" "Because" he says, "it takes hard work to succeed in business."

What else does Robert attribute to his success? It's very simple – he gives every customer what they want. "You must say yes to the customer, and then behind closed doors you figure out how you're going to do it." Robert also attributes his success to a very supportive wife. In 28 years of marriage, she has listened to his many frustrations. He explains, "You can't keep it all in, you need to be able to vent to someone who will listen and who understands."

Currently his business has four full-time employees, including Robert, his daughter, and two deaf technicians. The operation seems to run smoothly, but it's still hard for me to imagine him being successfully self-employed all these years. Now he has his daughter to interpret for him, but what did he do when his daughters were just babies and he had no one else? I ask, "What if there was a problem, or what if a customer was unhappy?" He smiles, "I got friends, employees, or whoever was available, to translate the orders for me. Most of the time I didn't have to talk to my customers because my service was so quick. I would provide overnight service. Customers were so happy, they didn't care I was deaf."

Darlene stops interpreting and says, "I remember at a very young age, maybe 8 or 9, talking to customers over the phone. I would call them and tell them when the rolls would be delivered." Robert adds, "Yes, I feel bad about that, you shouldn't have to have your children speak for you." He seems partly sad and partly angry. "I feel I have missed out on a lot not being able to hear. I can't hear lawyers or accountants. And I think most of the time I get a raw deal. I have to be very careful how I come across so they won't think I'm stupid." He continues, "I don't want them to think, 'why am I wasting time with him?'"

Finally, Robert attributes his success to a basic belief in himself. "My father thought I was a hell-raiser, a trouble-maker. I don't think he thought I would amount to much. But I always had a belief in myself. I wanted to prove I could do it."

And he did.

Daniel McGee
Graphics Technologies

Dan McGee speaks with the ease of someone totally comfortable with himself. After just a few minutes of conversation, I can tell he is an extremely articulate and fascinating man, with tremendous insight and a positive outlook that is refreshing and contagious.

Perhaps his outlook was partly shaped by the vulnerability of his health. Dan McGee has Sickle Cell Anemia, a blood condition where red blood cells sickle, harden, and take on odd shapes preventing the blood from clotting normally. The disease causes extreme pain, swelling, fatigue, and eventually destroys the organs of the body, causing death. Sickle Cell Anemia is a hereditary disease which effects primarily African-American males. Most who have the disease remain bed ridden and suffer profoundly throughout their lives.

Dan McGee is luckier than most. For some reason his Fetal Blood Factor has remained high throughout his life, keeping him from the rigors of the disease. When talking with Dan, you sense that he really appreciates his fortuitousness. "I have been able to do many things that most people with this disease cannot do." Which is to say that Dan McGee has led and will continue to lead a productive, "normal" life. For Dan this includes owning and operating his home-based business, Graphics Technologies.

Dan is not immune from the effects of the disease. He has experienced extreme swelling and pain and has spent days in bed. His energy is limited and he must design his lifestyle around his disability. Operating his business from his home gives him the flexibility he needs to remain healthy. "In the early morning I am the most productive," says the entrepreneur who starts his day at 5:00 a.m. "I can rest when I need to because my office is in my home. Also, working from home keeps me in touch with everything that's important to me - my family, my work, and my health."

Dan established Graphics Technologies in 1994, and since then, volume has grown slowly but steadily. The business provides large scale presentation graphics for architects and contractors. Dan takes the design from the architect or builder and then displays it visually in a way that customers, business owners, investors, or bankers can easily understand. He loves his work.

After graduating with a degree in Architectural Design, Dan worked as a designer in many capacities before starting his business. Getting a solid education did not come easy to Dan who took the Civil Service Exam right after high school and failed miserably. He describes his high school education as "extremely inferior" and was apprehensive about his future and his lack of readiness for the job market.

So, in 1966, Dan joined the Air Force. He explains, "It was during the Vietnam War, and the military was recruiting like crazy. That's why I got in with the Sickle Cell Anemia." He viewed serving in the military as a positive alternative to what was happening in his home town of Detroit at the time. He remembers sitting in a theater in the Philippines watching a burning landscape on the screen. It was Detroit – the riots of 1967 – and Dan McGee watched from afar as his neighborhood went up in flames. "That was so weird, I thought 'man I'm safer here than I would be at home.'"

During his stint with the military, Dan completed extensive technical training and became a flight-line mechanic. After four years of service, he returned home and considered again the advantages of a civil service career. He took the exam, this time scoring an impressive 90%. He applied for a job as a mail carrier for the Post Office, which would secure his future with solid pay and good benefits. But at the eleventh hour, Dan decided that the post office, while promising financial security, did not offer the stimulation he needed. He had a drive to do something creative. So he attended a local community college, received an associates degree in Commercial and Graphic Arts, and proceeded to receive his four-year degree in Art History and Media Production. His initial goal was to become a television camera man, but he went back to school again for a degree in Architectural Design.

Dan talks openly about his struggles with Sickle Cell Anemia and the depression he's experienced. "My health condition became the core of my existence." He explains, "There were times when I suffered excruciating pain. But I think the depression was more debilitating."

Dan credits his daughters with helping him change his outlook. Eventually it was his ambitions that became the core of his existence. He says, "You have to put something else first in your life. You need to find something you love, because love will lead to passion, passion will yield drive, and drive will yield success." He continues, "I lived a long time before coming to the realization that there are things in life bigger than you, that there's a power source beyond you."

Dan McGee believes that everyone has limited physical energy. He believes that we must have access to a power source that keeps us going, and that that power source comes from something you love. His advice to potential entrepreneurs is to "keep searching until you find that which you have passion for." For Dan McGee his passion is his family, his work, and his business.

Outside it's getting darker, and suddenly I become aware of how long we've been talking and how much I've enjoyed the conversation. So, I keep the interview going. I ask, "What other advice could you offer to potential entrepreneurs?" He responds, "It is not enough to love the business you're in, you have to love being in business. The more you 'get into' the business of being in business, the more successful you will become." He adds, "Don't just chase money. Money is a by-product of doing the right thing for enough people. My business took off once I stopped thinking about money and began thinking about my customers. "Also important," he adds "is practice, practice, practice. You must continue to hone your skills. Talents will fade if not kept fresh, sharp, and crisp."

I first met Dan McGee three years ago. I remember it well because I was impressed with a particular comment he made. At the time, I was encouraging business owners with disabilities to pursue government contracts and subcontract opportunities as disadvantaged businesses. I explained to Dan that the government and its general contractors must meet certain "quotas" for doing business with disadvantaged business enterprises (DBEs). I further explained that these DBE's are usually minority businesses and may, in some circumstances, be enterprises owned by a person with a disability. I told Dan that as a minority person with a disability, he would be an excellent candidate, But Dan McGee wasn't interested, he said "I want out of that pigeon hole. Anything you achieve will be discounted. That's why I'm glad what I do is visual. No government assistance helps me do what I do. It is my skill that gets me jobs." He adds, "That's why I am happy being self-employed. I was never very good at office politics. By being my own boss, I am judged on nothing more than my skill. I approach people fairly and honestly and I expect the same in return. My business may not be the most successful enterprise, but for now I'm right where I want to be."

Carol Backus
Shear Magic

In 1994, Carol Backus was homeless, living in a shelter with no possessions and no income. Her predicament resulted from what appears to be a combination of bad choices and undesirable circumstances. Married and divorced three times and wiped out by a hurricane in 1992, Carol's life has been plagued with bad luck and bad timing.

Although she was educated in commercial art, Carol worked in a number of diverse fields including dress making, upholstery, sign painting, and construction. She had a talent for working with her hands and never had a problem finding work. That was until shortly after the hurricane, when she fell and broke her hip.

After her accident, Carol continued to work until the pain got so bad she could hardly walk. "I can't believe how much pain I was in." She shakes her head, "I don't know how I could stand it. Imagine your knee pressed on a cheese grater. That's how it felt. I was taking pain killers, but they didn't help."

Like many working Americans, Carol didn't have health or disability insurance. She applied for General Assistance and Social Security benefits, but was turned down, and after months without any income, and no money to pay rent, she found herself with no where to go. "I was so depressed. I was always so independent and self-sufficient. I couldn't understand or rationalize why this was happening to me. I felt hopeless." It was then that Carol made several attempts to end her life. She tried taking an overdose of pain killers. But her plan was thwarted when she was discovered, hospitalized, and sent to a homeless shelter.

While at the shelter, Carol was able to get the help she needed and she began to feel hopeful. She remembers, "They helped me get emergency housing through the Department of Social Service. The local churches kicked in money for a security deposit, and although rent was $400 a month, my landlord accepted $100 a month until I was able to get back on my feet." She also found an attorney willing to work with her and after six months finally began receiving General Assistance.

As the months rolled by, Carol's condition deteriorated and the doctors informed her she was in need of a complete hip replacement. She was still without health insurance however, and had to wait a year before the state vocational rehabilitation services finally succeeded in getting Medicaid to pay for her surgery. Carol put the time she spent waiting to good use. She began sewing children's clothes and repairing toys for kids in her neighborhood. She purchased toys and dolls at resale shops, mended and repaired them, and then before the Christmas holiday, donated the toys (340 of them) to the Salvation Army. The following year, she continued her good will and ended up donating almost 700 toys to the charity. When the local paper published an article on her good works, people began bringing her their own toys and clothing. Last year Carol mended and donated 1313 toys for disadvantaged children. "The work gave me a purpose and I enjoyed it. It was an opportunity for me to use my creativity. I thought about the children who would receive the toys and play with them. I know what it's like to be poor, to be broke," she says, remembering the day, not too long ago, when she had nothing.

Much has changed for Carol Backus, whose work for underprivileged children has turned into a thriving small business. She started a business making reparations to clothes and furniture. She realized that if she was able to repair toys and clothes for children, she could do the same for adults and charge them for it. Initially business was slow. In her first month, Carol's sales were only $400. But by the end of her first year, she was taking in $3,000 a month. She now owns her own home with a barn in back, which she uses as her workshop. In three years, Carol Backus has virtually turned her life around. She continues to repair and donate toys and although she still experiences pain, she monitors her physical activity by carefully balancing her business, her charity work, and her family life. The business, she says, "Helps me keep my sanity. It helps keep the focus off the pain."

Carol has a number of insights into what has made her successful. "First," she says, "You have to focus on something positive. Negatives will kill you. If there's something you can do to solve a problem, do it. If there is nothing you can do, forget about it. Why would anyone start repairing junk toys? It was my way of doing something positive." She continues, "Be willing to spend a lot of hours, and you really have to like what you're doing. There are sacrifices. You don't have as much recreation time." Finally she says, "Stick to it and believe in yourself. You need to know you can succeed despite all the obstacles."

Even when she considers all the hard work, time and energy spent, Carol is happier now than she's ever been. "I'm not afraid of anything anymore because no matter what comes my way, I know I will survive."

CHAPTER 2

Lessons Learned from Successful Entrepreneurs

The entrepreneurs in chapter one had certain characteristics in common that contributed to their success. These characteristics are the fuel that starts the entrepreneur's engine and that moves them from the initial idea to start-up and eventually to success.

Much can be learned by understanding what traits successful entrepreneurs hold in common, and why some people succeed and others do not. I have seen many individuals with severe disabilities who succeed because they are focused, confident, and driven; and others, with minor impairments, who remain trapped by their feelings of worthlessness and despair. Usually it is the individual's attitude that influences their ultimate success or failure.

The lessons in this chapter were derived from the thoughts and words of the successful entrepreneurs profiled in the previous chapter. The characteristics, traits and behaviors compiled in the following lessons are the essential building blocks to success. They are strategies which if practiced, will help potential business owners like yourself reach their goals.

Lesson #1: Have Confidence - Believe in Yourself

Building self-confidence is arguably the greatest challenge for people with disabilities, who may see themselves as different, unable, or incapable of success. In fact, lack of confidence often presents an even greater barrier to a person's success than their disability.

Psychologists and other experts have written plenty about self-confidence and its importance in accomplishing goals and achieving success. For most people, confidence is cultivated early in childhood. Studies show that when children are raised in a safe, loving, nurturing environment, they will likely be trustful of the world and confident in their ability to function in it. But what if during childhood you never developed a basic trust or belief in yourself? Does this mean you are destined to fail? The discussions with the entrepreneurs suggest that the answer is no. Al Vickery, raised in a troubled and unhealthy environment, clearly lacked the nurturing environment that fosters confidence and trust. Al, through life experiences, learned to believe in himself.

So, a belief in yourself does not have to be developed in childhood (although it certainly helps), and it is not an absolute, i.e., you either have it or you don't. Most people believe in themselves to some degree, but will also experience moments in their life when they are less confident than others. This is true no matter how safe and nurturing a person's childhood may have been. Heidi Van Arnem describes herself as "confident and self-assured" at 16, but felt "worthless" after she became paralyzed. Only after she began focusing on her accomplishments and goals, did she begin to regain her confidence and self-worth.

Henry Ford said "Think you can. Think you can't. Either way you'll be right." To a great extent, a person's thoughts will dictate whether or not they will accomplish their goals. This quote, and the stories in Chapter 1, suggest that people can learn or re-learn confidence by thinking positively, staying focused, and being optimistic about the future.

Every one of the entrepreneurs profiled in Chapter 1 indicated that an important reason for their success was their belief in themselves. This belief, or confidence, is a deep trust in yourself and your abilities. Believe that you have the basic tools you need to survive and thrive, and you will.

Lesson #2:   Focus on What You Can Do, Not on What You Can't Do

The great explorer, Sir Walter Raleigh said "I can't write a book commensurate with William Shakespeare, but I can write a book by me." A common tendency of all human beings is to compare themselves to others; to be painfully aware of their limitations – of what they cannot do; and at the same time, disregard or minimize what they can do. Many people with disabilities struggle with feelings of inadequacy because they cannot always do what other people can do, at least not in the same way.

Dennis Figiel, owner of National Millwork, says that people with disabilities must learn to accept their limitations. He advises: "Focus on what you can do, not on what you can't do." When the focus is placed on what can be done, confidence and motivation result.

Jessica Poisson struggled with feelings of inadequacy because she was dependent on her husband's income. She didn't feel productive or useful. When Jessica began to focus on her skills and abilities, her confidence and self-worth grew. She knew she had the ability, the talent, and the motivation to succeed.

Lesson #3:   Find a Purpose

Dan McGee, owner of Graphics Technologies said, "You have to put something else first in your life. You need to find something you love, because love will yield passion, passion will yield drive, and drive will yield success."

Too much focus on a person's health or disability creates an imbalance in their life, leading to depression, and feelings of worthlessness. To achieve success in business and in life, focus must be placed on something other than one's health or circumstances. Time spent dwelling on one's limitations is time wasted, because usually one has little or no control over it. This is not to say that a person should not take care of themselves and manage their health and/or disability. It is important to recognize what your limitations are, and how you will make accommodations in order to live a happy, fulfilled life. As Dan McGee put it, "Your disease is a part of you, you are not a part of it. It is a real factor in your life, but not the core of your existence."

Lesson #4:   Work Through Depression - Move On

Depression is a dreadful condition that affects many people for all kinds of reasons. For some, it is caused by a chemical imbalance, and in these situations medical treatment is necessary. Others experience depression as a temporary and debilitating condition that strikes when some catastrophic event occurs. In other words, depression is triggered by a loss, a major disappointment, or any event that has a profound impact on a person's life. Experiencing depression after a catastrophic event is normal, but remaining in a depressed state impacts a person's ability to lead a successful life.

When depressed, a person views the world negatively. Often a realistic assessment of oneself, the world, and their ability to function in it, is difficult to grasp. Problems can become bigger than they really are. The entrepreneurs profiled in Chapter 1 talked about their depression and how they worked through it.

Dan McGee struggles with Sickle Cell Anemia, but said that he believes his depression was more debilitating. He addressed his depression by making his illness a peripheral part of his life, rather than the core of his existence. He found something more important to be the center of his life. For Heidi Van Arnem and Dennis Figiel, depression is avoided by not dwelling on their disabilities. They remain too busy to spend time thinking about their problems or their limitations.

Successful entrepreneurs come in all shapes and sizes, but no matter what their particular situation may be, they all possess the ability to quickly move on. They focus on their goals and when they have achieved one goal, they are satisfied until the next goal is achieved, and that satisfies them until the next one after that is achieved, and so on, and so on....leading to Lesson #5.

Lesson #5:   Keep Motivated – Stay Busy!

There is nothing more motivating than deadlines. Customers need their widgets, employees need their paychecks, suppliers need their money, and baby needs a new pair of shoes. Once in business, there is nothing more motivating than the day-to-day challenges of meeting deadlines, satisfying customers, and meeting financial obligations. But what about prior to business start-up, when all you have is the idea and there is little, if any, pressure to pursue it. According to Heidi Van Arnem you "have to just do it."

Heidi Van Arnem says "successful business owners are doers, not thinkers." She believes that you can think too much about what you're doing. You can easily over-analyze the right way to do this or do that. When it comes right down to it, you just have to get going. You will make mistakes. That is an essential part of the learning process. All people in business make mistakes, but they never get anywhere unless they keep moving forward.

Successful entrepreneurs motivate themselves by staying busy. They set goals and take steps each day to meet those goals. Even if the steps seem small or insignificant, they keep moving forward. Carol Backus decided to repair toys for children to keep busy and do something positive for the community. She enjoyed the work and it passed the time while she was waiting to have her surgery. She couldn't walk, had too much pain for other activiites, but sewing was something she could do and something she enjoyed.

Carol could never have known where her small project would lead. Her primary concern was keeping busy. She needed to focus on doing something positive to take her mind off her pain and her desperate financial situation. Finding something positive and constructive to do, no matter how seemingly insignificant, is anything but insignificant, because it is helping you move a step closer to success.

Lesson #6:   Be Determined

There are many obstacles for entrepreneurs, disabled or not; one needs to develop a business plan, find financing, hire the right people, pay taxes and find customers. To succeed, an entrepreneur must remain determined to overcome every obstacle that presents itself.

As a person with a disability or chronic health condition, you may confront any number of possible obstacles in pursuit of your dream of owning your own business. One obstacle may be the opinions of others as to your ability to run a business, given your current physical condition. You may encounter disapproval from family members, skepticism from bankers, or criticism from advisors. While this resistance may be difficult to acknowledge, it should not be ignored. Objections of naysayers have value because they force aspiring business owners to consider all the potential drawbacks. Sometimes these objections allow the entrepreneur to see a problem, which, if not solved, could eventually prove devastating to their business and financial situation.

Armed with a belief in oneself, almost anyone can accomplish all of the necessary tasks that starting a business involves, assuming of course that the idea has merit and that the owner possesses the necessary skills. Determination without consideration of the owner's abilities and limitations is ludicrous. The business owner must have a clear idea of how limitations will be accommodated. For example, Robert Collinge of R & C Grinding believed he had the skill and ability to succeed in his own business. He did have a major obstacle–he could not hear his customers. Robert was not oblivious to his limitations, he was well aware of the impact his deafness could have on his business. Still, he maintained his conviction that if he offered a better service than his competitors, customers would come. As evidenced by his success, Robert was right.

The moral here is, if your determination is tempered with a dose of reality and you still want to do it and believe you can, then do it!

Lesson #7:   Be Disciplined

By and large, success in business does not happen without discipline. Dennis Figiel turned a fledgling business into a thriving one. How? By disciplining himself. Dennis spent years preparing himself to run a small business. He attended night school to learn accounting and financial management. Then after working days and weekends as a musician, he didn't spend his money, he saved it, so that he and his brother could buy the business and expand it.

Discipline requires making short-term sacrifices in order to achieve long-term gains.

Business ownership is a long haul. It often takes years before any real profits are generated. It is discipline through these lean years that pays big dividends down the road.

In their book *The Millionaire Next Door*, Thomas Stanley and William Danko reveal how America's 3.5 million millionaires accumulated their wealth. One of the strategies highlighted in their book is the principle of "living below your means." The book profiles many entrepreneurs who are millionaires because they live a frugal lifestyle. They succeed, in part, because they are willing to forego certain extravagances, even when they can afford them, in order to save and invest for their future. Their discipline in the short-run leads to financial success in the long-run.

Lesson #8:   Work Hard

Robert Collinge has not succeeded in business because he has a rare talent or gift. He is successful because throughout his 24 years in business, he has worked very, very hard. Implementing an overnight service not only meant more customers for R & C Grinding, it meant Robert Collinge had to spend long evenings away from his family making sure the job got done, and it got done right. Robert's reality was that he had to work harder than his competitors to compensate for his disability. You may say, that doesn't seem fair. However, as the entrepreneurs in Chapter 1 will tell you, life's not fair, and the only way to compensate for life's inequities is by working hard.

This is not to say that business owners shouldn't have some level of skill or talent in their chosen field. Robert Collinge possesses mechanical aptitude and Jessica Poisson is a whiz at computers. Having aptitude helps and is usually necessary. However, aptitude or talent alone cannot make you successful.

Some people with disabilities or chronic health conditions lack the stamina to work 16-hour days. Does this mean they cannot be successfully self-employed? Absolutely not! Hard work is a relative thing. For some, it means working 6-hour days, for others it means putting in 16-hour days. The business itself and the owner's ultimate goal will define how hard the owner must work to achieve success. It is always true however, that the more one puts into something, the more they'll get out of it.

Lesson #9: Overcome the Fear of Failure and the Fear of Success

Many people believe that because they are physically limited, they are unable or incapable of succeeding as a business owner. They believe the demands and challenges of business ownership are too significant for people with physical constraints. The entrepreneurs in the previous chapter and the thousands of others who have succeeded in business are evidence that this notion is false. However, that is not to say that business ownership may not be a scary proposition.

Probably the most obvious fear associated with starting a business is that it will fail. On the other hand, many people with disabilities also silently harbor the fear that the business will succeed. Success could mean the loss of Social Security or disability benefits when their disability income is replaced by revenues generated from the business. When disability benefits are discontinued, this can also mean that medical benefits are discontinued as well. This is often a rational, justifiable fear. However, the Social Security Administration has created many programs for people who receive benefits to get back into the work force without prematurely losing financial or medical benefits. More will be discussed on this in Chapter 8. For now, it is important to understand that while the loss of disability benefits is a legitimate concern, it can also be used as an excuse. If, while starting a business, the owner plans to continue to receive benefits and/or utilize government programs, they should view them as temporary tools needed to achieve long-term goals. Succumbing to the fear of losing benefits is the same as fearing success, since technically benefits won't be lost unless some level of success is achieved.

Deciding to start a business is a risk. To a great extent whether or not you are willing to accept the risk depends on your personal situation, health issues, and the confidence you have that your business will succeed. And, of course, your ability to face your fears.

Lesson #10: Deal Constructively with Your Anger - Be Positive

When you have a chronic illness or a disability, there are a number of things to be angry about. Many individuals feel angry that this (disease, accident, etc.) happened to them and they feel angry about the attitudes of people who see only their illness or disability and can't look beyond it. Unfortunately, people with disabilities or chronic health conditions will encounter people who think they can't do something simply because they have a disability or physical limitation. And, unfortunately no one possesses the power to control the thoughts and attitudes of others. However, what can be controlled is the response one has to these thoughts and attitudes. Dennis Figiel said "the toughest thing about having a disability is people's attitudes. It's frustrating." He adds, "If you have an attitude, they will have an attitude," and you won't get what you want.

Generally speaking, most people will keep an open mind about you and your abilities. This is true even if they have made some initial assumptions about your disability. If you come across positive, knowledgeable, and motivated, generally people will give you the benefit of the doubt. Conversely, coming across bitter and defensive, decreases your chance of changing a person's initial bias. So, keep a positive approach to life and to people, and move another step closer to success!

Lesson #11: Seek Independence, But Don't Be Afraid to Ask for Help

We live in a culture that puts tremendous importance on independence. When we think of America, we think of independence. We think of John Wayne – the strong, quiet loner. This characteristic is so imbued in many Americans that some people resist asking for help of any kind. This is partly good and partly bad. Good, because as one solves a problem they develop analytical skills and the internal coping skills of strength and determination. The bad side of being too independent is that total reliance on inner resources can lead to isolation and disconnection.

There are many ways to be independent. One can be financially independent, emotionally independent, or physically independent. Often because of a person's physical characteristics, total physical independence is an impractical goal. Help may be needed to lift or move things, to get from place to place, or to communicate. For many people asking for help is difficult albeit necessary.

The successful entrepreneurs profiled in the previous chapter were fiercely independent, and in some cases, too independent. Dennis Figiel realizes now that he should have started using a wheelchair sooner. He said that he forced himself to walk because he told himself he *had* to walk. His stubbornness took a toll on his health and kept him from attending social events and interacting with people. He said, "I didn't want to go anywhere if it meant asking for help. I wanted to be independent, but I was hurting myself physically and socially. There's a fine line between being determined and being stubborn."

While the entrepreneurs profiled in Chapter 1 needed independence, they came to view independence in a new way. They recognized that accomplishing their goals – successful self-employment and financial independence – would take more than just their own resources. Most of these individuals were able to ask for help when they needed it. Many sought out the assistance from their family or friends, and identified resources in the community, mentors and support systems to provide assistance.

The financier, Charles Schwab said, "The best place to succeed is where you are with what you have." In other words, no matter who you are or what obstacles you may face, you still have the potential to succeed. The key to success is knowing *how* to get what you need in order to accomplish your goals. Successful business owners are well aware of where they need help and are not afraid to ask for it. In fact, they come to realize that asking for help often leads to new relationships and new opportunities because people generally like to help, to provide input, or share their expertise. This process of reaching out, asking for help and giving help brings people together. It keeps us from isolation.

Also, beware of maintaining total emotional independence while starting a business. It is an extremely trying time and a number of different emotions are experienced. The instinctive response may be to go through it alone. Resisting this instinct is critical. The entrepreneur must realize that all problems cannot be solved alone. It is important that feelings of frustration, worry, confusion, and elation are shared with trusted friends and family members who will listen and offer sound advice when needed. An excellent example is Robert Collinge who considers being able to vent to his wife one of his greatest business assets. Realizing you may need help from time to time can be an important step toward financial independence.

Lesson #12: Utilize Technology and Adaptive Devices

The use of technology is an essential part of managing almost any business. From the assembly line to the computer, technology has shaped our lives and continues to change the way we get things done. Businesses are often the first to incorporate new technologies with the intention of lowering costs and increasing productivity. Even the smallest of businesses can benefit from the many time-savings devices developed over the years.

Dennis Figiel advises those interested in starting a business to fully utilize technology. Technology can equalize the playing field, often making it possible for people to compete. Basic office technology including a fax machine, copy machine, answering machine and a computer can improve customer service, enhance a company's image, increase productivity, and lower costs. Technology advancements are tools; tools to help the entrepreneur do their job better, more efficiently, and with greater accuracy. Just as a builder uses proper tools to build a house, a business owner must use the proper tools to build a business.

For people with disabilities the need for technology may not be limited to business tools such as fax machines and computers. Depending on a person's disability or health condition, adaptive devices may be needed to successfully operate the business. There are assistive devices for almost every kind of disabling condition including hearing, visual and mobility impairments.

Many devices exist which make it possible for business owners with mobility impairments to efficiently use personal computers. For example, headsets using ultrasonic signals allow the user to control the computer through head movements. Joy sticks and trackballs give computer users with a limited range of motion the ability to activate a computer with greater ease and comfort. Voice recognition software was the solution for Jessica Poisson, making it possible for her to use a computer through spoken commands.

Adaptive devices such as these are quite common, and can help you solve a plethora of possible business problems. If you are interested in more information about computer and adaptive technologies, these sources may help:

ABLEDATA
An on-line database of technology and assistive devices.
web site: www.abledata.com, or call
The National Institute on Disability and Rehabilitation Research
1-800-227-0216

Job Accomodations Network
West Virginia University
P.O. Box 6080
Morgantown, West Virginia 26506-6080
Telephone/TDD: 1-800-526-7234 (U.S.) 1-800-526-2262 (Canada)
web site: janweb.icdi.wvu.edu

Lesson #13: Take Advantage of Community Resources

Carol Backus used community resources to get her life back in order, and eventually to start her business. She obtained assistance from local churches, shelters, government agencies, neighbors and friends who helped her access financial resources, a job, and suitable housing. She used the business community for advice and counsel and gathered information about her competitors.

It is important for the new business owner to remember that there are people out there with past experiences that parallel their current dilemmas. Meeting with experienced business owners at local Chamber of Commerce meetings or at trade association conferences can be an excellent source of ideas, information, and contacts. There are potential mentors in every community who can offer sage advice.

Business owners learn from their competitors by staying abreast of new products and services. This allows them to develop an informed marketing strategy or product/service niche. Owners can hone their skills by taking courses and seminars. Universities, community colleges, and some Chambers of Commerce offer courses or seminars on everything from using a personal computer to developing a marketing plan.

There are many ways to access information to help you manage your business. Heidi Van Arnem learned strategies for managing her travel business by absorbing everything she could find on personnel and financial management. She found the information she needed at her local library and immersed herself in learning. Today, business owners can access information via the Internet or the World Wide Web. The Internet allows the business owner to access data, how-to information, and even information about their competitors from their homes or offices by getting on-line.

Getting information and support is also important to managing one's health. Jessica Poisson credits her on-line Lupus support group with offering invaluable advice and counsel, contributing greatly to her total well-being. Non-profit organizations that target specific disabilities or health conditions, such as United Cerebral Palsy, the MS Society, or the Learning Disabilities Association, are champions of the issues facing their members, but are also excellent sources of knowledge, training, guidance, support and sometimes financial resources to help solve problems and meet immediate needs.

The Last Word on Lessons and Learning

As an aspiring entrepreneur, it is important for you to understand what it takes to succeed in a small business enterprise. Success in business is not unlike success in any endeavor; it requires a commitment of time, energy and resources. And it requires a commitment to grow, develop and learn. The entrepreneurs profiled in this section are examples of what can be achieved with perseverance and the willingness to learn and grow.

After reading the previous chapters, you probably have a good idea of what qualities you need to cultivate to achieve success in your life and in your business. Do you need to work a little harder, stay more focused and disciplined, or overcome your fear of failure? In each of us there is room for improvement. Only if you are highly committed to your goals will you make the effort to change what you need to change to be successful. Those who succeed not only learn what it takes to succeed, but they take the steps necessary to achieve their goals. In other words, successful entrepreneurs put what they've learned into action!

Armed with an awareness of what it takes to succeed and a willingness to take action, you too can succeed in business. In the following pages you will learn the technical aspects of running a business. First, you will learn if business ownership is right for you and if your business idea is feasible. Then you will learn how to set up your business legally, how to write a business plan, and how and where to go for financing. Finally, you will learn about resources to help you accomplish your goals and strategies for keeping your successful enterprise afloat. This book provides potential business owners with all the basics of preparing for and starting a business enterprise. However, an in-depth understanding of many of the concepts introduced is beyond the scope of this book. Therefore, each chapter includes a listing of references used and sources of additional information.

PART TWO

GETTING STARTED:

"More powerful than the will to win
is the courage to begin."

Unknown

CHAPTER 3

Choosing The Opportunity
That's Right For You

People with disabilities and chronic illnesses often discover that in order to work, they must be self-employed. They arrive at this conclusion for many reasons. Some pursue self-employment because they have spent years trying to find a job or years trying to keep a job. Others require the flexibility and autonomy that self-employment offers. In each case, the person acknowledges that self-employment offers them the best opportunity to earn a living while managing their health. If this applies to you, you may have been searching for a business opportunity that meets your financial needs and is consistent with your personal goals, skills and characteristics. In this chapter, you will find suggestions for identifying the right business opportunity for you.

Start with Your Resume

Your search for business ideas should start with your resume. What do you have experience doing? What jobs, hobbies, projects, or activities have you been involved in that could lead to potential business opportunities? Consider new ways of providing an old service. In your past jobs, what did you think should have been done differently? Robert Collinge started R&C Grinding because he believed his former employers were not responsive enough to their customers. He based his business on the premise that faster service would bring in customers.

What if you cannot do the work that you have experience in because of an injury or a health condition, what do you do then? Consider how your experience may be transferred to similar types of industries or related services. For example, if you have experience as a secretary, but because of your disability, are no longer able to type, you may consider starting a temporary placement service for clerical support workers.

Jessica Poisson is an excellent example of transferring skills to a related business or industry. After being diagnosed with Lupus and Carpel Tunnel Syndrome, Jessica's doctor told her that her career with computers was over. But Jessica found a way to transfer her computer acumen to a viable business that was compatible with her physical limitations.

The key to identifying opportunities is keeping your mind open to all possibilities.

Talk to people in your industry, read trade journals, keep up with current trends and changes in the market place. It may take some time, but remain patient and keep searching. Spend time networking with people who are likely to be good sources of ideas or information, or work on projects that will help expose you to opportunities. Carol Backus went from homeless person to successful business owner by spending her time constructively. Her good will efforts created attention from the media and ultimately spawned the idea for her business. You never know where a contact or an activity may lead.

Consider Your Skills and Interests

Every person has something to offer; something to contribute. To become self-employed, you must determine if what you have to offer has market value. In other words, will someone pay you for it? What marketable skills do you possess that can be transformed into a successful business? Do you have management or leadership skills? What about problem-solving or communication skills? Be aware of these skills as you consider various opportunities.

Interests and hobbies are an excellent source of potential business ideas. If you are involved in a hobby, there may be a market niche related to that hobby that remains untapped. Brainstorming sessions with family members or friends can help to sort out ideas and identify market opportunities.

There are numerous publications which offer business ideas and give useful insight about how other entrepreneurs have achieved success. For example, a business idea established in one area of the country can often be duplicated in another. When considering potential business ideas, it is helpful to visit your local library. Libraries have useful books, periodicals, and research manuals which can provide ideas and the information needed to investigate potential business opportunities. The resources listed in the reference section of this chapter may also help generate ideas.

Business expos are excellent for networking and developing business contacts, but are also a good place to generate business ideas. Keep talking to people and investigating ideas. Again, you never know where an activity may lead.

Franchises and "Packaged" Business Opportunities

Some franchise opportunities offer an ideal alternative to starting up a new, unknown concern. With a franchise, the franchisee is buying the right to use the franchised name, the expertise of the franchiser, and a concept which has already been proven successful in other markets. Most franchisers offer extensive training to owners, as well as ongoing managerial support. In addition, many provide the research needed to demonstrate market demand. These supports make franchises generally less risky than other ventures and may increase the availability of financing. In most cases, franchises require a considerable financial investment. As the franchisee, you pay a franchise fee and usually some percentage of sales or royalty in return for the company's proven management approach and ongoing guidance.

Franchises are regulated nationally by the Federal Trade Commission, and must file notice with the state's attorney general office where they intend to do business. The purpose of these regulations is to protect the consumer, or franchise buyer, from business opportunities which are operating illegally as franchises.

When purchasing a franchise, the buyer purchases the "right" to operate the business over a specified period of time. Most buyers assume that when they purchase a franchise they are buying a business. A franchise exists when the franchiser gives the franchisee the right to distribute services, while using the franchiser's trademark, logo, or advertising.

Some companies sell what are sometimes referred to as "vertical computer services" or "packaged" businesses. These are not franchises, they are packages that often include computer hardware and software and some instructional materials. Companies selling vertical computer services claim to sell "proven" business opportunities, but usually offer no training, no support, and probably will not offer an exclusive geographic territory. Therefore, you could be competing with dozens of other businesses in the same area who purchased the same package. Because the information they provide can be found at your local library, these packages usually offer no greater opportunity than you could create for yourself. Companies who sell packaged business opportunities often prey on the vulnerability of those individuals who are looking for ways to make money quickly.

Prior to investing in any franchise or packaged business opportunity, be sure to investigate the company thoroughly. The franchiser is required by law to provide the franchisee with a set of FTC documents. These documents include disclosure statements of past dealings, past and pending experiences with litigation or bankruptcy, and any fees, royalties or other franchise obligations. The disclosures also include financial statements of the franchise and the actual franchise agreement.

Potential franchise buyers should obtain a listing of all franchises currently operating. Contact existing franchise owners and gather information regarding the business opportunity. Ask specific questions. Are existing franchise owners making money? What are the pitfalls? What kind of support was provided by the company? Did the opportunity meet the owner's expectations? It is also a good idea to visit one or more of the franchises. Also, contact the Better Business Bureau and the Attorney General's office to see if any complaints have been filed against the company. This is particularly important if the company is unknown to you.

Finally, be careful of "get rich quick" schemes. If it sounds too good to be true, it probably is. Question everything. Be sure to read the fine print of the franchise agreement and be sure you know just what you are paying for. Once you have decided on a franchise, seek out legal representation before signing anything!

Home-based Business Opportunities

Home-based businesses are one of the most significant trends of the 90's. There are literally thousands of businesses which can be successfully operated out of the home.

Having the luxury of never having to commute to the office, not to mention flexible work hours and access to the comforts of home, make the home-based business an attractive option for many individuals with disabilities and chronic health conditions.

The decision to start a business from the home is often financial. Home-based businesses generally require less overhead and investment capital. Starting from your home allows you to keep costs low initially until you establish the level of demand needed to support the expense for office space, clerical support, utility costs, and the other costs associated with operating a business.

Tax advantages are among the many advantages of operating a home-based business. It is possible to take deductions on rooms or space you use for business purposes. This is typically a pro-ration of utilities, maintenance, and house payments based on a percentage of the floor space used and the time you spend in your home office. (An IRS Form 8829 must be filed. All other expenses will be reported on Schedule C as in any business.)

Despite the many advantages, there are problems associated with operating a business from your home. First, there is the issue of space. It is critical that your work area be separate from your living space. Family members must recognize this as your space and appreciate your privacy. Phone lines should remain clear during business hours, and if necessary another line installed. An answering machine or answering service is absolutely essential so that important calls are not missed.

Zoning restrictions may be an issue depending on local ordinances and the type of home-business operated. Generally, ordinances that focus on parking, traffic, and noise restrictions will be relevant to home-based business owners. Some communities may disallow hiring employees who will work inside the home. To avoid problems, you should contact your local zoning office for information on zoning regulations.

Another challenge facing home-based entrepreneurs are the frequently experienced feelings of isolation and loneliness. They often miss interacting with co-workers and dread spending so much time alone. To combat loneliness and isolation, the home-based entrepreneur needs to plan business networking and social activities. They need to make an extra effort to be part of the community and to feel connected.

Time management is also an important consideration. When doing business from home, it is a good idea to schedule undisturbed time so that you can focus on the task at hand. Each week give a copy of your schedule to your family. Ask that you be interrupted only when absolutely necessary.

Purchasing an Existing Business

Purchasing an existing operation can have many advantages. Existing businesses generally have an established market, a suitable location, trained employees, and a proven profit potential. Having an existing customer base usually translates into steady cash flow. Therefore, buying a business often provides greater financial stability than establishing a business from the ground up.

A serious, prospective buyer must evaluate the financial condition of the company they are interested in. To do this, request financial statements and tax returns from the owner, and review them with your accountant or financial advisor. You should be able to answer the following questions before entering into an agreement:

- What is the general financial condition of the business?
- What trends do you notice?
- Are sales increasing or decreasing? What factors may have resulted in sales fluctuations i.e. new competitors?
- Are there any unusual changes in expenses? What caused these changes?
- Are accounts receivable increasing? Ask to see an accounts receivable aging schedule. Are their any uncollectable accounts?
- Is inventory in good condition? Is any inventory damaged or obsolete?
- Is the real estate and machinery in good condition? Should appraisals be obtained?
- Is the business paying accounts on time? What is their relationship with suppliers? What are the terms of credit with suppliers?

Non-financial aspects of the business must also be considered. Who are the key employees? Will all or any key employees remain? How do your skills compare with the skills of the present owner? If need be, will the present owner be available as a consultant after the business changes hands? It is usually advisable to have this as part of the contract.

Evaluating a business is complex. Depending on the size and nature of the business, there could be hundreds of issues which need to be considered. Generally, these will fall into the following categories:

1. Financial stability of the business
2. Past and future profit potential
3. Market demand for the business – location, competitive advantage, and existing customer base
4. Goodwill and other intangibles
5. Other considerations include; economic conditions, government regulations, or any other factors which may impact business operations

Your accountant can help you evaluate the business and advise you regarding the fairness of the asking price.

Also, before you buy, request a Tax Clearance Letter from the Department of Treasury and obtain a statement from the seller that all taxes have been paid.

Who Will Be Your Customers?

No matter what type of business you start, there must be a demand for the product or service you sell. Entrepreneurs must research the marketplace thoroughly and be reasonably satisfied that a market exists for the business they plan to start.

How does one go about researching their market? Market research doesn't have to be expensive or fancy. It is simply the process of finding objective answers to questions that all business owners must answer. Such questions include: Who are my customers? What are their needs? What are their buying patterns? Who are my competitors? Where are they located? What are their pricing strategies?

Answers to these questions determine:

- Where you will locate your business
- Your pricing strategies
- Your promotional strategies
- Your hours of operation, and most importantly
- Whether or not prospective customers will buy your products—if there are no customers, there is no business

There are many ways to research the market potential of a proposed business. You can talk to potential customers, industry experts, or owners of similar businesses outside your market area. Before starting her business, Carol Backus contacted owners of upholstery businesses to obtain information about pricing and advertising. This information proved invaluable to Carol, helping her price appropriately and avoid paying for ineffective advertising. Prospective business owners can gain a wealth of knowledge from others who have ventured before them. Libraries are an excellent resource for start-up businesses. Associations, trade journals, and government agencies can provide data on specific industries and demographic trends. Chapter 6 will provide more detail on market research sources and strategies.

Assessing the Risks

Most people have a perception of starting a small business as terribly risky. However, the risks associated with starting a small business vary depending on the business type, the amount of investment capital required, and the sacrifice, both personally and professionally, the owner makes in order to start his/her own business.

Perhaps the most perplexing myths about small business ownership are the statistics involving failure rates. Statements such as: "Four out of five small businesses fail within the first five years of operation," are assumed to be totally valid. Yet recent studies suggest that the outlook of small businesses is not that dismal. According to a 1994 Dun & Bradstreet census of 250,000 businesses, almost 70 percent of all the firms that started in 1985 were still around in 1994. This same study pinpointed the true failure rate at less than one percent of all businesses per year!

It is also important to note that statistics such as these do not make a distinction between creating a part-time self-employment opportunity and starting a full-scale business. Some business opportunities may be established initially to supplement another source of income, or to create a job opportunity. In this case, the individual has no plans to hire employees and may never move the operation out of his /her home. Other businesses are established on a full-scale, where the business owner operates full time, and is paid a salary from revenues immediately. In each situation, the individual is a self-employed business owner. However, there are tremendous differences in the level of risk involved, both financial and personal.

The message here is to listen with skepticism to the naysayers who believe small business success is unrealistic or unattainable. Each potential entrepreneur must evaluate their idea on its own merit and, according to many experts, chances are good that with proper planning most businesses will succeed. Consider the words of a D&B economist, "If four out of five small businesses failed every five years, Main Street in every town in America would look different after very short periods of time."

Still, prospective business owners must remember that many new businesses do fail, especially when the business owner is unprepared or uninformed. A prospective business owner must fully understand the limitations as well as the opportunities of business ownership. The following chapters will provide the prospective business owner with the tools needed to evaluate their idea and to prepare for the path that lies ahead.

References and Resources

Desmond, Glen, and Faulkner, Monica, *The Ideal Entrepreneurial Business For You*, Wiley & Sons, 1995.

Edwards, Sara and Paul, *Working from Home*, Tarcher/Putnam, New York, 1994.

Edwards, Sara and Paul, *Teaming Up; The Small Business Guide to Collaborating with Others to Boost Your Earnings Potential and Expand Your Horizons*, Tarcher/Putnam, New York, 1997.

Ellis, Gwen, *101 Ways to Make Money at Home*, Servant Publications, 1996.

Forbes, Christine, *"The Homebased Psyche,"* Entrepreneur Magazine, March, 1990, pp. 76-81.

Glieson, Kerry, *The High-Tech Personal Efficiency Program*, John Wiley & Sons, 1998.

Hyatt, Jashua, *"Should I Start a Business?"* Inc., February, 1992, pp. 48-58.

Johansen, John, *How to Buy or Sell A Business*, U.S. Small Business Administration, Office of Development, Publication Number 2.029.

Knight, Brian, *Buy the Right Business at The Right Price*, Upstart Publishing, 1990.

Martin, Thomas, *Valuation Reference Manual, The Business Owner Series*, Martin Communications, Inc. 1994.

Bank Of America Small Business Reporter, *How to Buy and Sell a Franchise*, 1987.

Patterson, Marni, *Doing Business on the World-Wide Web*, Crisp Publications, 1997.

Powers, Mike, *How to Open a Franchise Business*, Avon Books, 1995.

CHAPTER 4

THE FEASIBILITY STUDY:

A Self Assessment to Determine Business Feasibility

Almost everyone comes up with a good idea at least once in their life. The key is knowing if your idea has real market value. It is important that the potential entrepreneur assess the potential of his/her business idea. In other words, is there a market for the product or service and can it be sold at a profit? Furthermore, an individual who comes up with a "good idea" does not necessarily possess the skills and characteristics needed to successfully operate a small business. The feasibility study can help determine if the owner, as well as the business, has what it takes to succeed. Assessing initial feasibility is recommended as the first step since it can eliminate the additional work of developing a business plan, seeking financing, and the disappointment of following through on an idea that is not likely to succeed.

Successful entrepreneurs learn to take calculated risks. They seek answers to questions and learn ways to minimize the risks involved with starting a new venture. The business plan and the feasibility study are both important tools to minimizing risk and ensuring success in business. The business plan includes specific, detailed information about the owner's plan. The business plan is a management tool, but it is also a sales tool since it is often used to persuade potential investors or funders to invest. The elements of the business plan will be discussed in Chapter 6.

The feasibility study identifies potential pitfalls or critical flaws in the business concept. The feasibility study is important because it functions as an objective assessment of the proposed business and the owner's readiness to operate the business. As a potential entrepreneur you should seek out information that not only supports your plan but which challenges the feasibility of it as well. This critical analysis allows you to consider honestly the strengths and weaknesses of your venture.

Prior to starting a business, a person must first be able to say to themselves: *"I know myself, what motivates me, and what I need in order to be productive, successful, and happy. I understand what it means to own a business, and I have a clear picture of what my day-to-day life will be like once I start my business."*

Many people are attracted to the prospect of owning their own business because they like the idea of being their own boss. However, many do not consider the time and physical demands placed on a business owner, and find themselves working excessive hours for which they are not adequately paid. Some people may not be fully aware of what motivates them or what makes them happy. Being in business for yourself can be isolating, stressful, time-consuming, and frustrating. The nature of your business, where it will be located, and whether or not you will have employees will impact how well the business fits your personality and lifestyle needs. Understanding yourself and your day-to-day responsibilities as a business owner will help you form realistic expectations about what it means to own your own business.

Before investigating the feasibility of your idea, it is well to consider your goals and to consider how your proposed business fits into your lifestyle and long-term plans.

Goal Setting

It is a well known fact that written goals are more likely to be attained than those that remain unwritten. Therefore, it is critical that potential business owners take some time to assess and reassess their goals for the short-term and the long-term.

A helpful process for goal-setting and evaluating goals is to list both personal as well as business goals. Start with your personal goals. These are goals that relate to your family, church, hobbies, travel and any other activities which occupy your free time. Separate these goals into short-term (1 to 2 years) and long-term (3 to 5 years) goals.

Next, prioritize your goals by assigning a "1" to the most important goal, a "2" to the next important goal, and so on.

Next, write down your business goals. Business goals address your work or financial objectives. Business and financial goals include; How much money will you make? When will you retire? When will your business turn a profit? As with your personal goals, separate business goals into long-term and short-term goals and prioritize business goals from most important to least important.

Now carefully review your goals. Are your business and personal goals compatible? For example, if one of your goals is to spend more time with your family, is it feasible for you to establish a restaurant which will take years of working long hours? When conflicting goals occur, consider how you prioritized these goals. Are you willing to sacrifice the achievement of one goal in order to accomplish a more desirable goal?

You must also consider how your disability will impact your goals. For example, if you have a health condition which is adversely impacted by stress, you should consider the impact the business may have on your health.

The goal-setting process will help you evaluate your desire to start a business when weighed against the other possible options that life brings. Business ownership can be rewarding, but it also requires sacrifice. The time devoted to establishing and running a business is time taken away from some other activity. If the lifestyle changes resulting from the business have not been considered, it can mean disaster for the business and the owner!

After you've considered both your goals and priorities, you can then assess the feasibility of your proposed business. First, a potential entrepreneur or business owner must answer two questions:

1. *Do I possess the skills and personal characteristics to run a business?*
   An assessment of your skills and characteristics is needed to determine what skills and characterisitics you possess, and if business ownership is right for you. Consider the business you are starting, and if you have the skills, qualifications, and characteristics to make the business work.

2. *Does my proposed business possess the characteristics of a successful business operation?*
   Can you demonstrate a demand for your product or services? Does your business require significant resources to establish? If so, do you have the capacity to access the necessary funds? As the owner, do you have the necessary technical and operational skills to run the business?

The feasibility study considers both the individual and the business concept when assessing business viability. It is a tool that not only determines if business ownership is appropriate for you, but determines if and when additional skill-building or more information is needed.

Assessing Personal Skills and Characteristics and Business Feasibility

People often think of successful business owners as born entrepreneurs. However, those who succeed in business often possess characterisitics quite unlike the "typical entrepreneur." Researchers have found that personality traits of successful entrepreneurs differ from the personality traits of successful managers. "Entrepreneur-types" are creative, independent thinkers. They tend to be passionate about their ideas, and have a broad vision for the future. Because of their enthusiasm, entrepreneur-types tend to be starters, but are not always good at the day-to-day task of making an idea work. "Manager-types" on the other hand, usually excel at the day-to-day aspects of running a business. They are organized, reliable, and strategic.

Despite the diverse characterisitics of managers and entrepreneurs, each type has the potential to succeed in business. It is important that the entrepreneur or business owner be aware of their strengths and weaknesses and be willing to make changes in behaviors when necessary.

While it is commonly known that our basic personality traits are developed very early in life, it is also known that we have tremendous power to change or alter many behaviors as we grow and develop. If we understand what traits or characteristics are necessary in order to achieve our goals, we can make changes which will result in positive outcomes.

In Part One of this book, we learned how successful entrepreneurs achieved their goals, specifically what skills, characteristics, and work habits they developed that contributed to their success. In this section you will assess your own skills, characteristics and work habits. This personal assessment will help you ascertain if business ownership is right for you.

The following is a list of skills and characteristics which research has shown are important to business success. Each characteristic heading includes a definition of the characteristic and a list of questions for you to answer.

Answer "yes," "no," or "sometimes" to each question. Then give yourself an overall score using the following scale:

If you answer "Yes" to a majority of the questions in a category, give yourself a final score of "P":

P = The entrepreneur and/or the proposed business possess this characteristic

If you answer "no" to many of the questions in a category, give yourself a final score of "D" or "I":

D = The entrepreneur needs to develop this characteristic,

I = More information is needed.

When assessing your personal characteristics with respect to the proposed business, it is important to distinguish when there is need for development or where additional information must be gathered. When you answer "no" to a question, indicate whether you need to change a behavior "D" or if you need to gather more information "I". The extent to which you already possess these characteristics and are able to make the changes necessary to develop your weak areas, will impact your ability to succeed in business.

Problem Solving

People who succeed in business have the ability to identify a problem, identify the need for assistance, use available resources, work cooperatively with a variety of people, and make use of consultation.

Can you identify the resources needed to get a job done?

Are you willing to learn new techniques and ideas and are you able to adapt to change?

Are you able to effectively solve problems?

Can you prioritize work?

Score: _____

Optimism

Successful business owners are generally optimistic about their future. They have a basic feeling that things will go well for them.

Do you believe you can accomplish what others tell you you can't?

Do you have a positive view of the world, or do negative thoughts and feelings impact your outlook on life?

Do you believe that things will go well for you?

Do you believe you have control over your future?

Score: _____

Getting Things Done

Successful business owners are "action" oriented. They take steps every day that will get them closer to accomplishing their goals.

Are you hard working?

Are you task oriented?

Do you make daily to-do lists and follow them?

Are you goal-oriented?

Do you tend to focus on a project until it gets completed (or do you leave projects unfinished)?

Score: _____

Taking Risks

Successful business owners are risk-takers. They are willing to try new things and are able to accept failures as well as successes.

Are you a risk-taker?

Are you willing to risk your personal assets if necessary?

Are you generally among the first to try new technologies or new ways of doing things?

Are you a self-starter (or do you tend to need direction from others)?

Score: _____

Communication and Interpersonal Skills

Communicating your ideas, values, directions and goals will be important for long-term success in business. Business owners should possess the ability to communicate effectively – both verbally and in writing.

Do you generally like people?

Can you work well with all types of people?

Do you have lots of friends?

Are you effective at communicating your ideas both verbally and in writing?

Do you feel comfortable selling yourself or your ideas?

Score: _____

Commitment/Desire/Persistence

Starting a business requires considerable time and energy well before the benefits of hard work can be realized. It is important that an individual pursuing business ownership have a strong commitment to the business and a high degree of persistence to overcome obstacles – there will be many!

Are you highly committed to starting your business?
Do you persist if you cannot solve a problem right away,
(or do you tend to give up)?
Can you give specific examples of obstacles you have overcome to start your business?

Score: _____

Stress Management

Business ownership often creates stress in one's life. Those who succeed as business owners are able to remain cool under pressure.

Can you work well under stress (or do you tend to become
easily flustered or frustrated)?
Can you physically handle stress (or do you fear that stress
will adversely impact your health)?
Do you focus on those problems you can control and tend
not to worry about things you cannot control?
Are you able to handle multiple demands or projects
simultaneously?

Score: _____

Leadership

Those who succeed in business often possess the elusive quality of
leadership that allows them to influence people, accept responsibility and make decisions.

Are you willing to accept responsibility for business failures
as well as successes ?
Can you make well-informed decisions and act on them?
Do other people respect you and follow your lead?
Can you stick by your decisions (or do you often second-
guess yourself)?
Do you negotiate for a better outcome or just accept what
comes to you?
Are you persuasive?

Score: _____

Management Skills

The U.S. Small Business Administration cited lack of management
expertise as the number one reason for business failure.
Management expertise encompasses the ability to organize and
manage time and resources, communicate effectively, and to analyze situations and make sound business decisions. A successful
business has access to expertise in the following areas: financial

management, marketing and promotion, operations, personnel management, and knowledge of legal and accounting issues. If the business owner does not have an understanding of these areas, they must hire personnel, purchase expertise, or utilize other resources at their disposal.

Are you organized?

Do you keep close control over your spending and the financial management of your home and personal finances?

Do you plan your day in advance and are you careful to make the most of every minute?

Can you readily find objects you need (or do you spend too much time looking for things)?

Have you ever managed a business, an office, or a large project?

Score: _____

Technical or Operational Skills

Knowledge of the industry is vital to business success. A business owner must understand the environment in which they plan to operate and must also possess the technical skills required to provide the product or service.

Do you have experience in the type of business you want to establish?

Can you perform most of the essential functions of the business?

Will you enjoy the day-to-day activities of the business?

Score: _____

Market Demand

An assessment must be made regarding the level of market demand which exists for the product or service. An existing customer base, the size of the potential market, any unique competitive advantages, the number of competitors, and the degree to which the owner can cost effectively implement a sound marketing strategy all factor into the assessment of market demand. During the initial feasibility stage, basic information regarding market demand should be gathered. If the idea appears to have potential, further information can be gathered during the business planning process.

Do you know who your customers will be? What are their characteristics?

Do you know your competitors and their strengths and weaknesses?

Do you know where the business will be located?

Have you determined a pricing strategy?

Do you know how you will attract prospective customers? (Advertising, direct sales, media, etc.)

Do you understand what effects, if any, industry changes will have on your business?

Score: _____

Personal Credit/Financial Solvency

This characteristic assesses your ability to pay your bills and maintain a positive credit rating.

Do you generally pay your bills on time?

Have you requested a copy of your credit report? If so, is it positive?

If there are derogatory marks on your credit report, are they health-related?

Score: _____

Analyzing the Results

If you answered "yes" to most of these questions, you are probably well-suited to, and ready for, small business ownership. If you answered "no" to many of the questions, you may have given yourself one or two D's (need for development) as a final score. This means that you need to develop these areas, or re-consider your decision to become self employed.

If you need to change or develop a characteristic there are many opportunities to do so. The first step in making a change is understanding the behavior you want to change. Some characteristics are more difficult than others to change, and some may even be impossible. It is difficult for most of us to look honestly at ourselves and realize that we are who we are, and are not likely to change. It is important to remember that there is no "right" way to be. We are all unique and all make special contributions to the world.

In completing the questionnaire, you may have answered "no" to some of the questions simply because you didn't have the information. For example, you may not have access to the information on your credit report, or you may not have obtained information about your competitors. A "no" generally indicates that some action is needed prior to starting your business. This may involve gathering information or adjusting a behavior. For example, you may have answered "no" to the question, "Do you make daily to-do lists?" This should prompt you to start making to-do lists, and to begin following them.

In analyzing the questionnaire results you need to consider the type of business you are starting and if a particular characteristic is important to its success. For example, the questionnaire may reveal that you're not a risk-taker. However, if your business is a home-based, part-time venture, with no employees, and requires only a small investment, you may not need to be a tremendous risk taker. In other words, some of these characteristics may not be critical for your particular business.

In some situations, an individual's lack of skill in one area can be offset by excelling in another area. Robert Collinge would certainly answer no to being able to communicate effectively. But even though he wasn't able to communicate in the usual way, he found a way to make his business work by providing what his customers wanted, working hard, and excelling at the technical aspects of his business. Therefore, your own health and disability considerations must be taken into consideration, and if you do not possess a particular characteristic, consider how important the characteristic is, and if there is a way to be successful without it.

There are some business and personal characteristics that are critical no matter what type of business you start. For example, every business must have customers. There must be someone who will buy your products and services. This is true even if you operate a small, one-person, home-based business.

Research has shown that five of the characteristics included in the assessment are significant factors in the successful operation of a business. These five attributes are:

1. Commitment/Desire/Persistence
2. Management Expertise
3. Technical Skills
4. Market Demand, and
5. Credit History and Financial Solvency[2]

In determining whether your business idea is feasible, you should give greater weight to these five characteristics since lacking in one or more could seriously impede your ability to succeed.

Assessing Your Current Financial Situation

Usually a person's financial situation will influence their purchasing decisions. In other words, the resources you have, or are likely to get, will determine if you buy the Pinto or the BMW. The same is true when starting a business. Understanding your current financial situation will help you establish realistic goals.

For many individuals, income from another source can cover monthly expenses, i.e. a spouse's paycheck or disability benefits. Others must rely on revenues or profits from the business to pay monthly bills. Knowing what is needed each month is an essential step to assessing business feasibility. Assess your current financial situation, by completing the Personal/Family Budget (Form #1). This form reveals the level of net business income you need to pay your monthly bills.

---

[2]Goodman, Barbara, and Herzog, Roseanne, *The Business Assessment Scale*, Goodman, Herzog and Associates, 1994.

Next, complete the Personal Financial Statement (Form #2). This form identifies what resources you have to contribute to the business. (A similar form will be used by your banker to determine your loan viability.)

Obtain a copy of your current credit history. This will reveal your history of paying creditors. It is difficult to establish a business with a poor or inadequate credit history. Therefore, before you seek financing, previous credit problems should be remedied. If you have filed bankruptcy or have poor credit, don't despair – you are not alone. Many individuals with disabilities or chronic health problems, who have experienced long periods of hospitalization as well as sudden, dramatic changes in income have difficulty paying bills in a timely manner. If you have a sound reason for your credit problems, many lending institutions will take this into consideration. This is especially true if you can demonstrate the ability to keep current on existing obligations.

Form 1: Personal/Family Budget

Monthly Non-Business Income
- Spouse's Salary _____
- Investment Income _____
- Social Security _____
- Other income _____
- Retirement Benefits _____
- Less Taxes _____
- Net Monthly Income _____
- **Total Monthly Income** _____

Monthly Non-Business Expenses
- Rent/Mortgage _____
- Utilities _____
- Homeowner's Insurance _____
- Property Taxes _____
- Home Repairs _____
- Groceries _____
- Telephone _____
- Tuition _____
- Transportation _____
- Child Care _____
- Medical Expenses _____
- Clothing _____
- Insurance Premiums:
  - Life, Disability, Auto, Medical _____
- Miscellaneous:
  - Entertainment, Vacation,
  - Gifts, Dues, Fees, etc. _____
  - Auto Loans _____
  - Consumer Debt _____
- **Total Monthly Expenses** _____

Monthly Surplus/Deficit:
(Income-Expenses) _____

Of the five critical elements of the feasibility assessment (listed on page 51) obtaining access to financing is probably the easiest to remedy. If your business has tremendous market potential, if you have the management experience, technical skills, the commitment and desire, you can in many cases, identify the resources needed to start your business. In Chapter 7, you will learn various strategies for getting the money you need to start your business.

If your business requires more capital than you have access to, you may need to dramatically scale down your initial plan. Once in business, it is easier to obtain financing (as long as market demand can be demonstrated from actual sales). However, do not start the business without sufficient capital. Inadequate working capital can be terminal to many small businesses. Careful planning is needed to anticipate the levels of revenues generated and expenditures incurred in your first and second year in business. Financial projections are used for this purpose and are discussed later in Chapter 9.

Form 2: Personal Financial Statement

Assets
 Cash   _____
 Stocks, Bonds, Other Securities _____
 Accounts/Notes Receivable _____
 Life Insurance Cash Value _____
 Rebates/Refunds _____
 Autos/Vehicles _____
 Real Estate _____
 Vested pension/Retirement Accounts _____
 Other Assets _____
 Total Assets _____

Liabilities: _____
 Real Estate Loans _____
 Auto Loan Balance _____
 Notes Payable _____
 Taxes _____
 Other Liabilities _____
 Total Liabilities _____

Net Worth
 (Total Assets-Total Liabilities) _____

Conclusions

The decision to start a business may be one of the most important decisions of your life. The decision requires serious consideration of all the risks and sacrifices. You, the potential business owner must realistically assess your characteristics with respect to the type of business being established and any resulting changes in lifestyle the business will create.

Ideally, a prospective business owner will already possess most of the skills listed in the previous pages, but if they do not, they must acquire the necessary skills or identify a source outside themselves to bring these skills to the business. Partnerships are often formed with one individual who possesses a high degree of technical skill and another who possesses the needed management skills.

The feasibility study takes time. It requires seeking out information from a variety of sources and it requires careful assessment and consideration of all the factors – both personal and professional. Once the feasibility study is completed, you should have all the necessary information to make a decision whether or not to pursue your business.

After answering the questions in this chapter, you may decide that you are not ready for business ownership. You may decide to postpone starting your business until you are able to find a partner or gain more experience. Do not expect there will be a perfect time or a perfect situation. Inherent in starting a new venture are unknowns. Learning as you go is an inevitable and necessary aspect of long-term success.

CHAPTER 5

The Basics of Business Ownership

Every business owner, no matter how small their business, must determine how their business will be structured, what tax obligations they are required to fulfill, and what level of protection is needed to avoid exposing the business to unnecessary risk. This chapter provides the basic essentials regarding these fundamental aspects of starting a business. Decisions you make in the following areas may very well impact long-term business survival.

Choosing a Legal Structure

The legal structure of a business is determined by its size, market, and the products and services it provides.

Sole-Proprietorship: The simplest of all legal forms of an organization is the sole-proprietorship. In this legal form of doing business, the owner generally performs most key functions of the business and does not share control of the business with anyone.

Sole proprietorships must file a D.B.A. (Doing Business Under an Assumed Name) with their local county clerk's office. Sole proprietorships are not considered as separate legal entities. The owner and the business are considered one and the same for legal and tax reporting purposes.

Partnership: A partnership is an association of two or more persons to carry on as co-owners in business for profit. The partners should execute an agreement, in writing, setting forth the guidelines under which the partnership will operate and/or dissolve. It is advisable to consult with an attorney to assist in the formation of this type of entity.

Partnerships must file a U.S. Partnership Return of Income (Form 1065). This form is generally for informational purposes only. Each partner reports his share of the profit or loss on his/her individual tax return.

"C" Corporation: The corporation is the most formal and most complex of all legal structures. To establish a corporation the owners must file Articles of Incorporation with the appropriate state agency. The Articles of Incorporation specify the purpose or purposes for which the corporation is formed, the total authorized shares of the corporation, the classes of such shares, (i.e. common/preferred), and the address of the corporation's registered office.

Corporations must file an income tax return (Form 1120). A corporation and its owners are separate legal entities.

Subchapter "S" Corporation: This form of corporation is a tax designation. The Internal Revenue Code permits a corporation to be taxed at the share holder level. Profits and losses are reported on the tax returns of the owners and are taxed at the individual rate rather than the corporate rate. The corporation must file Form 1120 which is generally for information purposes only.

Like the "C" corporation, the owners of the "S" corporation share ownership through stock and the business is managed by a Board of Directors. Also like the C Corporation, the owner's liability is generally limited to the amount of capital contributed unless the owner acts as guarantor of corporate debt.

There are certain requirements that must be met for a corporation to be eligible to elect an "S" Corporation status. For more information contact the IRS and request publication 589.

Limited Liability Company: Many states have adopted a new form of legal ownership – the Limited Liability Company (LLC). The LLC has been designed to provide business owners with the flexibility and tax advantages of a partnership, and the protection against personal liability of a corporation.

The LLC in most states is treated as a pass-through entity for federal tax purposes and will not be subject to federal income taxes. Like the Subchapter S corporation, all profits will flow directly to the owners of the business.

This form of business ownership is especially desirable for those businesses which have traditionally been established as partnerships, such as real estate development operations, professional firms, and joint ventures formed for specific projects.

Unlike the Subchapter S corporation, the LLC may have an unlimited number of owners and there are no restrictions on the types of persons or entities permitted to be owners. In addition, the LLC may make allocations of income among its members and may make contributions of property on a tax-free basis. And unlike a limited partnership, all members of the LLC have limited liability. In a limited partnership, there must be at least one general partner who has unlimited liability.

To obtain additional information on the LLC and for guidance on which legal structure is right for your business, consult with an attorney who is well versed in corporate structuring.

Licenses, Permits, Regulations

Licenses & Permits

Some businesses and occupations require a license. Licensing regulations vary from state to state, but businesses and occupations most likely to require licenses include: doctors, dentists, architects, veterinarians, employment agencies, and marriage counselors. Depending on the state, there may be many more. Business owners should check with their state's Department of Commerce, Department of Licensing and Regulation, or Business Ombudsman office to obtain information on licenses and permits relevant to their industry.

Business permits may be required for various construction, operating, production, or waste disposal procedures. Again, contacting the appropriate state agency is the first step toward compliance with all regulations.

Zoning Restrictions

When starting or expanding a business, you must consider any zoning and building restrictions that apply to your situation. Business owners can obtain zoning guidelines by contacting their city assessor's office or township clerk.

When purchasing a building or facility, the local building inspector should be contacted to identify applicable construction codes, including barrier free design codes, electrical, mechanical, and plumbing codes, and any and all other codes which may be relevant to the construction of new facilities.

Environmental Regulations

Most states have strict environmental regulations and licensing requirements. Generally businesses that are engaged in processes or practices involving major alterations to the landscape must comply with strict governmental regulations. A special license is required for companies that engage in the following activities: building near waterways or wetlands, emitting substances into the air, discharging waste into the water, disposing or processing solid waste, or generating, hauling or disposing of hazardous waste. Those engaging in these activities must follow strict government guidelines. It is important that new business owners obtain the necessary information from their state's Department of Natural Resources.

Trademark, Copyrights, Patents

Trademarks

A trademark is the "brand name" by which we identify the goods or services of a particular manufacturer, distributor, or provider. The U.S. Patent & Trademark Office defines a Trademark as "a word, phrase, symbol or device, or any combination other than a trade name in its entirety, adopted and used to identify goods made or sold or services provided by a business and to distinguish them from similar goods made or sold by others." Registration of a trademark gives the owner of the mark certain privileges. Trademarks may be registered at the state level and with the U.S. Patent and Trademark office for use throughout the United States.

U.S. Patent and Trademark Office
Washington, D.C. 202311
Telephone (703) 557-5168

Copyrights

A copyright enables its owner to exclude others from reproducing certain works such as books, musical compositions, technical drawings, and computer programs. A copyright Certificate of Registration is obtained by filing an application with the Register of Copyrights. There is a small filing fee of $20.

> Register of Copyrights
> Library of Congress
> Washington, D.C. 20559

Patents/Inventions

Many people with disabilities and chronic health conditions have come up with product ideas for the purpose of making their lives easier. These products could be used by others with disabilities who, like the inventor, are looking for more efficient ways to get things done. In some cases, products invented for people with disabilities could have wide-spread appeal well beyond the disability community. The general public is often eager to buy products that make their lives easier as well.

There are two steps the inventor must take when developing a new product:

1. Protect their idea legally, and
2. Determine if their idea has market potential.

Inventors protect their ideas with patents. A patent is a government grant to an inventor that gives him/her the right to take legal action against others who, without the prior consent of the owner, make, use, or sell the invention covered by the patent during the time the patent is in force. A patent may be obtained by filing an application with the U.S. Patent and Trademark Office.

> U.S. Patent and Trademark Office
> Washington, D.C. 20231
> Telephone: (703) 557-5168

Many individuals with patented inventions have difficulty obtaining the start-up capital and the manufacturing expertise needed to get their idea off the ground. Often inventors presume their idea will sell and fail to properly evaluate the market demand of their product. This lack of information makes finding capital or a manufacturer extremely difficult.

Many states have programs centers that assist inventors. Some offer evaluation services, which review product ideas and assess their market potential. An example of one such program is the Wisconsin Innovation Service Center. You can contact them at 414-472-1365 or on the www at http://wisbus.uww.edu/innovate/invent.htm.

Inventors should beware of companies who sell their expertise regarding patents and inventions. Many of these companies make promises they can't keep and often charge exhorbitant prices for their services. When seeking assistance with your new invention confer with people in organizations whom you trust. Federal and state funded programs such as the Small Business Development Center or SCORE (Service Corp. of Retired Persons) in your area can provide names of reputable resources in your community.

Taxes: Federal, State and Local

The importance of keeping current and correct tax records cannot be understated. Failure to comply with tax requirements and deadlines can result in the assessment of substantial penalties and interest. Additionally, the IRS has the power to seize assets and terminate business operations in the event of serious delinquencies in tax payments. Ignorance is almost never an acceptable explanation, so the business owner must be aware of tax regulations and requirements.

Federal Employer Identification Number: All IRS forms filed require a federal employer identification number (FEIN) or commonly referred to as the "Tax ID Number." If your business is a corporation or a partnership, or if you plan to hire employees, a FEIN must be obtained by filing a form SS-4 with the IRS.

Income Taxes: Different income tax requirements are applied to different types of legal organizations, which were reviewed earlier in the chapter. When assessing the appropriate legal structure, tax requirements should be taken into consideration.

Payroll Taxes: Any business with employees must comply with federal and state payroll requirements. There are four types of payroll taxes:
- Income Tax Withholding (Federal, State, and Local if applicable)
- Federal Social Security Tax (FICA)
- Federal Unemployment Tax (FUTA)
- State Unemployment Tax

(Additional information is provided in the next section, Hiring Employees.)

Single Business Tax: Corporate entities and individuals conducting business in a particular state may be required to pay a single business or franchise tax. This tax requirement varies from state to state so it is necessary to contact your state treasury office.

Sales Tax: Most states require businesses to collect sales tax from purchasers of tangible goods. The business is required to keep accurate records of transactions and to remit funds in accordance with established guidelines. For more information, contact your state treasury office.

Hiring Employees

Unemployment Insurance: Unemployment insurance protects workers who lose their jobs due to staff layoffs or cutbacks. Employers must pay both state and federal unemployment taxes. The funds used to pay unemployment benefits are covered by accumulated taxes paid on employees' wages during their employment.

Federal Unemployment Insurance (FUTA) is collected by the IRS. When an employer files its employer identification number, the IRS will send the necessary forms for filing and paying unemployment insurance.

Income Tax Withholding: All employers with one or more employees must withhold federal income tax from wages paid to their employees. Most states also require income tax withholdings. For additional information contact your state's treasury office and the IRS (1-800-829-1040).

Social Security Taxes: The federal law also requires that employers withhold social security taxes from employees' wages. These taxes are paid to the IRS along with a matching amount paid by the employer.

Workers' Compensation Insurance: Workers' Compensation Insurance is required in almost every state. Workers' Compensation protects the worker when an injury occurs on the work site or as a consequence of a work activity. Most employers obtain workers' compensation insurance from commercial insurance companies. Premium rates vary dramatically depending on the type of industry and the employer's track record. It is wise to shop around for a competitive rate.

Employees vs. Independent Contractors

Many business owners try to lower costs by hiring individuals on a contract basis. The issue of contract vs. employee relationships is often confusing. An independent contractor is not subject to withholding, FICA or unemployment taxes on the amount s/he receives for a job. Additionally, a potential employer is held responsible for the actions of an employee but may not be held liable for the acts of the independent contractor. Your business would require the independent contractor to be bonded or insured.

Prior to establishing an independent contractor relationship, you should be aware of the criteria established by the IRS for hiring contract labor. This list of twenty or so factors can be obtained from your local IRS office.

Note: Laws governing business requirements and regulations vary from state to state, therefore it is important to contact local agencies for information and to seek out the advice of attorneys and accountants when needed.

Managing the Risks

What is Risk Management? Insurance authorities define it as "the management of uncertainty concerning loss." That is, how the business owner chooses to handle the risk or chance that his/her business will suffer as a result of some unforeseen circumstance. Business owners should be concerned with five major types of common business risks:

1. Changes in economic, market, and technological conditions,
2. Losses from theft, shoplifting and bad debt,
3. Disasters caused by weather, geological conditions, hazards, etc.
4. Liabilities arising from negligence or other actions, and
5. Death or disability of key executives.[3]

---

[3]Van Voorhis, Kenneth, *Entrepreneurship and Small Business Management*, Allyn and Bacon, 1980.

The first business risk, "changes in economic, market, and technological conditions" cannot be insured against. It is up to the owner(s) to be current on economic conditions and technological changes and how these may impact market trends.

The last four business risks are insurable. In each case, the business owner has two choices; they can decide to purchase insurance or they can choose to live with the risk. In some situations, the business owner may decide that the risk is so minimal that insurance is not warranted. The purchase of insurance to remove a risk may be too expensive to be realistic. The business owner must balance the magnitude of each potential loss and its probability of occurring with the cost of insurance coverage for that loss. The owner should ask questions regarding possible risks: "What would happen to this firm if such-and-such happened?" If the results would be absolutely devastating, even if a very small probability exists, the owner should seriously consider insurance coverage.

Establishing the proper legal structure, protecting your idea and effectively managing the risks associated with your particular business are necessary steps to take prior to getting your business off the ground. Careful consideration of the issues discussed in this chapter may prevent future disputes, litigation, and financial loss.

This chapter provided a simple overview of issues relating to legal structure, taxation, and risk management. These topics are complex and could fill a book by themselves. Before making serious decisions that could impact the future of your business, it is important to seek the advice of experts whom you trust. Lawyers, accountants and insurance professionals can provide guidance in these areas. While their fees may seem at times prohibitive, these professionals are likely to save you money in the long term.

References and Resources

Dent, Gregory, and Johnson, Jeffrey, *Tax Planning Made Easy for the Self-Employed*, John Whiley and Sons, 1996.

Frasier, Lynne Ann, *The Small Business Legal Guide*, Sourcebooks, Inc., 1998.

Freidman, Robert, *The Upstart Small Business Legal Guide*, 2nd Edition, Upstart Publishing, 1998.

Incorporating a Small Business, U.S. Small Business Administration Management Aid Number 6.003.

Mendelson, Steven, B., *Tax Options and Strategies for People with Disabilities*, Demos Vermande, 1996

Schmedel, S., Morris, K, and Siegel, A., *The Wall Street Journal's Guide to Understanding Your Taxes*, Lightbulb Press, 1994.

CHAPTER 6

The Business Plan: Charting Your Success

The business plan is a tool for planning, communicating, and organizing your idea. Preparing a business plan is an important step because it forces the owner to establish goals and clearly outline how these goals will be met. Chapters 4 and 5 provided the fundamental or critical issues that every prospective business owner must consider. In those chapters, your business goals were defined, your business idea and personal skills were assessed, and some of the details regarding legal structure, taxation, and risk management were considered. Now it's time to put this information in writing.

Many lending institutions require that a business plan be submitted along with a loan application. The business plan communicates to the lender how the owner plans to turn the idea into a profit making enterprise, and how the loan will be repaid. The value of a well thought-out business plan, however, extends far beyond the search for initial investment capital. The business plan is important for existing businesses because it helps to identify market areas and to plan for expansion and growth. Many successful business owners use their business plan as a management tool to gauge their progress and assess their performance. Once goals and objectives are established, business owners should occasionally revisit these goals and use them as indicators for charting future benchmarks.

Writing a business plan does not have to be a stressful or complicated process. You probably already have most of the information needed to complete your plan. Just build on the information gathered in the previous chapters, use the outline on the following pages, and write as clearly as possible. Before long, a comprehensive and organized document will emerge.

There are many variations of business plan outlines, but most include the elements on the following pages. In Appendices G, H, and I you will find samples of business plans for three types of businesses – retail, manufacturing, and service. Use the outline on the following pages and these sample plans to develop a business plan for your business.

The Business Plan Outline

Cover Page

Include the business name, address and phone number, the owner(s) name, the title of the document, and date.

Executive Summary or Statement of Purpose

The Executive Summary gives the entrepreneur an opportunity to *sell* the idea to a lender or investor. It includes all the key points discussed throughout the plan and provides compelling reasons why the business and the owner will be successful in the proposed business venture. The points addressed in the executive summary are:

- The purpose for writing the plan
- The owner's goals for the business and benchmarks used
- If financing is being sought, an indication of how much is needed, how the funds will be used, how the funds will be repaid, and what the terms of the loan requested will be
- Your reason for starting the business
- A brief statement about the market opportunity
- A brief summary of the owner's qualifications
- A statement about why the business will be successful

Table of Contents

This section should be included for easy reference to your plan.

Business Description

The business description includes basic information about the business.

- What is the type or nature of the business – is it service-based, retail, or manufacturing?
- What is the product or service to be sold?
- What is the legal structure of the business?
- Who owns the business?
- What is the method of distribution for the product or service?
- What is the status of the business - new, take-over or expansion?

The description should provide the reader with some basic knowledge and understanding of your business and how it functions.

Market Analysis

The business plan must include reliable information regarding the market to be served. An expansion of the information gathered during the feasibility stage will generate answers to the following questions:

- What is the size of the market and the present and projected population of each market segment?
- What are the needs, or perceived needs, of the market?
- How will my product or service satisfy these needs?
- How will prices be determined?
- What types of data/sources were used to gather information? i.e. census data, surveys, magazine articles, published research, and/or focus groups.

There are many ways to gather market data. Marketing research from both primary and secondary sources can be found in published books, magazines, surveys, and census data. Information found in these resources may be used to demonstrate the demand or need for your business. For example, if you are establishing a retail clothing store, secondary data may include articles on recent trends in clothing purchases. Information from retail associations, such as average sales volume, profit levels, and inventory turnover may also be useful. Telephone directories can be used to estimate the number of competitors in your area. Traffic patterns, which provide statistics regarding traffic flow, may be helpful in evaluating potential business sites. Secondary research materials can be found at most libraries. Relevant information can also be obtained from trade associations, government agencies, and colleges and universities.

Primary research is information gathered directly from customers or potential customers. Surveys, telephone interviews, focus groups, and questionnaires are frequently used to gather primary information. Primary research is critical when introducing a new product or service to a market area. For example, if you plan to sell your "tasty new diet cookies" in local specialty shops, you should get opinions of the taste by providing samples to potential customers and interviewing them. (It would be important that taste testers not know that these cookies are your recipe and that you are planning to market them. You should appear as a market researcher interested in only objective information-good or bad).

If you do not feel equipped to perform the research yourself, there are professional market research firms who provide this service for a fee. Paying for reliable information up front could identify deficits in your plan and result in savings down the road.

Competition

It is important to make a realistic assessment of the strengths and weaknesses of your competition. Information from competitors is used to identify your product/service niche, establish pricing strategies, determine your location, or any number of other strategic decisions you must make prior to starting your business. This section of your plan should answer the following questions:

- Who are my competitors?
- Where are they located?
- What is their size?
- What are their strengths and weaknesses?

A competitive analysis is important when evaluating your strategic options. The analysis should include basic information about each of your competitors including: number of years in business, key managers, and pricing and promotional strategies. Critically and objectively analyze the operations of your competitors in comparison to yours. What can you learn from them? Can you anticipate any future actions they might take?

In some cases (but not many), a new business will not have "direct" competitors.

Direct competitors are companies that sell the same or a similar product or service that your company sells. "Indirect" competitors sell a substitute product or service. In other words, the customer may buy a substitute product/service with a similar result.

A business may not have direct competitors if their product or service meets a new, not previously defined need. If by manufacturing a new product, a company actually 'creates' a need and if it is the only company which can meet the need, then it may be operating in an environment free of direct competitors. For example, assume a pharmaceutical company introduces a new drug that treats an illness that was until now untreatable. This company would have no direct competitors. If however, the condition had previously been treated using homeopathic remedies, these remedies would be considered as indirect competition, even if the new drug produces much better results.

Caution should be taken when assessing your competitive situation. Owners of small businesses routinely underestimate their competition, and consequently overestimate the demand for their products or services. There are direct or indirect competitors in practically every type of business. One way to determine if you have competitors is to ask yourself: "Are my potential customers getting their needs met presently by using another product or service?" If your answer is yes, than you have competition. It doesn't matter if the competitor's service is significantly different or inferior, competition still exists and should be included as part of the business plan.

Competitive Advantage

Every new business should have at least one competitive advantage. If it does not, the owner must question the market value of the product or service, and the rationality of starting the business. Competitive advantage can be a lower price, more experienced personnel, a better location, or higher quality products. Many companies have a competitive advantage through new products which have been developed and patented.

Marketing and Promotional Strategies

In this section, indicate what methods can be used to expand your current market share, what special promotions will be offered to customers, and how promotional strategies will be tracked. Also provide a detailed advertising budget.

Provide specific examples of how you plan to attract your target market. What kinds of promotional strategies or techniques will be implemented to attract potential customers to your product or service? Television, radio, news print advertising, direct sales calls, telemarketing, brochures, trade shows, and direct mail are all examples of promotional strategies.

Location

For many businesses, physical location of the business plays a critical role. In others, the business location will be irrelevant. If the former is true, than a section should be included about the location and why the location will benefit the business and meet the needs of the customer base.

Questions to answer:

- What is the layout and what are the physical features of the building?
- What renovations are needed?
- Is parking adequate?
- Is the building visible to potential customers?
- Is the building on a main street and what is the traffic flow?
- What type of businesses are in the area?
- Is there much business turnover in the area?

Answers to these questions will help you determine if you have identified the right location for your business.

Management

The owner's ability to manage the new business is an important criteria for success. In this section, demonstrate your ability to manage the proposed business by including the following:

- A personal and work history of the owner(s).
- The duties and responsibilities of the owner(s).
- How business operations will be managed.
- Goals and objectives, in measurable terms, of the owner(s) and manager(s), and a plan for how these will be reviewed.
- The salaries to be drawn by the owner(s) and manager(s), and
- A list of key outside advisors and resources.

Include current resumes of owners and key managers.

Personnel

This section specifies how you will attract and keep good employees. A personnel plan reveals information on the personnel needs of the business and, for existing businesses, gives a profile of the employees, including their background and specific areas of expertise.

- What critical functions are performed by employees?
- How many people will be hired?
- How much will they be paid?
- Will benefits be offered?
- How will employees be identified and selected?

Provide job descriptions and qualifications needed for each job classification.

Operations Plan

An operations plan is usually included in plans for manufacturing businesses. This section describes the production process. Non-technical language should be used so that any banker or investor can understand the basic process of manufacturing the product.

Financial Plan

The financial plan includes information about the financial condition of your business or proposed business. If you are seeking a loan to start or expand your business, this section is probably the most important. It is critical that the information provided be as complete and accurate as possible.

The following financial documents should be included in your business plan:

1. Beginning balance sheet and projected balance sheets for two years
2. Projected income statements for two or three years
3. Cash flow projections for two to three years
4. A personal financial statement listing all personal assets and liabilities for each of the owners (If you are applying for a loan, most lending institutions require you to complete their personal financial statement)
5. The amount of capital to be invested and the sources and uses of funds.

For more information on managing the finances of your business, refer to Chapter 9, in the next section.

Completing the Plan

Preparing a business plan can seem daunting, but the process is absolutely do-able for almost any adult. If the thought of preparing a business plan makes you anxious, try to break down the plan by section, and attempt to complete one section at a time. Once the preparer understands the elements of the business plan, the process becomes less overwhelming. When preparing the plan, consider how it will be used. If the plan is to be used primarily as an internal management document, then it is likely to be a detailed document. However, if the plan will be used to obtain financing, it is not necessary that every detail of your business be included. Lenders and investors generally do not need or want to read a lengthy document. A business plan of 10-15 pages is usually sufficient. Also, if you use the plan to attract financing or investment capital, sell your business by focusing on the strengths and opportunities of your venture.

The plan should include your clearly defined goals and should specify how you intend to accomplish these goals. A lender who does not understand your business, and how and why it will be successful, will probably not approve your application for financing.

Examples of business plans for three types of businesses – service, manufacturing and retail are provided in the appendices. The businesses are fictional. They are provided for use as guides. You will note that the plans vary in scope and size. Generally speaking, the more complex the business, the more detail necessary for the business plan.

If you'd like assistance with your plan, there is local help available. SBDC's (Small Business Development Centers) or SCORE (Service Corps. of Retired Executives) consultants can help by reviewing your plan and identifying potential pitfalls and obstacles. SCORE offers an on-line counseling service so you can get answers right from home. To obtain more information, check out their web site: www.score.org.

References and Resources

Burton, E. James, and McBride, W., *Total Business Planning: A Step-by-Step Guide with Forms*, Wiley & Sons, 1991.

Corello, Joseph and Hazelgren, Brian, *The Complete Book of Business Plans*, Sourcebooks, 1995.

Eliason, Carol, *The Business Plan for Homebased Business*, U.S. Small Business Administration Office of Business Development, Management Aid Number 2.028.

Business Plan for Retailers, U.S. Small Business Administration Office of Business Development, Management Aid Number 2.020.

Business Plan for Small Manufacturers, U.S. Small Business Administration Office of Business Development, Management Aid Number 2.007.

Business Plan for Small Construction Firms, U.S. Small Business Administration Office of Business Development, Management Aid Number 2.008.

Malburg, Christopher, *The All-In-One Business Planner*, Adams Media Corporation, 1994.

Zuckerman, Laurie, B., *On Your Own: A Women's Guide to Building a Business*, Upstart Publishing, Second Edition, 1990.

CHAPTER 7

Finding $$$ To Start Your Business

So you have determined that your idea has potential, you have thoroughly researched your market, and you have completed a business plan. Now it's time to find the funds needed to start your business.

Finding money may not be as difficult as you might think. Plenty of opportunities exist for enterprising individuals who remain tenacious in their search. This chapter provides a variety of funding alternatives – some conventional and some not so conventional, as well as strategies for getting the capital you need to get up and running. The following pages include both funding options available to the general public, as well as funds specifically for people with disabilities and chronic health conditions.

General Sources of Financing

Personal Income, Family, Friends

In recent years, loans for small business start-ups and expansions have become easier to access, still most lending institutions resist financing higher risk, start-up ventures. This is why most aspiring entrepreneurs look to their own finances or assistance from relatives or friends to obtain the necessary funds to get their venture up and running. A recent Inc. magazine study of the fastest growing companies in the U.S. revealed that start-up capital for more than half of the businesses came from the owner's personal savings. Funds from family members comprised 10 percent, while bank loans and charge cards accounted for only 7 percent.

When borrowing from friends or relatives, it is wise to establish clear expectations regarding the risks involved and the method of repayment. It is not uncommon for relationships to sour as a result of financial disputes. Therefore, a written, legal contract is a necessity. The document should include a repayment plan, time frames, and a process for handling disputes.

Partners

Partnerships may be a constructive form of collaboration and an excellent way to raise start-up or expansion capital. Partners often bring much more than money to a business. They are business associates, personal acquaintances, or informal contacts who share similar business goals and who recognize a market opportunity when they see one. They often add knowledge, skills, and their own circle of business contacts. Partners can be excellent cheerleaders or coaches, helping to motivate each other to set benchmarks and meet deadlines.

Entrepreneurs are usually innovative and creative, but often lack focus and organization. Partners often bring skills that turn an idea into a viable business. Wise entrepreneurs assess their skills, abilities, and personality traits and identify potential partners who complement these characteristics and who bring needed skills and abilities to the operation.

Unlike family or friends, partners are not interested in investing because they care about you, they are interested in investing because they believe in your business and expect to gain some financial return. They may share your vision for the company and may have the same degree of passion and commitment. For this reason, partnerships are often more desirable than borrowing money from family and friends.

Contrarily, partnerships have a down-side. They can be tenuous at times and disputes between partners can devastate a vulnerable new business. A partnership is like a marriage, the parties must share the same vision and goals and have the same basic philosophies regarding business management. The wise entrepreneur will avoid jumping into a partnership before engaging in discussions which illuminate the goals, personal habits, characteristics, beliefs, and management style of the potential partner. Prior to signing any papers, both partners should understand their role in the business and know what decisions, if any, can be made unilaterally.

Banks

You may have heard it said that "banks lend money to people who need it the least." Many banks avoid making small business loans because of the risks and the costs associated with processing business loans of small amounts. Loan base limits may be as high as $100,000 or as low as $20,000 depending on the bank. Loan officers try to avoid small loans that require large amounts of investigative work. This is especially true if the loan is considered by the banker as risky, such as loans for start-up businesses. To counteract inadequacies in a loan proposal, the entrepreneur should have a carefully prepared and well organized business plan.

Some banks have centralized decision making. Therefore, the loan officer receiving your application may not have the authority to approve the loan. He or she must "sell" the idea to a committee or decision maker that you will never meet. The loan officer can be your champion if you sell your business in a clear and convincing manner. Provide the loan officer with information that presents compelling evidence that your business will succeed.

If you need a loan to start your business, you should be knowledgeable about how the bank will evaluate your proposal. There are a number of factors or criteria banks and other lending institutions use to make lending decisions.

First, the lender will evaluate your credit history. If your credit history reveals a record of slow payments or a bankruptcy, the problem should be remedied if at all possible. Regular payments to creditors is important, as is keeping current on all existing debts, and lenders should be provided an explanation as to the cause of any credit problem. Obtain a copy of your credit report and attempt to clear any erroneous information. Your explanation of a credit flaw (up to 100 words) can be added to your credit file. A lender may make exceptions to poor credit if the explanation appears reasonable and if the proposal looks solid otherwise.

Second, the lender will evaluate your ability to repay the loan. This assessment is based on the cash flow of the borrower. For start-up businesses with no previous track record, the banker will identify other sources of income such as a spouse's pay check or income from disability checks or worker compensation. Banks do consider Social Security benefits as income and cannot use 'lack of long-term employment' if it is due to a disability as a reason for denial.

Be prepared for the banker by providing all the necessary financial documents. Tax returns, balance sheets, income statements, proformas, and a personal financial statement will be required. Understand these documents and know your numbers. Be able to explain where you came up with them and why they are realistic. If you have these documents prepared in advance, the loan officer will be impressed and grateful. Also, remember to build loan payments into your proformas.

Third, the lender will evaluate your ability to secure the loan. The lender will look at existing assets and the assets to be acquired with loan proceeds. Generally, the lender will approve loans which can be fully secured. The bank's value of collateral is rarely what an asset is actually worth. Banks use resale or liquidation value rather than book value to determine the amount of collateral required. The liquidation value is what the bank would get if it were forced to sell the asset. For example, if a business owner seeks a loan to finance the purchase of inventory, the inventory value assessed by the bank, for collateral purposes, will be much less than the actual value of the inventory. The best collateral is a certificate of deposit because it can be easily transferred into cash. The worst collateral is specialized machinery which has limited application and which cannot be readily sold.

To mitigate the risk for loans that lack sufficient collateral, bankers often make use of the SBA's loan programs. These loans will be discussed in greater detail later in the chapter.

Fourth, the lender will consider the business idea and current market conditions by asking if the timing is right for this type of business, what sort of competitive environment exists, and what the industry trends appear to be. Again, your business plan will prove valuable to the lender by answering some critical questions. Be careful not to present your business as 'too good to be true.' Bankers are not likely to believe information that appears one-sided or embellished. For starters, a competitive analysis should include both positive and negative aspects of your competitor's operation.

Finally, the lender will consider the level of personal risk taken by the business owner.

It is rare to see a bank finance 100% of the required capital needed to establish a venture, especially if the business owner has little or no previous experience with the lender. Consequently, in most cases, the borrower should be prepared to make a personal investment.

Home Equity Loans

Home equity loans borrow against the equity from your home. Most home equity loans come with variable interest rates and usually offer relatively low rates. Home equity lines of credit require the borrower to use their home for collateral, placing the borrower's home at risk if the loan is not repaid. When home-equity financing is being considered, shop for the best interest rates and payment terms possible.

Credit Card Financing

When initial cash needs are minimal, entrepreneurs often turn to their credit cards to finance new ventures. This is especially true in periods where interest rates are low. On those occasions when very low introductory rates are offered to attract new customers, credit card companies can be an excellent, albeit limited, source to finance a small business. Credit card rates can be as low as 5.9% and are usually offered for 6 months to a year. After the special offer is over, however, interest rates soar to as high as 20%. So using credit cards to start a business should be done only to finance short-term needs and only if cash will be available within a couple of months to pay off the debt.

SBA Loan Programs

The U.S. Small Business Administration (SBA) is a federal agency created to provide technical and financial assistance to the nation's small businesses. The SBA offers a number of loan programs which are usually made as guarantees through a participating SBA lender or bank. The SBA makes funds available to businesses that cannot obtain financing through normal lending channels.

The SBA over the past several years has ebbed away from providing loans to individuals*, and instead has moved towards a more risk-averse, guaranteed lending strategy. Under the guaranteed lending program, the business owner applies at a participating SBA lending institution. If the application looks good to the banker, s/he will send the documentation to the SBA. If approved by the SBA, the loan amount is then guaranteed by the Small Business Administration.

---

*The only direct loan programs available in recent years are the Handicapper Assistance Loan (HAL) Program and the Disabled Veterans Loan Program. However, congress has not appropriated funds for these programs and when funds are available, they are extremely difficult to access.

7(a) Loan Guarantee Program

Section 7(a) of the Small Business Act authorizes the SBA to guarantee loans to small businesses that cannot obtain financing through normal lending channels. The program is designed to promote small business formation and growth by guaranteeing long-term loans to qualified candidates.

This program is delivered through commercial lending institutions. Loans are available for many business purposes, such as real estate, expansion, equipment, working capital, or inventory. The SBA generally will guarantee up to 80 percent of the loan amount.

LowDoc - Low Documentation Loan Program

The LowDoc (low documentation) loan program resulted from a recent initiative by the SBA to make their lending programs easier for banks to access. This program reduces the paperwork involved in the application process for loan requests of $100,000 or less, thereby making it easier for banks to participate in making loans of smaller amounts. The SBA uses a one-page application and relies primarily on the strength of the applicant's character and credit history.

There are other loan programs available through the Small Business Administration under the 7(a) Loan Guarantee Program. For additional information on SBA loan programs, call the SBA Answer Desk – 1-800-8-ASK-SBA. The SBA TDD number is (202) 205-7333.

Small Business Investment Companies (SBIC)

Small business investment companies exist to supply equity capital, long-term loans and management assistance to qualified businesses. The privately owned and operated SBIC's use their own capital and funds borrowed from the Small Business Administration to provide financing to small businesses in the form of equity securities and long-term loans. SBIC's are for-profit lending institutions that specialize in "small" business financing. Only firms that are identified as small are eligible for financing. The SBA defines a company as small when its net worth is $6 million or less and its average net (after tax) income for the preceding two years does not exceed $2 million.

Some SBIC's specialize in providing lending opportunities to specific industries or to small businesses owned by socially or economically disadvantaged persons. SBIC's are primarily interested in financing existing companies with some proven track record. If you are trying to finance a start-up, this is probably not a good place to start. To obtain more information about SBIC's, contact the SBA office nearest you.

SBA Micro Loan Demonstration Program

In 1991 the SBA created a new program to help women, minorities, and low-income entrepreneurs obtain business loans. The program lends money to intermediary lenders who in turn, lend the money to special, targeted populations. The "micro" loans cannot exceed $25,000 and are typically higher risk loans. These programs relax loan criteria and therefore will approve loans from individuals who have less than perfect credit, limited collateral, and lower levels of income.

There are currently 109 intermediary lenders operating in the United States. For a complete listing of these programs see Appendix D.

Leasing Companies

An increasingly popular way to finance equipment and furniture is through leasing companies. Leasing is a way to obtain needed equipment without tying up cash. The business owner, instead of borrowing the cash needed to purchase the equipment, makes arrangements with a leasing company who purchases the items. The equipment is leased to the business owner for a set period of time. The title of the property is retained by the leasing company.

While leasing generally costs more than purchasing, it is also tax deductible, is generally not depreciated, and may not be listed as a liability on the business' balance sheet. Like banks, leasing companies do extensive credit checks on applicants, but may be willing to accept a higher level of risk in return for higher interest rates.

Venture Capital/Private Investors

Venture capitalists seek opportunities that have a high potential for growth and a high return on their capital. These investments are made on an equity basis, and investors, in effect, become co-owners of the business. Investors frequently take part in the management of the business and may require a controlling interest.

Investors seek a high return within a relative short period of time. Their intent is to sell their share of the business back to the entrepreneur or to other investors. Venture capital is usually invested in high tech ventures or new products where entry into the market place is expected to yield high returns.

Private investors may invest in businesses of all types and sizes. These individuals, often referred to as "angels," are usually wealthy members of your community who are willing to risk capital to finance small businesses. Those successful in attracting investors usually have had some previous contact with a potential investor, either through a family member, friend, or as an acquaintance.

Life Insurance Policies

Life insurance policies are an often overlooked type of financing. Most life insurance policies can be borrowed against at very competitive rates. Insurance companies generally perform less pre-screening than banks and therefore may accept candidates with less than perfect credit.

Economic Development Grants and Loans

Some local governments offer grants or loans to businesses that create jobs in their community. Many of these programs pool funds from several banks to make higher risk loans to new businesses. These are usually operated through Economic Development Offices and are available only to candidates with business operations within the city or county lines. Grants may be available for businesses interested in moving to a particular location, but this is usually the case only if the business will create a number of jobs in the community.

To find out about loan opportunities in your area call or write the Economic Development Planning Commission (202) 482-2873. Room H3719 Herbert C, Hoover Building, Washington, D.C. 20230. Or contact your local Small Business Development Center or Economic Development Office.

Farmers Home Administration

Farmers Home Administration (FHA) loans are available to existing and start-up businesses which operate in rural communities. Business and industry loans may be made in any area outside the boundary of a city of 50,000 or more and its immediate adjacent urbanized areas with population density of no more than 100 persons per square mile. Priority is given to applications for projects in open country, rural communities, and towns of 25,000 and smaller.

Loans are made in the form of a loan guarantee whereby the agency contracts to reimburse the lender for a maximum of 90 percent of the principal and interest. Applicants apply for these loans through private lenders. The rates are generally competitive.

The Farmers Home Administration has offices in nearly every rural county in the United States. FHA offices are listed in telephone directories under the U.S. Government, U.S. Department of Agriculture. You may also write the FHA headquarters: Farmers Home Administration, USDA, Washington D.C. 20250.

U.S. Department of Agriculture Rural Business and Industry Loans

The Business and Industry Loan Guarantee Program guarantees loans by eligible local lenders to businesses to benefit rural areas. The primary purpose is to create and maintain employment and improve the economic and environmental climate in rural communities. The program approves larger projects that generally require a minimum of $500,000 and typically guarantees losses on up to 80 percent of the original loan amount. Inability to obtain other credit is not a requirement.

Loan proceeds can be used for working capital, real estate, and machinery and equipment. The loan applicant must first obtain approval from a participating lending institution. Final decisions are made at the state level by the Rural Business Cooperative Service of the USDA.

Small Business Innovation and Research Grants

Small businesses with new product ideas may qualify for federal Small Business Innovation and Research (SBIR) grants. These grants allow companies to research a product idea without risking company resources. If the idea fits the federal government's priorities and meets its criteria for funding, a company could research an idea, develop prototypes, test and evaluate the product, and market the innovation and the government pays the tab! The SBIR program involves 11 different federal agencies that make grants specifically to small companies for research and innovation projects.

Companies are initially eligible to receive Phase I funding up to $50,000 for researching the product idea. Upon completion of Phase I companies may be eligible for up to $200,000 in Phase II funds for use in developing and test marketing the concept. To obtain information on SBIR grants contact an SBA office or Small Business Development Center near you.

Loans and Grants for Persons with Disabilities and Chronic Health Conditions

Few states have established loan funds specifically for start-up and existing businesses owned and operated by people with disabilities and chronic illnesses. And many persons with physical limitations, like other entrepreneurs, find bank financing out of their reach.

Fortunately there are other options. On the following pages, non-traditional financing alternatives are provided. These programs differ in terms of interest rates offered, loan terms, and eligibility requirements.

Micro-loan Programs

Many small, disadvantaged businesses have difficulty attracting start-up capital. To address this problem some states have developed micro-lending programs that specialize in granting small, micro loans specifically to low-income persons with special needs, or other disadvantaged groups.

Micro-loan funds are generally targeted to a specific geographic area, sometimes spanning several counties, sometimes only a small community. These programs are established by local community develop corporations (CDC's) and local economic development groups. They are frequently funded with state funds or foundation grants. Many receive funding via the SBA Microlending Demonstration Project.

Several micro loan funds exist which specifically target people with disabilities. The New Jersey Micro-loan and Non-profit Development Fund, was established in 1993 to provide start-up and expansion loans to New Jersey Entrepreneurs with Disabilities. The program is now located within the New Jersey Community Loan Fund. Several other states have or are in the process of creating loan funds. Maine, Michigan and Pennsylvania are among the other states that have a micro-loan program specifically for business owners with disabilities.

Veterans Administration

The Veterans Administration offers vocational rehabilitation services for veterans whose disability is service connected. Veterans with serious employment disabilities may receive self-employment assistance. Veterans who qualify for assistance, typically people with the most severe disabilities, are considered to require self-employment in order to achieve a positive rehabilitation outcome. These veterans may receive comprehensive training, inventory or supplies, essential equipment, technical assistance through the period of start-up, and incidental services such as business license fees.

Vocational Rehabilitation Programs

Each state has an agency which provides vocational assistance to persons with disabilities. These vocational rehabilitation (VR) agencies offer a variety of services including training, assistance with college tuition, and help purchasing assistive technology for the job site. Some vocational rehabilitation programs offer their clients financial assistance to establish small businesses. Generally these "grants" come out of a counselor's case management funds, and are usually for relatively small sums of money.

To qualify for vocational rehabilitation services individuals must have a disability that causes substantial problems in becoming employed or maintaining employment. Vocational rehabilitation services are available to individuals with a wide range of disabilities. The agency has no upper age limit for those who may qualify, so seniors with special needs may be eligible to receive services.

In some states, persons with visual impairments may be served through a separate agency. Provision of services is based on state and federal funds availability. Clients with the most severe disabilities are served first when limited resources make it impossible for the agency to serve all clients.

In the following chapter, we will review strategies for pursuing VR funding. If you're interested in obtaining vocational rehabilitation service through your state, contact your state office to get the number and location of the office nearest you. See Appendix B for a listing of state vocational rehabilitation offices.

Plan for Achieving Self Support (PASS)

Individuals who are eligible to receive SSI (Social Security Income), may also be eligible for the PASS program. This program allows an individual to set aside income for the purpose of starting a business. More will be said about PASS plans in the next chapter.

Foundations

Foundations rarely offer grants to individuals for the purpose of starting a business.

Some foundations offer scholarships or specific educational programs to individuals, but foundations generally fund only non-profit 501(c)3 corporations for specific projects. If you are interested in grant opportunities available through foundations, the following guides may be helpful:

> Directory of Grants for Organizations Serving People with Disabilities
> Directory of Computer and High Technology Grants
> Directory of Building and Equipment Grants

These directories may be found at your local library or you can contact the publisher: Research Grant Guides, Inc., P.O. Box 1214, Loxahatchee, Florida 33470 for information on these and other grant guides.

Local Non-Profits

Local non-profits can be a source for a disadvantaged business owner who seeks funding for a specific purpose. If you're having trouble raising funds to purchase equipment, consider approaching a local non-profit organization for a contribution. Kiwanis Clubs, Lions Clubs, and the like, may be interested in supporting a business venture which may result in the owner's independence from social security benefits.

Note: While foundations do not generally make grants to individuals, they do make grants to non-profit organizations. For example, if you have an idea for a business that could potentially create jobs and train unemployed workers consider approaching a non-profit to partner with you on the project. The non-profit organization could submit an application for funding to the foundations which may, if approved, generate sufficient capital for your project.

Corporate Giving

Many corporations donate used equipment and furnishings to community organizations, churches, and local residents. Contact large to medium-sized companies in your area and inquire about the possibility of receiving donated equipment. Be prepared to sell them on your need for the items. You may find that a corporation routinely donates used equipment to a local charity. If so, contact the charity to see if they have donated equipment that is not currently in use. If they have no immediate need for the equipment, they may be willing to donate it to someone who can put it to good use.

Some companies only give to non-profit, 501(c)3 organizations. This allows the company to take a tax deduction for the charitable contribution. If this is the case, contact a local non-profit and request that they act as a pass-through organization for the donated goods. The corporation donates the equipment to the 501(c)3, non-profit corporation, who then donates the equipment to you.

Corporations outside your community should not be ignored. Computer manufacturers give away thousands of dollars of used or out-dated equipment each year. Write the corporate headquarters and clearly explain your situation and your equipment needs. You could be surprised by the result! For a listing of companies, addresses and contact names, visit your local library.

Note: State and local governments also give away used and outdated equipment. Check with your local city/county clerk or your state ombudsman.

Finding Money

Many entrepreneurs struggle to find adequate financing to start their business. This may be especially true for entrepreneurs with disabilities who may encounter obstacles due to insufficient cash flow or unsatisfactory credit. Inability to access funds may result from discrimination or apathy on the part of service providers, bankers, or loan fund administrators who do not believe people with disabilities or chronic health conditions have the stamina or capacity to operate a successful small business. Entrepreneurs must arm themselves with a strong conviction that they will succeed. They must be prepared to approach a number of possible funding sources, and to consider many different combinations of funding.

Many entrepreneurs find that to get their business up and running, they must start on a shoestring. Controlling costs is a natural and healthy part of doing business. However, undercapitalization is not healthy, and if you are attempting to start out on much less than you hoped – be careful. Most experts agree that undercapitalization is one of the most common causes of business failure.

If you have been unable to secure funding from the sources listed in this section, there are other options. First, review your list of start-up costs. Is there equipment on the list that could be leased rather than purchased? Can you use less expensive products with fewer features? Include those costs that are absolutely necessary and eliminate any extraneous costs. For example, your business plan may include fees to hire an advertising consultant. In your contingency plan, you may opt for a friend helping you design promotional materials in-house. As long as the end result looks professional, you will save money and not risk losing potential customers. As you consider what to pare down, consider what impact, if any, the savings will have on future sales.

Strategies for managing cash can help entrepreneurs "find" money to start or expand their business. Many new businesses can start on a shoestring if they are able to carefully manage when cash comes in and when cash goes out. Here is where your cash flow projections (Chapter 9) come in handy. Business owners can often predict when payments will be received for services rendered. Prudent managers will wait until there is sufficient cash flow to purchase new supplies. This may seem obvious, but some business owners carry a personal tendency to seek immediate gratification into their businesses. New business owners may have to cast off their old habits of reckless spending and replace them with a more spartan approach.

Some businesses can actually create cash flow by requesting a down payment for services. This is common in the building trades, but there is no reason why consulting businesses, desk-top publishers, editors, artists, etc. could not successfully implement the same strategy. Any service that requires several days to complete could potentially command a down payment.

Some small businesses can rely on suppliers to extend credit for as long as 60-90 days. By collecting on receivables sooner and by extending accounts payables longer, business owners can create additional cash flow. Here your customers and suppliers are actually extending you credit by allowing you to hang on to your money longer and by allowing you to access their money sooner. In doing this, you must be careful not to alienate your customers or suppliers. The lines of communication must be kept open and mutual trust must be established.

Bartering can be used instead of cash to purchase office supplies, construction services, consulting, and many other products and services. Bartering is simply the process of providing a product or service in exchange for another product or service. No money is exchanged. Barter companies or associations exist in almost every community and offer an excellent alternative to businesses short on cash.

Many strategies for improving a company's management of cash are discussed in more detail in Chapter 9, Money Matters: Managing Business Financials. However, it is important to note here that by expanding cash reserves, a business can eliminate or reduce the need for debt financing or investment capital. If owners of new and expanding businesses view finding money as a task which involves looking *internally* as well as *externally*, they will keep their costs contained and increase their chances of survival and growth.

References and Resources

Applebaum, Julie, *"The Secret of Getting Bank Loans,"* Wealth Magazine, 1990, pp. 36-38.

Arnold, Nancy, *"Self-Employment Curriculum for Vocational Rehabilitation Counselors,"* University of Montana Rural Institute on Disabilities.

Federal Trade Commission/Facts for Consumers, *"Home Equity Credit Lines,"* Bureau of Consumer Protection.

Goldstein, Arnold, S., *Starting on a Shoestring*, Wiley & Sons, 1995, Third Edition.

Lister, Kate, and Harnish, Tom, *Finding Money: The Small Business Guide to Financing*, John Whiley and Sons, 1995.

Metts, Robert L. and Nansea, National Rehabilitation 1996 Switzer Monograph, *Contact List of Self-Employment Strategies in the United States.*

Posner, Bruce, *"How to Finance Anything,"* Inc. Magazine, April, 1992, pp. 51-62.

Stoltz, William, J., *Start up Financing: An Entrepreneurs Guide to Financing a New and Growing Business*, The Career Press, 1997.

CHAPTER 8

Getting Assistance From Government Agencies

People with disabilities and chronic health conditions may be eligible to receive benefits or services furnished by state and federal agencies. Services provided by government agencies can be valuable tools that can help people access financial resources, medical care, housing and transportation. When we think of government assistance, we often think of the social service programs that help disadvantaged people access basic living needs. But government social service programs do much more than provide basic needs, they make it possible for people to get an education, receive training, and find jobs. They also provide assistance to disadvantaged individuals interested in self-employment.

One of the most significant criticisms of government programs is that they discourage people from entering or re-entering the work force. For example, many entrepreneurs with disabilities remain dependent on Social Security, not because they need the monthly income, but because they need the medical coverage provided through the medicare program and cannot afford to pay the exorbitant prices of private medical insurance. Today, programs exist which allow a person with a disability to return to work or become self-employed without fear of prematurely losing their benefits. These *Work Incentive* programs were established to help people with disabilities enter or re-enter the workforce by protecting their entitlement to cash payments and by protecting Medicare, until they can support themselves.

Work Incentives exist primarily to help you make the transition from receiving benefits to being employed or self-employed. Work incentives are available within the Social Security Administration, the Department of Veteran Affairs, the Internal Revenue Service and the Department of Health and Human Services. This book details work incentive programs available through the Social Security Administration, however you can learn about other work incentive programs by contacting the appropriate agencies. By mastering these resources, you can establish a business without fear of prematurely losing your benefits.

Social Security Administration

Persons with disabilities may be eligible for two programs administered by the Social

Security Administration: 1) SSDI Social Security Disability Income and 2) SSI Social Security Income. SSDI is available to individuals who have 'paid into' the program. These are individuals who have been employed and have paid social security taxes. SSI is available to those individuals with disabilities who have not paid into SSDI. Individuals with disabilities may qualify for both.

Supplemental Security Income benefits those who become disabled prior to having a substantial work history. If you are disabled and your income is below the Federal Guaranteed Minimum Rate of $494 per month, you are eligible to receive SSI. Note: $494 is the 1998 rate, The Federal Guaranteed Minimum Rate changes each year.

The SSI program is a needs-based program and generally places a $2,000 limit on the value of property you may own. Those who own more than $2,000 in assets must sell their assets and use up this income prior to becoming eligible for SSI. There are two exceptions. A person with a disability receiving SSI may own a house and a vehicle worth more than $2,000, however, there are limits to how valuable these assets can be. Each state has established value limits on these assets.

Unlike SSI, SSDI beneficiaries do not have to sell any personal property prior to becoming eligible. The SSDI program is not a needs-based program. SSDI is a pension program, based on the Federal Insurance Corporation Act taxes you paid the government when you were working. These pension taxes, known as FICA, are based on the amount you paid during the 40 quarters of your last ten working years.

When determining eligibility for SSI or SSDI, the Social Security Act defines disability as:

> "...the inability to engage in any substantial gainful activity by reason of any medically determinable physical or mental impairment which can be expected to result in death or which has lasted or can be expected to last for a continuous period of not less than twelve months, or in the case of an individual who has attained the age of 55 and is blind...inability to engage in substantial gainful activity requiring skills or abilities comparable to those of any gainful activity in which he has previously engaged with some regularity and over some substantial period of time...An individual shall not be considered to be under a disability unless he furnishes such medical and other evidence of the existence thereof as the Secretary may require."

The Social Security Administration (SSA) mandates the involvement of a medical professional in determining the nature of the disability. Also the SSA specifies that a person is only considered disabled when their disability precludes them from achieving substantial gainful activity, which is defined as..."the performance of significant and productive physical or mental work for pay or profit. The substantial gainful activity (SGA) level is countable earnings over $500 per month for non-blind beneficiaries and $810 per month for SSDI beneficiaries who are blind."

The Social Security Administration deducts from gross earnings the cost of items a person needs in order to work and the value of support a person needs on the job due to the impairment, before deciding if the work is considered substantial gainful activity.

Using Work Incentive Programs

Work incentives make it possible for you to continue to receive benefits as you work toward a long-term career or business goal. The work incentive programs are useful because they allow an individual to accumulate resources, over and above the threshold required to initially qualify for benefits, in order to achieve a longer-range vocational goal. One such program, the Plan for Achieving Self Support (PASS), allows individuals to set aside income toward a pre-specified and pre-approved goal so that they continue to qualify for benefits while, at the same time, continue to save money for their long-term goal.

The following is a list of work incentive programs available to individuals receiving SSI (Social Security Income) and SSDI (Social Security Disability Income).

Work Incentives for SSI Recipients:

- **Earned Income Exclusion** - This incentive allows earned income to be excluded when figuring the SSI payment amount. The SSA excludes the first $65 of earnings in a month plus one-half of the remainder. This means that one-half of a person's earnings are counted when figuring his/her SSI payment amount.

- **Blind Work Expenses** - For self-employed, visually impaired persons, these expenses include those that are necessary in order to earn income. Some examples include: dog guide expenses, transportation to and from work, Federal, State, and local income taxes, Social Security taxes, attendant care services, visual and sensory aids, translation of materials into Braille, and professional association fees.

- **Plan For Achieving Self-Support (PASS)** - The PASS can help people acquire needed capital to start a business by allowing them to set aside income and resources while still remaining eligible for benefits. A PASS can help a self-employed individual establish or maintain SSI eligibility and can increase or help maintain the individual's SSI payment amount as the person gains the capacity for self-support.

  A PASS plan can only be established when an individual is earning a source of income other than SSI. The primary purpose of the PASS is to allow an individual to earn money or acquire resources without the fear of losing benefits.

  When establishing a PASS, a self-employed individual who earns a profit (excess over expenses) that exceeds SGA, can remain eligible for SSI payments and continue Medicare coverage. The excess revenues are set aside in a PASS account to be used specifically for the business. Suppose a self-employed auto mechanic establishes a business on a shoestring but is still able to earn a monthly profit of $200. If he/she is to remain in business new equipment and tools will be needed. The $200 excess can be set aside in order to purchase the tools at a future date. The owner will remain eligible to receive regular monthly SSI payments.

A PASS can be established to exclude any resources that become available to you after you have been on SSI, such as an inheritance or legal settlement. Resources set aside in the PASS are not counted when determining a person's eligibility for SSI or in calculating the amount of the SSI benefit. In other words, some individuals who may not have qualified for SSI because they exceeded the resource limit, can become eligible if a PASS is written. For example, if an individual has assets exceeding the established limit of $2000, they are not eligible for SSI. However, if by writing a PASS they show how these assets are necessary for achieving their plan for self support, these assets may not be considered as regular assets and the individual may then be eligible to receive SSI and take advantage of the benefits of the PASS program.

To qualify for the PASS plan, a business plan must be completed, which demonstrates how the business will lead to self-sufficiency. If the plan is denied, there is an appeal process through the Social Security Administration. Obtaining legal representation may improve your chances for approval. The application for a PASS plan is available at your local SSA office.

- **Property Essential to Self-Support (PESS)** - This work incentive pertains to the $2,000 asset limit established by the Social Security Administration as an eligibility standard. When determining the $2,000 eligibility limit, the SSA allows an individual to exclude certain resources which are essential to the person's means of self-support. The PESS is commonly written along with a PASS to protect benefits when property held by an individual is needed to maintain or achieve self-support.

If your business requires an investment of capital which you currently have or will have, a PESS should be written. If your business requires ongoing expenses in which your current resources will not cover, a PASS should be written.

Work Incentives for SSDI Recipients:

- **Trial Work Period** - The Trial Work Period allows a person to work and earn income for up to nine months. There is no limit on the level of earnings, and, during this period the individual is still eligible to receive benefits. For self-employed individuals, the Social Security Administration only counts those months you earn over $200 or work more than 40 hours per week.

  Earnings are based on profits not gross revenues. Therefore, the business must show a profit of at least $200 before that month will count against the trial work period.

  Also, the Social Security Administration may still pay benefits after the nine month trial work period has expired for up to 36 months if you can show that you are earning no more than $500 a month.

Work Incentives under SSI and SSDI

- **Impairment-Related Work Expense.** Impairment-related work expenses are incurred as a necessary function of one's job. They are unavoidable, necessary expenditures such as transportation and medical costs.

  If impairment-related items are required and paid for by a self-employed individual, they can be deducted from earnings and are not included when computing Substantial Gainful Activity (SGA). This is the case even when these items are also needed for non-work activities. Impairment-related work expenses are deductible for both SGA and SSI payment purposes when:

  ✔ The expense enables a person to work.
  ✔ The expense is reasonable.
  ✔ The expense (for SGA purposes) was paid for in a month in which the individual is or was working.
  ✔ The expense (for SSI payment purposes) is paid in a month in which earned income is received or work is performed.

  Examples of Deductible Services:
  - Attendant Care Services
  - Transportation Costs
  - Medical Devices
  - Assistive Devices
  - Residential Modifications
  - Routine Drugs and Routine Medical Services

- **Section 301** - Continued Payment under a Vocational Rehabilitation Program. Section 301 applies to individuals receiving SSI or SSDI who have reached medical recovery and are no longer considered disabled by SSA. Section 301 ensures that SSI and SSDI benefits continue if, at the time the disability ceases, the person is participating in an approved vocational rehabilitation program.

  If your small business is being sponsored by an approved vocational rehabilitation program, you will continue to receive benefits until your vocational program is considered complete. This is when it appears likely that your business will begin to earn a profit or when you can rely on regular paychecks. This time frame should be discussed with your vocational rehabilitation counselor and clearly indicated in your Individual Written Rehabilitation Plan (IWRP).

These work incentive programs and your own resourcefulness should lessen your fears of losing benefits. Businesses are established to make money and you should feel reasonably confident that your proposed venture can generate enough income to pay business expenses with sufficient excess to pay yourself. Earning a profit won't come overnight. Most businesses earn a profit after two or three years. Work incentives allow you to develop your business, establish a client base, and acquire assets needed to expand while continuing to receive benefits.

Vocational Rehabilitation

Each state has a vocational rehabilitation agency that serves free of charge all qualified individuals with disabilities. Vocational Rehabilitation programs were created to assist individuals in obtaining the skills and education needed to successfully join the workforce. These programs will provide assistance with training, work accommodations, and sometimes job placement.

Title I of the Federal Rehabilitation Act refers to eligibility criteria for vocational rehabilitation (VR) services. The act defines an eligible person with a disability as "any individual who has a physical or mental disability which for such individual constitutes or results in a substantial handicap to employment and can reasonably be expected to benefit in terms of employability from vocational rehabilitation services..." The state VR agency is responsible for making its own evaluation of the existence of a disability as well as an individual's capacity to benefit from VR services.

Each rehabilitation customer is teamed with a trained rehabilitation counselor who provides guidance and support as the customer pursues their vocational goals. The rehabilitation process begins with an assessment of the individual's skills, abilities, and interests. The individual and rehabilitation counselor explore possible obstacles to employment and determine when additional assessments are needed. Once the investigative work is completed, the customer and the counselor develop and agree upon an Individualized Written Rehabilitation Program (IWRP), which includes an employment goal and any services required to meet that goal. The rehabilitation counselor monitors the customer's progress and provides limited follow-up services once they're on the job.

In addition to its other services, rehabilitation programs may provide assistance to individuals interested in self-employment, including developing start-up businesses. Vocational rehabilitation programs vary from state to state with respect to their attitudes, policies and procedures regarding self-employment as a vocational goal. Many rehabilitation programs have resisted exploring self-employment as an option because they feel the expense and the risk is too prohibitive. In recent years however, VR agencies have begun to see the benefits to self-employment for their customers who are unable to find work, or who simply believe that self-employment offers their best chance for financial independence and job satisfaction.

Individuals who succeed in obtaining financial assistance from their state rehabilitation program know how to be their own advocate and are generally assertive and professional in their approach to the agency. It is important to approach your rehabilitation counselor with a clear idea of what you intend to do and how you intend to do it. Many VR programs require a business plan and some may require an investment be made by the individual before they'll consider making an investment into a business enterprise. Also, most VR programs require you to demonstrate the feasibility of the business, and may refer you to a Small Business Development Center or private consultant for help in this area.

It is impossible to know how your state's VR agency will respond to your request for financial assistance to start a business. It is probable that how your request is received depends upon the rehabilitation counselor assigned to your case. Depending on the attitudes and perceptions your counselor has regarding small business, you may or may not garner much support for your venture. Still there are many excellent vocational counselors who are open-minded, creative, and resourceful enough to provide you with the support you need to get started and be successful.

Many rehabilitation counselors view self-employment as a last resort. In other words, if there are no jobs available for you or if your disability precludes you from working in a traditional employment setting, then and only then, will they consider providing self-employment assistance. It will be your job to convince your rehabilitation counselor that self-employment is the best vocational option for you, even if you probably could find a job working for someone else.

If you are not satisfied with the way your counselor is approaching your plan for self-employment, try meeting with his/her supervisor. If this tact does not work, most agencies have a Client Assistance Program to address the concerns of agency clients. It is important however, to make sure that the agency's reason of refusal is not due to a flaw or limitation in your plan. They may have a solid reason for not supporting your business and you would be wise to carefully consider their objections and perhaps alter or revise your plan if necessary.

Furthermore, while many rehabilitation agencies provide grants for business start-ups, there are limitations. Each state has a budget, which dictates the level of assistance they can provide. Also, they have specific eligibility criteria, which dictate the services they provide and to whom. Therefore, their refusal to support certain ventures may be a function of the agency's budget constraints or eligibility criteria.

Getting What You Want From Government Agencies

While trying to start your business, you may wish to access resources available within federal, state, and local governments. In addition to Vocational Rehabilitation Services and the Social Security Administration, entrepreneurs with disabilities may access funds through the U.S. Small Business Administration, Department of Commerce, Department of Agriculture, Economic Development Authorities, and other government agencies that sponsor loan or grant programs.

Because of delays, bureaucratic red tape, endless paperwork, and not so friendly attitudes of some government workers, receiving benefits and services from governmental agencies can be frustrating, time-consuming, and down right exasperating. Many entrepreneurs, given the choice, opt not to pursue services offered through government programs. They choose instead to identify resources – both technical and financial – from private sources within their communities. However, despite the shortcomings of government programs, they do offer valuable services and resources. And for individuals with limited incomes, working with government agencies may be the best source for financial and technical assistance.

There are productive and unproductive ways of working with government agencies. Succumbing to frustration and anger by raising your voice is one example of being unproductive. Generally, those who succeed in getting what they want remain calm and even-keeled, despite the frustrations they encounter. There are no guarantees that VR or any other agency will assist you with your business, however, you can increase your chances by following these rules:

1. Make the counselor, case manager, or the agency represenentative you are working with comfortable with you and your business idea. Do this by providing information which supports your idea and your contention that self-employment is the best vocational option for you. Try to establish a good relationship with your counselor. Share information about yourself. Be forthright and honest.

2. Be responsive. You may be asked to submit what you feel is a lot of unnecessary information. However, it is important that you provide the information, and do so *in a timely manner.*

3. Be professional. Present your idea in an organized and professional

manner. Be prepared to answer questions relating to your plan. And be enthusiastic and convincing in your responses.

4. Be patient. Dealing with government agencies takes time. There are many procedures which must be followed. And your rehabilitation counselor or case worker may not have had much experience working with individuals interested in small business ownership. They may need to be educated along the way. It is important to be aware of the agency's procedures for dealing with self-employment and it is also helpful to assist your counselor with the learning process.

5. Be persistent. Persistence is essential for working with vocational rehabilitation programs and other government agencies. Keep in touch with your agency contact on a regular basis, but also give them space to do their job.

6. Be reasonable. Do not make unrealistic demands on your counselor or the agency. Remember, your counselor may have hundreds of individuals on their case load. Making unreasonable demands will alienate them and will likely work against you.

Federal and state governments offer valuable services and information that can help entrepreneurs start, manage, and expand their small business. For lists of government resources and programs refer to the following appendices:

Appendix B: State Vocational Rehabilitation Offices and State Services for the Blind

Appendix C: Small Business Development Center State Offices

Appendix D: SBA Micro-Loan Programs

Appendix J: Free or Low Cost Government Services, Resources and Information

References and Resources

"A Guide to the Federal Work Incentives," Prepared for the Annual Convention of the American Association of Spinal Cord Injury Psychologists and Social Workers. September, 1994.

Red Book on Work Incentives. Department of Health and Human Services, Social Security Administration, SSA Pub. No 64-030, June, 1991.

A Desktop Guide to Social Security and SSI Work Incentives. SSA Pub. No. 05-11002, January, 1997.

PART THREE

MANAGING FOR SUCCESS

"Only through the experience of trial and suffering
can the soul be strengthened, vision cleared,
ambition inspired, and success achieved."

Helen Keller

CHAPTER 9

Money Matters:
Managing Business Financials

Business owners often dread the financial aspects of business management. However, it is almost impossible to run a business without understanding basic financial concepts. Many business owners would just as soon delegate all tasks involving finances to someone more knowledgeable. But even those who hire bookkeepers and accountants need to have a general handle on the financial condition of their business.

After reading this chapter you will begin to feel at ease around financial concepts and begin to understand and analyze financial statements. The financial documents necessary to complete a business plan are included, as well as the financial concepts that are important to planning and managing a small business. Blank forms are provided (Appendix F) as well as a glossary of financial terms (Appendix E) in case you encounter unfamiliar terms.

This chapter reviews many of the critical principles of managing the finances of your business. However, the information provided on the following pages is by no means a complete review of these topics. If, after reading Money Matters, you still have questions, check out the resources listed at the end of the chapter, contact your local library, talk to your accountant, or seek assistance from your local SBDC or SCORE office.

Financial Statements

Balance Sheet

The Balance Sheet (or Statement of Financial Position) is a "snapshot" of a company's financial condition at a particular point in time. This statement represents the debt, assets, and net worth of the business, and is a general indication of how well the business is managed.

The balance sheet portrays the Basic Accounting Formula: Assets = Liabilities + Owner's Equity. Assets and liabilities are separated by subgroups. The first asset subgroup is *current assets*, the first liability subgroup is *current liabilities*. Current assets include cash or those assets that will turn into cash within a year, such as accounts receivable. Current liabilities are obligations that must be paid within a year. The second subgroupings are *long-term assets* and *long-term liabilities*. These are assets, fixed or long-term, not to be turned into cash anytime soon, or liabilities – obligations not due within a year.

Form #3 shows the elements of the balance sheet and can be used to complete projected balance sheets. Business Plans furnished in the sample business plans in the appendices will help you gain a better understanding of how to complete a balance sheet for your own business.

Business plans for start-up ventures often include projected or proforma balance sheets. Projected balance sheets include a start-up balance sheet created to calculate the expected balance on the starting date, as well as a projected balance for two years. When projecting assets and liabilities, a prospective owner should consider the future plans of the business. What is the expected growth of the business? What assets will be acquired? How will these assets be capitalized?

Form 3: Projected Balance Sheet

BUSINESS NAME:	YR	YR	YR	YR
ASSETS				
Current Assets				
Cash				
Marketable Securities				
Accounts Receivable				
Inventory				
Prepaid Expenses				
Other				
Total Current Assets				
Fixed (Long Term) Assets				
Building & Equipment				
Less Accumulated Depreciation				
Net Buildings & Equipment				
Land				
Other				
Total Fixed Assets				
Goodwill				
Total Assets				
LIABILITIES				
Short-Term Assets				
Accounts Payable				
Long-Term Assets				
Notes Payable				
Other				
Total Liabilities				
OWNERS' EQUITY				
Common Stock				
Retained Earnings				
Total Equity				
LIABILITIES & OWNERS' EQUITY				

Income Statement

Income Statements, also referred to as Profit and Loss Statements, set forth the revenues and expenses of the business. This statement gauges how well the business is doing, or will do, in selling products or services, keeping costs down, and maximizing profits.

As part of the business plan, a projected income statement is used to forecast revenues and expenditures monthly, quarterly, or yearly depending on the nature of the business, the level of seasonality, and the expected growth patterns. Form #4 can be used to project the revenues and expenses for your business. Examples of income statements can also be found in the sample business plans provided in the appendices.

Cash Flow Projections

Cash flow projections, also known as *proformas* are used to anticipate the cash needs of the business. Cash flow projections are generally estimated on a monthly basis for one or two years.

The cash flow projections are an important planning tool because they allow business owners and lenders to anticipate cash inflows and outflows, and to determine what level of working capital is needed prior to start-up. Proformas can help you predict when the business will need additional cash, and can help the owner avoid unanticipated cash flow problems.

The cash flow proforma is continuous, like a check book. The ending balance of the first month becomes the beginning balance of the second month, and so on. Complete the projected cash flows for your business using Form #5, or create your own form using any computer spreadsheet program.

When developing financial proformas, it is best to use a computer spreadsheet program. This will allow you to see how variations in anticipated revenues/cash inflows and expenses/cash outflows will impact your profitability and cash position. By using spreadsheets, business owners can easily create "what if" scenarios that allow them to understand how various contingencies will affect their bottom line.

Personal Financial Statement

The personal financial statement furnishes the assets, liabilities, and net worth of the business owner. This document allows the lender to evaluate the credit potential of the business based on the net worth of its owner(s). The personal financial statement (Form 2) was covered in Chapter 4. See Appendix F for additional forms.

Sources and Uses of Capital

Business plans for new businesses often include a listing of the expected sources of capital and how the funds will be used. First, you must list the capital needs of your

Form 4: Projected Income Statement

BUSINESS NAME:

	Mo.1	Mo. 2	Mo. 3	Mo. 4	Mo. 5	Mo. 6	Mo. 7	Mo. 8	Mo. 9	Mo. 10	Mo. 11	Mo. 12	TOTAL	RATIO
Revenues														
Sales														
Less Discounts														
& Allowances														
Net Sales														
Less Variable (Cost														
of Goods sold)														
Materials														
Labor														
Other														
Gross Profit														
Operating Expenses														
Acctg & Legal Fees														
Advertising														
Salaries/Wages														
Bad Debt														
Depreciation														
Entertainment														
Insurance														
Loan Payment														
Office Supplies														
Postage														
Printing														
Repairs and Maint.														
Rent														
Telephone														
Travel														
Miscellaneous														
Other														
Total Expenses														
Before Tax Profit														
Less Estimated Tax														
Net Profit														

Form 5: Monthly Cash Flow Projections

BUSINESS NAME:

	Mo.1	Mo.2	Mo.3	Mo.4	Mo.5	Mo.6	Mo.7	Mo.8	Mo.9	Mo.10	Mo.11	Mo.12
Beg. Cash Bal.												
Cash Receipts												
Sales												
Collections from Credit Accounts												
Loan/Invested Capital												
Total Cash Receipts												
Total Cash Available												
Cash Paid Out												
Materials												
Labor												
Acctg & Legal Fees												
Telephone												
Advertising												
Bad Debt												
Dues & Subscriptions												
Entertainment												
Insurance												
Loan Payment												
Office Supplies												
Owner's Draw												
Postage												
Printing												
Repairs and Maint.												
Rent												
Supplies												
Taxes												
Utilities												
Total Cash Paid Out												
Ending Cash Balance												

business. For example, if you are interested in starting a lawn care service, the list of capital needs may look like this:

Uses of Funds

Landscaping Machinery and Equipment:

Pick-up Truck	$10,000

Lawn Mowers:

2 Toro Riding Lawn Mowers	3,000
1 Manual mower	800
Lawn Mower Accessories	400
Landscaping Tools and Accessories	1,000
Subtotal	$15,200

Office Furniture and Equipment:

Computer - IMT 286	$ 2,200
Desk - Zmart Model #A76	220
Chair - Zmart Model XET	300
Filing Cabinet	100
Typewriter - Panazonic (used)	200
Subtotal	$ 3,020
Working Capital	$ 8,000
Total Funds Needed	**$26,220**

Once the uses have been identified, the source(s) of funds must be determined. Let's assume you plan to invest $5,000 of your own money and your Aunt Mary agrees to loan you $6,000. You currently have $11,000 ($5,000 + $6,000) to invest. You've indicated that you need $26,220 to start your business. Therefore, you will need to come up with the balance: $15,220 ($26,220-11,000). You may choose to approach another relative, apply for a grant, or borrow the money from your local bank. In this case, John decides to submit his plan to XYZ bank.

Sources of Funds

John Smith	$ 5,000
Note -Mary Brooks	6,000
Note -XYZ Bank	15,220
Total	**$26,220**

When the sources and uses are included in the plan, the banker or investor knows how much is needed, what other sources of funds are available to the owner, and how the funds will be used.

Break-even Analysis

Break-even analysis can be a very effective business planning tool. Break-even determines the point at which revenue contributions will meet fixed costs.

Prior to explaining how break-even analysis works, some critical financial concepts need to be defined. The two most fundamental concepts to understanding break-even analysis are fixed and variable costs. These are the types of costs that businesses incur on a regular basis. *Fixed costs* are costs that remain constant with fluctuations in sales or production. Examples of fixed costs include; salaries, rent, insurance and other costs that tend to remain the same from month to month. *Variable costs* change proportionately with increases and decreases in business activity. Variable costs increase as more products are produced and decrease when less products are produced. Variable costs generally include raw materials, hourly labor, electricity, and maintenance. Some business costs have characteristics of both variable and fixed costs. It is up to the business owner to analyze the nature of their business costs, and classify them as variable or fixed accordingly.

The Break-even Chart (Fig. 1) explains how increases in units produced and revenues earned will impact variable costs. You can see that revenues increase at a faster rate than variable costs. This difference is referred to as the contribution. When the business reaches this point, the amount of contribution (the difference between revenues and variable costs) is equal to fixed costs.

Fig. 1

Source:
American Management Association

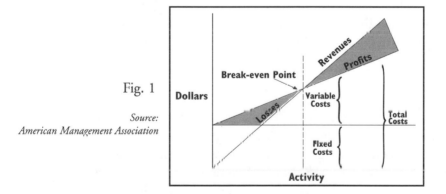

The break-even point can be calculated in either sales or units, and requires dividing the fixed costs by the contribution margin per unit. To illustrate, assume you have concluded that there is tremendous demand for your tasty diet cookies, and your research shows that customers will pay no more than $2.00 a dozen. You have estimated that your fixed costs for a dozen diet cookies will be $.90 a dozen, and that variable costs will be $.60 per dozen. (We will discuss later how to estimate costs and establish prices.)

Let's further assume that you expect to sell 5,000 packages of 12 cookies. First, determine the contribution margin: (Sales-Variable Costs)/Sales. $10,000 (5,000 x $2) - $3,000 (5,000 x .6)/$10,000 = $.70.

Then calculate the B.E.P. where:
Break-even point = Fixed Costs/Contribution Margin Percentage
$$\$4500/.70 = \$6428.$$

In other words, you need to sell $6,428 worth of cookies, or roughly 536 packages of a dozen in order to break even.

Break-even Equation

Break-even point = Fixed Costs divided by Contribution Margin

Where: Fixed Costs = Sales - Variable Costs
          Sales = your Projected Sales for the period
          Variable Costs = Projected Variable Costs for the period

Break-even analysis is an important analytical tool for business owners. Some companies depend on this tool to make strategic business decisions. For example, break-even analysis is helpful when projecting how much profit or loss would result if a company purchased additional equipment to increase production. Many business owners assume that by increasing production and sales, they will make more money. They often find out the hard way that increasing sales does not always result in increasing profits. Increases in production can cause changes in variable and fixed costs, which can sometimes reduce profitability. It is important that managers understand the implications of increasing production and sales. Break-even analysis provides advanced information to the business owner on the expected financial results for various levels of activity. Thus, business owners and managers are able to avoid rushing into projects without knowing their expected impact on profits.

Pricing

Identifying the appropriate price is one of the greatest challenges a new business owner will face. Pricing strategies vary depending on the nature of the business and the information the business has regarding competitors and customers. Market research can be useful in helping the business owner determine appropriate price ranges. Pricing involves knowing your costs (direct and indirect), what profit level is desired, and how important price is to your customers.

Entrepreneurs make many mistakes when it comes to pricing, some of the most common are:

- Pricing by undercutting competitor's prices or pricing at competitor's lowest price. This strategy does not consider costs, overall profit goal, and contribution margins. Many new business owners fail to consider that their competitors may have lower (per unit) costs, and by meeting their price, a new business may be selling at a loss.

- Undercharging due to either a lack of confidence or to overcompensate for a lack of experience. This generally occurs with consulting or service firms. When companies charge less than their competitors, the message to customers may be that they cannot perform the service at the same level of quality.

- Undercharging initially with the intent of increasing prices later. It is usually more difficult to raise prices than to lower them.

- Pricing to sell at a volume versus pricing to sell at a profit. As we will demonstrate, the percentage of profit desired is built into the pricing equation. To determine a price for your product or service, start by establishing a floor (or base) price and a ceiling price. The floor price is determined by total costs. This is the minimum at which you can sell the product or service. The market determines your ceiling price. This is the maximum price at which the market is willing to pay for your product or service.

Your pricing should include some intangible image factor, or market positioning. In other words; how do your customers perceive your products or services? If your price is too low, customers may perceive the quality as substandard. If priced too high, customers may not be able to afford the product, or may not perceive its value as worth the price.

Adopting a pricing strategy that is inconsistent with your position in the market sends customers an inconsistent message. If you advertise that you offer superior quality with the best service and warranty in town, but your prices are budget, customers will assume there's a catch. If you make claims that appear 'too good to be true' even if the claims may be true, potential customers may harbor suspicions and may question your integrity. Either consciously or subconsciously, people generally prefer to pay a price that they perceive as fair. If your price deviates too much from the perceived fair price, customers will go elsewhere.

For businesses that offer a variety of products, it is important to remember that different products may have different margins. The goal to pricing is to achieve overall dollar profit. Thus, while prices for some products may result in lower profit margins, prices for others should make-up the difference.

Example: Assume Worldwide Enterprises, Inc. sells three products with a profit goal of $30,000 on sales of $600,000. The profit margins may look like this:

Product	Sales	Margin	Profit
A	100,000	-2%	(2,000)
B	200,000	1%	2,000
C	300,000	10%	30,000
	600,000		30,000

Therefore, it is possible to sell a single product at a loss while maximizing profits.

There are several methods used to calculate prices. This chapter addresses the most frequently used methods.

Cost Based Pricing

1. First determine your costs, direct and indirect, of doing business.
2. Establish desired profit percentage goal.
3. Calculate the overhead allocation factor (OAF):

$$\text{OAF} = 1 + \frac{\text{Total Indirect Costs}}{\text{Total Direct Costs}}$$

4. Multiply cost of the item by OAF to determine total cost.

$$\text{Total Cost} = \text{OAF} \times \text{Cost of item}$$

5. Determine selling price by using profit percentage from budget.

Divide total cost by 1 – profit percentage.

$$\text{Selling Price} = \frac{\text{Total Cost}}{1\text{-Profit \%}}$$

Test your knowledge of pricing using the following example:

Acme Janitorial expects to generate sales of $10,000 in its first year of operation. Total costs are estimated at $2.00 per square foot of area cleaned.

Acme's Projected Income Statement

Sales	$10,000
Expenses	
Rent	$ 4,000
Labor	$ 2,000
Supplies	500
Advertising	600
Travel	400
Insurance	300
Dues	100
Misc.	500
Total Expenses	8,400
Profit	**$ 1,600** (15%)

a. **Determine the company's direct and indirect costs from the projected income statement:**

Direct		Indirect	
Labor	$2,000	Rent	$4,000
Supplies	500	Advertising	600
Travel	400	Insurance	300
		Dues	100
		Misc.	500
Total Direct	**$2,900**	**Total Indirect**	**$5,500**

b. Calculate OAF

$$OAF = 1 + \frac{\text{Total Indirect Costs}}{\text{Total Direct Costs}} \quad \frac{1 + 5,500}{2,900} = 2.9$$

c. Calculate Total Cost

$$TC = OAF \times \text{Cost of Item} = 2.9 \times 2.0 = 5.8$$

d. Calculate Selling Price

$$\text{Selling Price} = \frac{\text{Total Cost}}{1 - \text{Profit \%}} = \frac{5.8}{1 - .15} = \$6.82 \text{ /sq. ft.}$$

Acme Janitorial would charge $6.82 per square foot of area cleaned.

Suggested Going Rate

Suggested going rate is frequently used in retail businesses when the manufacturer suggests a retail price for products. The retailer has the option of using the suggested price or adjusting the price (usually downward) to reflect local market conditions.

Pricing Services

Timid undercharging usually occurs in the service industry where the service is performed by the owner. Undercharging is usually the result of a lack of confidence. The owner keeps the rate low to overcompensate for a lack of experience. Low prices are set during the early months of operation with the idea that they can be raised later on.

There are a number of problems with this strategy. First, lower fees may send a signal to potential customers regarding the value of your services. A lower price may give an impression of lower quality. Second, it is usually easier to lower prices than it is to raise them. New customers may be lost after prices are raised. It is usually smarter to compete on quality and customer service than to compete on price.

When calculating prices for service businesses, first determine the number of available billable hours. Start by eliminating time for holidays and business tasks that are necessary, but not billable. For example, assume Joe's Auto Repair is open 8 hours, 5 days a week. The total number of work hours per year is 52 weeks x 8 hours x 5 days – 2080. Subtract for holidays, training, administration, and marketing. Assume holidays and training consume a total of 4 weeks (160 hours annually). Administration and marketing requires a weekly time commitment of 12 hours (624 hours annually). That leaves 1,296 billable hours.

The next step is to determine your costs of doing business. First, start by determining the salary of the repair person or owner. The owner's salary should be comparable to wages paid to people working in the same type of job. Assume Joe is working alone and estimates his annual total costs will be:

Salaries

Owners salary - $250 per week	$13,000
Benefits/taxes @ 14%	1,820
Health Insurance $100/month	1,200
Subtotal	**$16,020**

Operating Costs:
Advertising
Car Expense
Depreciation on Equipment
Education and Training
Insurance
Professional Fees
Repairs and Maintenance
Supplies and Postage
Rent - allocate even if business is home-based
Utilities
Telephone
Other

Total Operating Costs Allocated to Repairs   **$10,325**

Total Costs   **$26,345**

Joe determines his hourly rate as follows:

$$\frac{\text{Total Costs}}{\text{Number of Billable Hours}} \quad \text{x} \quad \text{Desired Profit Rate}$$

$$\frac{\$26,345}{1,296} \quad \text{x} \quad 120\% \quad = \quad \$24.39$$

Then Joe called several small automotive repair shops in the area and found their hourly rates were between $25-$35. Joe decides to set his price in the middle, charging $30 per hour for his services.

Pricing Strategies for Small Manufacturing Firms

Generally speaking, small manufacturers should not compete on the basis of price unless they are *the* low cost producer. Smaller firms should compete on the basis of customer service, quality, delivery time, or value-added features of services.

Small manufacturers should consider using *product differentiation* as a competitive strategy. The process of differentiating your products in the market place can be accomplished through changes in product design, product performance, or financing arrangements. Products can also be differentiated by the level of service offered. Product differentiation is best utilized when price sensitivity is lowest. A buyer in a price sensitive market will likely choose the less expensive alternative with fewer features and services.

If the buyer uses a product infrequently, they tend to be less sensitive to price. For example, a company who buys office supplies on a regular basis tends to seek out the best deals. However, when this same company needs custom-designed computer software and hardware, they will likely choose the firm they believe has the best reputation or who will be the most responsive to their needs.

Pricing for Retailers

The key to understanding pricing for retail businesses is understanding markup. A retailer's markup is the difference between the cost of the merchandise and the retail price. If an item costs you $12 and you feel you can sell if for $20, your markup on that item is $8. Markup is often expressed in percentages. In the above example the percentage markup is 40% (the dollar markup/the retail price).

Image is important when determining pricing strategies. This is true for manufacturing and service businesses, but may be especially true in retail. The quality and selection of a retailer's merchandise, the store location, and the methods of promotion, will depend on how the business is positioned in the market. The market niche, or the customer base must be the focal point of all decisions, including pricing.

Pricing in retail stores must consider costs as well as market conditions. An optimal markup should be determined based on costs and profits desired. In short, market considerations will affect your pricing decisions, but using cost analysis for setting prices will help you maximize profits.

Recordkeeping for Small Business

Maintaining good business records is one of the critical ingredients of long-term business success. Many business owners avoid the daily task of tracking business activities. They often consider recordkeeping a hindrance or inconvenience that keeps them away from producing products or servicing customers. Sooner or later the business owner will learn that recordkeeping can save valuable time and money.

There are six characteristics of a good recordkeeping system. The system must be (1) simple to use (2) easy to understand, (3) reliable, (4) accurate, (5) consistent, and (6) designed to provide information on a timely basis.[4]

Recordkeeping involves tracking and organizing the cash inflows and outflows of the business. Most recordkeeping systems require four basic records: sales, cash receipts, cash disbursements, and accounts receivable.

The recordkeeping system starts with a General Ledger which categorizes accounts. A typical classification of Ledger Accounts include: Assets, Liabilities, Sales, Expenses, and Capital Accounts. Journal entries are used to record all business transactions. For example, assume ABC Corporation pays its supplier, XYZ Corporation, for materials purchased on credit. The transaction would be recorded as follows:

April 1, 1996	Debit	Credit
Cash		$104.50
Accounts Payable	$104.50	

Journal entries are posted to the General Ledger which keeps balances of individual accounts. The following is a simplified General Ledger for ABC Corporation.

---

[4]Cotton, John, *Record Keeping for Small Business*, US Small Business Administration Management Aid.

Assets
    100 - Cash in Bank
    101 - Accounts Receivable
    102 - Inventory
    103 - Supplies
    104 - Tools and Equipment

Liabilities
    200 - Accounts Payable
    210 - Notes Payable
    220 - Taxes Payable

Sales
    300 - Sales Revenues

Expenses
    400 - Salaries and Wages
    401 - Payroll Taxes
    402 - Rent
    403 - Telephone

At the end of each fiscal year, accounts are balanced and closed. Account balances are used by your accountant to compile an Income Statement and Balance Sheet.

Many businesses are turning to computer software packages which often simplify accounting procedures. Accounting packages walk you through the accounting steps so that previous accounting expertise is not required. Accounting packages such as Quick-Books and Peachtree can be valuable management tools, cutting your bookkeeping and accounting time in half. With computerized accounting, owners are able to generate financial reports, track time and inventory, write checks and pay bills.

Cash vs. Accrual Accounting

A business can use one of two forms of accounting – cash or accrual. Keeping books on a cash basis is the simplest approach, but is not appropriate for all types of businesses. Cash basis accounting is used by very small businesses when income or cash is received when the service or product is delivered. Accrual based accounting is generally appropriate when services are billed or when credit is extended to customers. It is defined as "a method of recording income and expenses when the item is earned or incurred, without regard as to when actual payments are received or made." Accounts receivable and accounts payable are necessary when using the accrual method of accounting.

Payroll

Generally businesses make payroll weekly, bi-weekly or monthly. Employees must complete a W-4 Form specifying their income tax withholding. The business owner deducts appropriate social security, FICA, and state payroll taxes from each check and makes regular tax deposits to their bank.

Regular payment of payroll taxes is required of all employers. Reports of individual payroll payments must be made to your state treasury and the IRS. Each employee receives a W-2 form at the year-end showing total withholding payments made for the employee during the calender year. Business owners should keep a file with accurate and current information on all employees and subcontractors including, addresses, social security numbers, telephone numbers, payroll records, and a name of who to contact in case of an emergency.

Depreciation

For some businesses, a schedule of depreciation must be kept. Depreciation allows a business to expense depletion of fixed assets over a period of time. Most small businesses depreciate assets using the straight-line method of depreciation. This method is based on the expected life of the asset and reports depreciation evenly over the useful life of the asset. For example, assume you purchase a truck for $20,000 that is expected to last five years. Using straight-line depreciation the vehicle would be depreciated at 20%, or $4,000 per year.

Depreciation expenses for many firms can be quite complex, therefore it is usually wise to seek advice from an accountant.

Financial Management and Cost Control

Successful business owners manage wisely the cash inflows and outflows of their business. This requires a day-to-day handle on cash flow, as well as a general understanding of the financial condition of the company. Sound financial management is critical to the long-term stability of any business. Even businesses which experience increasing sales volume can run into financial trouble. This occurs for a number of reasons. First, many business owners understand the technical or creative aspect of the business, but do not understand or appreciate the importance of managing finances. Second, many entrepreneurs are so engaged in the process of delivering the product or service, they fail to consider the financial consequences of selling at a price too low to make a profit. Third, business owners may not always be aware of how money is spent and often wasted.

Businesses experiencing depleting cash reserves often turn to the bank for financing. However, debt is usually not the answer to cash flow problems. Changing purchasing patterns, collection policies or pricing strategies may generate sufficient cash and eliminate the need for debt.

For example, I once worked with a woman who owned a small-town bar. She was seeking a bank loan to address her immediate and unanticipated cash flow problem. Because the business had prospered in the past, it was her opinion that her cash flow problem was due to a short-term slump in sales. Since business transactions were almost all in cash, and since there were few controls established to manage finances, it was difficult to assess the core of the problem. However, after some discussion, it was revealed that her new spouse was tending the bar quite frequently and often 'bought' drinks for customers, while helping himself to a libation or two at the same time.

Of course it is easy to see how over time this behavior could drain a business' cash reserves. Proper controls could reverse the situation and eliminate the need to obtain financing.

Sound financial management also involves managing growth and managing the 'quality' of sales. Many entrepreneurs sell without the ability to deliver or make delivery on time. Over-promising and under-delivering creates poor customer relations, which may require discounts be given to keep a customer happy. Successful business owners recognize when making a sale may not be in the best interests of their company. They understand that some deals are not worth the headaches, and are willing to bypass what may appear to be a "once in a lifetime" deal.

Managing growth also requires proper planning. Successful entrepreneurs utilize proformas to anticipate cash inflows and outflows and are able to plan for periods when cash reserves are low. This strategy takes the crisis out of managing the business and the worry out of making payroll.

Mastering Financials: Don't Stop Here

The purpose of this chapter was to acquaint you with the financial terms and concepts which are necessary to developing a business plan and helpful in managing a business. Here we discussed the crucial role and the elements of financial statements. We gave an overview of pricing strategies, as well as an explanation for computing a simple break-even point. This chapter was intended to be an overview. Thus, it probably will not provide all the information you need, and may not answer all of your questions. You can learn more by reading from this chapter's list of references and recommended resources, or by visiting your library, local book store, business college or Small Business Development Center.

References and Resources

Bender, James, *How to Use Financial Statements, A Guide to Understanding the Numbers,* McGraw-Hill, 1994.

Cotton, John, *Record Keeping for Small Business,* US Small Business Administration Management Aid.

Finkler, Steven, A., *A Complete Guide to Finance and Accounting for Non-Financial Managers,* Prentis-Hall, 1993.

Gill, James, *Financial Basics of Small Business Success,* Crisp Publications, 1994.

Hammel, Fred and Goulet, Peter, *Break-even Analysis: A Decision-Making Tool,* U.S. Small Business Administration Office of Business Development, Management Aid Number 1.019.

Holtz, Herman, *Priced to Sell: A Complete Guide to More Profitable Pricing,* Upstart Publishing, 1996.

Lennon, Victor, *What is the Best Selling Price,* U.S. Small Business Administration Office of Business Development, Management Aid Number 1.002.

Walker, Bruce, *A Pricing Checklist for Small Retailers,* U.S. Small Business Administration Management Aid Number 4.013.

Wilsted, William, *Pricing for Small Manufacturers,* U.S. Small Business Administration Management Aid Number1.005.

Zuckerman, Laurie, B., *On Your Own: A Women's Guide to Building a Business,* Upstart Publishing, Second Edition, 1990.

CHAPTER 10

Marketing as an "Investment"

Marketing is defined as the process by which companies attract and keep customers. The four key elements of marketing, product/service, price, distribution, and promotion, define how a firm will position itself in the market place. These elements establish the basis of the Marketing Plan which drives the marketing investments of the firm. Viewing marketing as an investment involves a commitment of time and resources towards gaining an understanding of customers, and how the firm can best meet their needs.

Business owners must be in touch with current market demands and industry trends. Information gathered from customers, industry sources, and even competitors is invaluable to maintaining a competitive advantage or market niche. Ongoing research, which involves gathering and analyzing market data on a regular basis is a must. This can be done by tracking customer orders, making profiles of customers, and documenting their purchasing patterns. This can also be accomplished through surveys of present and prospective customers regarding their experiences with the company. Creating an opportunity for customers to give feedback shows customers you care about quality and customer service and may disclose problems that can easily be remedied.

The activities of competitors must also be monitored. Pertinent information includes new products or services offered by competitors, new pricing or promotional strategies, or changes in location or distribution methods.

The Marketing Plan

Business owners who view marketing as an investment develop marketing plans that start by clearly defining their mission and target market(s) (or customers).

When a marketing plan is developed, promotional expenditures are carefully targeted and therefore marketing dollars are more prudently spent. The marketing plan may be simple or complex, depending upon the nature of the business, but usually incorporates the following elements:

- Mission Statement: One or two sentences that describe the chief function of the business, identifies its customers, and the specific company attributes that address customer needs.

- Market Analysis:
  Definition of Target Market(s) - Age, income, education, occupation, geographic location.
  Industry Trends - Products/Services available, prices, distribution methods, changes in technology.
  Competition - Products/services available, quality, customers served.
  Competitive Analysis - Strengths and weaknesses of competitors.

- Marketing Strategy:
  Detailed Positioning Statement - Unique Competitive Advantage.
  Promotion - Advertising, Direct Sales, telemarketing, public relations.
  Budget - Marketing/advertising budget as a percentage of sales.

It is one thing to develop a plan, it is another thing to follow it. Many business owners develop business and marketing plans only to show a banker or invester and then file them away. The marketing plan is only useful if you use it regularly to monitor the effectiveness of your strategies. If, as the owner of the business, you feel you do not have time to monitor the plan, delegate the task to an employee. If you are operating the business alone, be sure to set aside time weekly or monthly to refer to your plan and make amendments as needed.

Once you have developed a marketing strategy, stick with it until you are confident it is no longer working. If you've done your homework and know your customers, the strategy for reaching potential customers shouldn't be difficult to ascertain. Once determined, be consistent and persistent with marketing strategies. Avoid premature changes to your marketing program. When you find a successful formula, intensify it before you make changes.

Monitor the success of your marketing strategies by determining how your customers are hearing about your business. Tracking promotional strategies will reveal which strategies are working and which are not. Evaluate effectiveness in terms of dollars. In other words, which marketing strategies produce the most results for the least investment. But be prepared to invest sufficient time and financial resources in marketing your business. Potential customers will not buy from you if they don't know you're out there.

Public Relations - Advertising for Free!

As you develop your marketing plan, don't forget to include PR strategies. Public relations is an excellent way to get your company's name out there without spending a dime. Heidi Van Arnem's business, Travel Headquarters, benefitted considerably from free publicity. Capitalizing on the public's interest in seeing people overcome adversity, Heidi took advantage of this opportunity and turned her disability into an asset.

To begin your PR program, write a compelling news release about yourself and your business. Send it to your local media. Newspaper, television and radio editors are looking for stories about interesting people in their communities.

Creating a news release is extremely simple. Keep the content direct and to the point by using the five "w's" (who, what, where, when and why). Start the newrelease with the most important and interesting information and include more detail in the following paragraphs. The release should be double-spaced and should include a date, contact person, and location. For example, if you are writing a newsrelease to promote your grand opening, the first paragraph should have a description of the event, the date, time, and the place. After sending your newsrelease follow-up with a telephone call to make sure your release has been received and confirm that all the necessary information was included.

As part of your PR program, try writing articles for trade journals or local magazines. Articles help you establish a reputation as an expert in your field, which can be extremely valuable for promoting your business. Consider including camera-ready layout and a photo. Make it easy for the media to write about your business by giving a stimulating presentation in a professional manner.

Almost any business can be interesting if presented correctly. Think about what "hot buttons" to push. Do you provide a new or unique product or service? Or perhaps you offer a new twist to an existing product or service. Why did you start your business? Did you have obstacles? What did you do to overcome these obstacles?

After promoting your business locally, you may want to try the national circuit. There are literally thousands of potential news organizations who could be interested in your story, especially if it's connected in some way to a headline story. For example, if the leading story of the week is the latest research on the relationship between food preservatives and heart disease and you happen to sell organic herbs, contact the media with the scoop on how your products may help to reduce the risk of heart disease. Also, ask them to put your name on their list of experts to call when technical questions come up. This exposure can be on-going and extremely valuable. Make sure you're able to handle the demand that could result – this kind of exposure could bring in hundreds or thousands of orders!

Networking

People generally do business with people they know and like. The purpose of networking is to expand your circle of acquaintances, not necessarily to make a sales pitch. The key is to establish rapport by forming a connection or common ground. The potential of meeting prospective customers is only one benefit to networking. Meeting new people through professional circles can teach you about business resources in your community, forge opportunities to meet business advisors and mentors, and acquire valuable insight regarding suppliers and industry trends.

Most people network through social circles by attending parties, clubs, or sports activities. Others network through business or civic organizations by attending association meetings, volunteering to serve on committees of business organizations or non-profit agencies, or by joining service clubs, like the Rotary or Kiwanis.

Networking gives you the opportunity to get to know people in the business community. Generally, the more people you know, the more successful you become. This is especially true for service industries which depend on referrals from professionals or related service industries. For example, if you are starting a painting business and are relatively new to the area, you must identify people in the community who could be sources of referrals. Consider those in similar industries whose businesses are related to yours. You could join a local Building Contractor's Association and begin to network with building contractors, electricians, plumbers, and other contractors. You could also talk to paint suppliers and hardware stores and make an effort to get to know the owners and their employees. The more people you get to know, the more referrals you receive.

Sell, Sell, Sell

There is no more effective way to promote your business than direct sales. This is especially true in service industries where it is important that the customer come to know and trust the people who run the business. New business owners frequently purchase advertising and wait for customers to call. More times than not, this strategy does not work. Generally it is necessary for the business owner to become directly involved in the selling process. This means having direct contact with potential customers.

Few products or services sell themselves. Therefore, the business owner must become a salesperson and be prepared to convince a prospective buyer that their product or service will meet their needs. However, the owner/salesperson must first understand the needs of their customers. (The marketing plan should be used as a guide to understanding the needs of customers and the nature of the competitive environment.)

When buying a new product or service, the customer either (1) chooses your product instead of your competitors', or (2) chooses your product in order to satisfy a currently unmet need. In either case, potential customers must be convinced that your product or service will address their needs.

The first step to identifying the needs of your customers is to ask questions and listen. Listen to what prospective customers are saying and what they are not saying. Often prospects give reasons for not buying that may be perceived as a lack of interest, but may indeed indicate their need for additional information. Carefully listening to the objections of prospective customers can lead to clues regarding their needs, fears, and expectations. Through the process of listening and overcoming objections, salespeople become problem-solvers.

An effective sales strategy starts with setting sales goals. Sales goals are set in terms of dollars but are based on the number of units sold or hours billed. Every business has a maximum capacity. Service businesses must consider their personnel resources when establishing sales goals. How many hours per week are billable?

Retail and manufacturing firms must consider material as well as personnel resources. How many units can be produced in a given time? How much inventory is required to meet sales goals?

As you gain experience through operating your business, setting sales goals will become easier and more accurate. Businesses look to past performance to establish future sales goals. For example, if your first year sales were $50,000, your goal for the second year may be to increase sales by 20% or $60,000. Sales goals should be realistic and attainable given the market conditions and the business' internal resources.

Once goals are established, a plan should be put in place to evaluate sales performance. Depending on the business, weekly, monthly, or quarterly review of sales is important to gauge progress and to address problems. For a retail business, the number of weekly transactions and the average dollar amount per transaction are common checkpoints. Retail businesses expect to make sales transactions on a daily basis, so weekly averages are meaningful. For consulting businesses, sales reviews may be monthly or quarterly because the sales cycle is generally much longer.

A sales plan must include more than just goals in units and dollars. The plan should establish weekly goals of contacts made, letters sent, meetings scheduled and so on. This is especially true in service businesses that have long sales cycles. A weekly review of your progress is important to keep you on target.

It is useful to keep a file on customers and potential customers with a detailed log of contacts made, work completed, and personal information about the customer or potential customer. The more you learn about a particular customer, the more likely you are to make a sale.

Often the sales process begins with a telephone call. For this reason, it is useful to be skilled at creating rapport and building confidence through a telephone conversation. Using the telephone as a sales tool is often referred to as *telemarketing*. To be successful when prospecting potential customers, you must first determine the purpose of the initial phone call. Is it reasonable to expect that a sale will result, or is your purpose to provide information or schedule an appointment?

People are often skeptical of telephone sales. Therefore it is important to initially establish rapport and to immediately state the purpose of your call. Telemarketing activities can serve various purposes including:

- Generating and qualifying prospects
- Creating an awareness of the company
- Introducing a new product or service
- Reinforcing direct mail advertising
- Gathering market information
- Handling customer inquiries, and
- Selling a product or service.

Using the telephone as part of the sales process is an efficient and cost-effective way to access information. A telephone call can determine: the customer's needs, who in the company will ultimately make the purchasing decision, and the process by which purchasing decisions are made.

To establish an effective telemarketing campaign, set aside time each week to make calls. Keep track of calls made using a sales log. Telemarketing requires preparation, persistence, and commitment. Be prepared to handle objections and be prepared for rejection. But don't be discouraged. Develop a winning attitude - be energetic, enthusiastic, and confident!

Quality Customer Service

Companies keep good customers by providing quality customer service. This generally requires that customers receive quality products and services, at reasonable prices, in a timely and convenient manner. It also requires that their concerns be met with understanding and action.

Successful business owners agree that customers must be given better service than they expect. However, few companies succeed at providing quality customer service. A recent survey by the U.S. Office of Consumer Affairs reported that American businesses are not performing as they should when it comes to customer service. The survey revealed that one in four consumers is dissatisfied with the typical commercial transaction, and that they will complain to an average of 12 other people about poor service. This leaves much room for improvement for most businesses and it presents an opportunity for the emerging business to excel where their competitors may be lacking.

One benefit of being a small, new company is the ability of the owner to get close to the customer and to find out what they really need and want. Customers respond extremely well to being asked for input. In his book *In Search of Excellence,* Tom Peters surveys what he calls "excellent companies" in an effort to find out why they are top competitors. According to Peters, "Excellent companies are close to the customer. The customer intrudes into every nook and cranny of the business – sales, manufacturing, research and accounting." Excellent companies, according to Peters, listen to their customers.

Even though Robert Collinge can't hear, he managed to "listen" to his customers, and learned that faster service was what they wanted. He built his business by providing his customers with the quick turn around they needed. As you consider how you will compete for business, keep these words by Robert Allen, CEO and Chairman of AT&T in mind: "No matter how technology and regulatory changes effect the market, the winners will be people who remember they're in business to delight the customer. You can never be good enough at customer service."

References and Resources

Davidson, Jeffrey, *Marketing for the Home-Based Business*, Adams Media Corporation, 1990.

Edic, Martin, *Sales for the Self-Employed*, Prima Publishing, 1997

Gale, Bruce, *Managing Customer Value*, The Free Press, 1994.

Gandolfo, Joe and Korn, Donald Jay, *Sell and Grow Rich*, Dearborn Financial Publishing, 1993.

Gersen, Richard, F., *Marketing for Small Business*, Crisp Publications, 1994.

Hanen, Mack, *Consultative Selling*, Amacom, 1995.

Heibing, Roman, and Cooper, Scott, *The 1-Day Marketing Plan*, NTC Publishing, Chicago, 1992.

Inc. Magazine's 301 Do-it-Yourself Marketing Ideas, The Goldhirsch Group Inc., 1997

Martinet, Jeanne, *The Art of Mingling*, St. Martin's Press, New York, 1992.

McDonald, Malcolm, and Keigan, Warren, *Marketing Plans That Work*, Butterworth-Heinemann, 1997.

Roth, Charles, and Alexander, Roy, *The Secrets of Closing Sales*, Prentice-Hall, 1993.

Small Business Survival Guide, A Blueprint for Success, Prentice-Hall, 1993.

White, Sarah, and Woods, John, *Do-It-Yourself Advertising*, Adams Media Corporation, 1997.

Afterword

Success is accomplished by doing, one step at a time, all the tasks necessary to accomplish your goal. The entrepreneurs profiled in Part One of this book succeeded because they kept moving forward. Like many prospective business owners, they were apprehensive about their abilities and intimidated by all that it takes to succeed in business. But they maintained a belief in themselves and in their businesses, and moved forward with a 100% commitment.

Starting a business can be extremely demanding and immensely challenging. However, despite the challenges, business ownership is a realistic goal for almost anyone no matter what obstacles they face.

Persons with chronic health conditions and disabilities are ideally suited to business ownership. This is true for a number of reasons. As a person with a chronic health condition you may spend much of your time overcoming obstacles. You probably are accustomed to trying creative approaches to getting things done. You have learned how to be resourceful and to compensate for your limitations. Whether it's getting what you need from medical professionals or government agencies, or whether it's having to deal with the ignorance of the general public, you have learned to persevere and to persist.

It is the same qualities you've developed as a result of your illness or disability, which make you uniquely qualified for self-employment. These qualities of perseverance, patience, and resourcefulness will take you through the many events, turning points, and learning experiences of starting and operating a successful business. In short, business ownership is a journey that requires tremendous dedication, commitment, and perseverance. Who better than a person with a disability to take the journey?

Part 4

Appendices

Success:

The Progressive Realization
of a
Worthwhile Dream

Unknown

Small Business Resources for Persons with Disabilities or Chronic Health Conditions: (By State)

The following pages provide a listing of potential business resources, many offering financial assistance to business owners with disabilities and chronic health conditions. Because there are so few programs in the U.S. that specifically target entrepreneurs with disabilities, programs which provide assistance to low-income populations are included. Certainly not all persons with disabilities and chronic health conditions would fall into a low-income category, however, those that do need the most help from available resources. This listing is not exhaustive. It is possible that there are other programs that provide specific services to entrepreneurs with disabilities. Furthermore, this listing is accurate as of the publication date of this book. Names, addresses, and telephone numbers may change at any time. To identify other resources in your state contact your state ombudsman, commerce department, or statewide chamber of commerce.

Programs that provide services specifically for people with special needs are indicated with a ✔

Alabama

SBDC Auburn University
108 College of Business
Auburn, AL 36849
TEL: (334) 844-4220
FAX: (334) 844-4268

Services: Business training, consultation, assistive technology, and research. It provides the services of an SBDC and has experience assisting people with disabilities.

Arizona

✔ Research Institute for Special Entrepreneurs (RISE)
7656 Sonoma Way
Tucson, AZ 85743
TEL: (602) 744-8268

Services: Provides training programs for entrepreneurs with disabilities, individual consultation, referral services and international research.

Arkansas

The Good Faith Fund - Peer Lending Program

400 Main Street, Suite 118
Pine Bluff, Arkansas 71601
TEL: (501) 535-6233
FAX: (501) 535-0741

Services: Peer lending program operates much like a community based credit union. Members join peer-lending groups which consider and approve small business loans for their fellow member entrepreneurs.

✔ University of Arkansas, Research and Training Center in Rehabilitation

346 N. West Avenue
Fayetteville, AR 72701
TEL: (501)575-6417
Contact: Kay Shriner, Ph.D.

Services: Research in economic development and self-employment in rehabilitation counseling. Developing a micro-loan model for a local independent living center.

California

Arcata Economic Development Corporation

100 Ericson, Suite 100
Arcata, California 95521
TEL: (707) 822-4616
FAX: (707) 822-8982

Services: Provides technical assistance and loans to low income persons, women, minorities and dislocated workers in Arcata.

Coalition for Women's Economic Development

315 West 9th Street, Suite 705
Los Angeles, California 90015
TEL: (213) 489-4995
FAX: (213) 489-4090

Services: Assists low-income people achieve self-sufficiency through self-employment.

✔ Disabled Business Persons Association

9625 Black Mountain Road, Suite 207
San Diego, CA 92126-4564
TEL: (619) 586-1199
FAX: (619) 578-0637

Mission/Services: The DBA exists to guide people with disabilities to opportunities in self-employment, and to assist disabled people who are already in business. The organization provides information and referral, assistance with business plan preparation, as well as marketing, accounting, legal and other technical assistance.

✔ **Self-Employment for the Enterprising Disabled (SEED)**

26271 Tarrasa Lane
Mision Viejo, CA 92691

Services: Business counseling and training for entrepreneurs with disabilities. Business feasibility studies.

Colorado

Colorado Department of Social Services

140 East 19th Avenue, 2nd Floor
Denver, Colorado 80203
TEL: (303)894-7438
FAX: (303)894-7419

Services: Provides business, technical, and financial assistance for Denver Employment First participants.

Greater Denver Local Development Corporation

P.O. Box 2135
Denver, Colorado 80201
TEL: (303) 296-9535
FAX: (303) 297-0911

Services: Provides business loans to socially and economically disadvantaged entrepreneurs in Denver and surrounding areas.

Connecticut

Cooperative Fund of New England

108 Kenyon Street
Hartford, Connecticut 06105
TEL: (203) 523-4305
FAX: (203) 523-4305 (call ahead)

Services: Loan program for cooperatives and low-income, worker-owned businesses.

Hartford Economic Development Corporation

15 Lewis Street
Hartford, Connecticut 06103
TEL: (203) 527-1301
FAX: (203) 727-9224

Services: Loans to AFDC, low and moderate income residents. Loans available from $1,500 to $20,000.

Delaware

Wilmington Economic Development Corporation
605A Market Street Mall
Wilmington, Delaware 19801
TEL: (302) 571-9088
FAX: (302) 652-5679

Services: Loans to enterprises owned by low-income, disadvantaged persons in New Castle, Newark, Wilmington, Middletown, Odessa, and Townsend.

District of Columbia

Jubilee Jobs, Inc.
2712 Ontario Road, NW
Washington, D.C. 20009
TEL: (202)667-8970
FAX: (202)667-8833

Services: Technical assistance and small business lending to low-income persons in the D.C. metropolitan area.

Florida

Community Equity Investments
302 North Barcelona Street
Pensacola, Florida 32501-4806
TEL: (904) 433-5619
FAX: (904) 435-6987

Services: Provides technical and small business lending to low and moderate income people.

Georgia

Grasp Enterprises
10 Park Place South, Suite 305
Atlanta, Georgia 30303
TEL: (404) 659-5955
FAX: (404) 880-9561

Services: Provides technical and financial assistance to low-income dislocated workers and entrepreneurs.

Idaho

Panhandle Area Council
11100 Airport Drive

Hayden, Idaho 83835-9743
TEL: (208) 772-0584
FAX: (208) 772-6196
Services: Loans to low-income, disadvantaged individuals in Benewan, Bonner, Boundary, Kotenai, and Shoshone Counties.

Illinois

Chicago Association of Neighborhood Development Organizations
343 South Dearborn Street, Suite 910
Chicago, Illinois 60604
TEL: (312) 939-7171
FAX: (312) 939-7236
Services: Technical assistance and lending to low- and moderate-income individuals throughout Chicago.

The Economic Development Council for the Peoria Area
124 South West Adams Street, Suite 300
Peoria, Illinois 61602
TEL: (309) 676-7500
FAX: (309) 676-7534
Services: Technical assistance and micro-loans to low-moderate income residents of the county of Peoria.

Indiana

Eastside Community Investments
26 North Arsenal Avenue
Indianapolis, Indiana 46220
TEL: (317) 637-7300
FAX: (317) 637-7581
Services: Technical assistance and small business lending to low-income persons in east Indianapolis.

Iowa

✔ Entrepreneurs with Disabilities Program Iowa Department Of Economic Development
200 E. Grand
Des Moines, Iowa 50309
TEL: (515) 242-4948
FAX: (515) 242-4749
Services: Provides technical and financial assistance to help qualified individuals with disabilities become self-sufficient by establishing, maintaining, expanding or acquiring a small business.

Institute for Social and Economic Development

1901 Broadway, Suite 313
Iowa City, Iowa 52240
TEL: (319) 338-2331
FAX: (319) 338-5824

Services: Provides technical and financial assistance to low-income, ethnic minorities and women entrepreneurs in Iowa.

Kansas

✔ **Resource Center for Independent Living, Inc.**

210 N 9th Street
Osage City, KS 66523
TEL: (913) 528-3105
FAX: (913) 528-3665

Services: Business training, consultation, training materials and assistive technology for entrepreneurs with disabilities.

SBDC Washburn University of Topeka

1700 College
Topeka, KS 66621
TEL: (913) 221-1010 ext. 1305
FAX: (913) 231-1063

Services: Business training, consultation, and developing training material.

Kentucky - See Microloan Programs (Appendix D)

Louisiana

Northeast Louisiana University SBDC

700 University Avenue
Monroe, louisiana 71209
TEL: (318) 342- 1224
FAX: (318) 342-1209

Services: Provides technical assistance and micro-loans to low-income entrepreneurs.

Maine

Aroostook Company Action Program

P.O. Box 1116
Presque Isle, Maine 04769
TEL: (207)764-3721
FAX: (207) 768-3040

Services: Provides technical assistance and lending to low income individuals.

Coastal Enterprises

P.O. Box 268
Water Street
Wiscasset, Maine 04578
TEL: (207) 882-7552
FAX: (207) 882-7308

Services: Helps low-income residents of Maine by providing financial and technical assistance for small business.

✔ New Market Tech.

P.O. Box 724
Augusta, Maine 04330
TEL: (207) 287-7370

Services: Coaching and management assistance for new businesses. Business assessments and feasibility studies. Loans available to small businesses owned by people with disabilities.

Maryland

Council for Economic Business Opportunity

The Park Plaze
800 North Charles Street, Suite 300
Baltimore, MD 21201
TEL: (410) 576-2326
FAX: (410) 576-2498

Services: Loans for low-income and disadvantaged individuals in Baltimore, Ann Arundal, Carroll, Hartford, and Hopward Counties.

Massachusetts

✔ Council for Economic Action

One International Place, 17th Floor
Boston, Massachusetts 02110
TEL: (617) 439-2950
FAX: (617) 345-0556

Services: Provides technical assistance to disadvantaged populations, minorities, the physically disabled, and those living in low-income or disadvantaged areas.

Neighborhood Reinvestment Corporation: Neighborhood Enterprise Centers

80 Boylston Street, Suite 1207
Boston, Massachussetts 02116
TEL: (617) 565-8240
FAX: (617) 565-8494

Services: Provides technical assistance and peer lending to low-income women and people of color in over 180 neighborhoods nationwide.

Michigan

✔ **Disability Community Small Business Development Center**

Ann Arbor Center for Independent Living

2568 Packard Road

Ann Arbor, MI 48104-6831

TEL: (734) 971-0277

FAX: (734) 971-0826

TDD: (734) 971-0310

Services: State-wide program offering business counseling, training, government procurement assistance, and micro-lending on a limited basis. Publishes State-wide Directory of Business Owners with Disabilities. Business Feasiblity Studies.

Ann Arbor Community Development Corporation

2008 Hogback Road, Suite 2A

Ann Arbor, Michigan 48105

TEL: (734) 677-1400

FAX: (734) 677-1465

Services: Technical assistance and small business lending to low-income individuals, primarily women, in Washtenaw County.

Detroit Entrepreneurial Institute

455 W. Fort Street

Detroit, Michigan 48226

TEL: (734) 961-8426

FAX: (734) 961-8831

Services: Technical assistance, training and lending to AFDC recipients.

✔ **Grand Rapids Center for Independent Living**

3600 Camelot Drive SE

Grand Rapids, Michigan 49546

TEL/TDD: (616) 949-1100

FAX: (616) 949-7865

Services: One-on-one technical assistance, training and support.

Project Invest

Northwest Michigan Council of Governments

P.O. Box 506

Traverse City, MI 49685

TEL: (800) 692-7774

FAX: (616) 929-5012

Services: Self-employment training, coaching, and micro-lending for low-income individuals in northwest Michigan.

Minnesota

Arrowhead Community Economic Assistance
702 Third Avenue South
Virginia, Minnesota 55792-2775
TEL: (218)749-2914
FAX: (218) 749-2913
Services: To provide business assistance and loans to unemployed, low-income, and minority residents.

✔ CourageWorks
3915 Golden Valley Road
Golden Valley, MN 55422
TEL: (612) 520-0551
FAX: (612) 520-0577
Mission/Services: To assist people with severe physical disabilities for whom working at home in self-employment is the most appropriate employment choice. Provides business training, consultation, training materials, and assistive technology.

North Star Community Development Corporation
615 Board of Trade Building
301 West First Street
Duluth, Minnesota 55802
TEL: (218) 727-6690
FAX: (218) 727-6690
Services: Technical assistance and micro-loans to low and moderate-income persons in Duluth.

Northeast Entrepreneur Fund, Inc.
820 Ninth Street, Suite 140
Virginia, Minnesota 55792
TEL: (218) 749-4191
FAX: (218) 741-4249
Services: Provides technical assistance and micro-loans to unemployed and under-employed, low-income men and women in a 7-county region in northeastern Minnesota.

Mississippi - See Microloan Programs - Appendix D

Missouri

Human Development Corporation of Metro St. Louis
1408 North Kings Highway

St. Louis, Missouri 63113
TEL: (314) 367-5585
FAX: (314) 367-0766

Services: Provides technical assistance and small business loans to AFDC recipients in St. Louis and Wellston.

Montana

Human Resource Development Corporation
321 East Main Street, Suite 300
Bozeman, Montana 59715
TEL: (406) 587-4486
FAX: (406) 585-3538

Services: Provides technical assistance and small business loans to low-income persons, women and minorities in Gallatin, Park and Meagher counties.

Montana Department of Commerce
1424 9th Avenue
Helena, Montana 59620
TEL: (406) 444-3494
FAX: (406) 444-2808

Services: Provides technical assistance and small business loans to minorities, women, and low-income persons.

✔ Montana University Rural Institute on Disabilities
52 Corbin Hall
University of Montana
Missoula, Montana 59812
TEL: (406) 243-5467
FAX: (406) 243-2349
TDD: (406) 243-4200

Services: Research on rural rehabilitation services and self-employment for persons with disabilities. Develop, conduct, and evaluate appropriate training for VR counselors in the use of self-employment strategies.

SBDC Havre
Bear Paw Development Corporation - Fast Trac II
306 3rd Avenue
Box 170
Havre, MT 59501
TEL: (406) 265-9226
Fax: (406) 265-5602

Services: Business training, loans, consultation, assistive technology and research.

Nebraska - See Microloan Programs - Appendix D.

Nevada

Nevada Self-Employment Program
P.O. Box 50478
Reno, Nevada 89513
TEL: (702) 329-6789
FAX: (702) 786-8152

Services: Provides technical assistance and micro-loans to low and moderate income persons.

New Hampshire

New Hamphire Community Loan Fund
P.O. Box 666
Concord, New Hampshire 03302
TEL: (603) 224-6669
FAX: (613) 225-7425

Services: Provides technical assistance and micro-loans to low and moderate income people of Concord.

New Jersey

✔ New Jersey Disability & Non-Profit Loan Fund
20 West State Street, CN-835
Trenton, NJ 08625-0835
TEL: (609) 292-3860/(609) 292-3745
TTY: (609) 777-3238

Services: Loan fund for entrepreneurs with disabilities. Coordinates support systems from existing economic development programs and provides training for state vocational rehabilitation counselors on business start-up strategies. Loan amounts range from $2,500 to $50,000 based on demonstrated need and repayment capacity as well as experience of the candidate. The program also provides direct counseling and business planning assistance.

New Mexico

Women's Economic Self Sufficiency Team
414 Silver SW
Albuquerque, NM 87102-3239
TEL: (505) 848-4760
FAX: (505) 241-2368

Services: State-wide program offering technical assistance and micro-loans for low-income women and minorities.

New York

Alternatives Federal Credit Union

301 West State Street
Ithaca, New York 14850
TEL: (607) 273-4666
FAX: (607) 277-6391

Services: Provides loans and other business-related assistance to low-income persons.

✔ Onondaga Small Business Development Center

Onondaga Community College
EXCELL Building - Room 108
4969 Onondaga Road
Syracuse, New York 13215-1944
TEL: (315) 492-3029
FAX: (315) 492-3704

Services: Business training and counseling to assist people with disabilities achieve self-employment. Funding sources for people with disabilities have been identified. Also the handbook *Business Opportunity for Individuals with Disabilities* is available at no charge.

North Carolina

North Carolina Rural Economic Development Center, Inc.

4 North Blount Street
Raleigh, North Carolina 27601
TEL: (919) 821-1154
FAX: (919) 834-2890

Services: Technical assistance and micro-loans to low and moderate income persons in rural communities of North Carolina.

Mountain Microenterprise Fund

29 1/2 Page Avenue
Ashville, North Carolina 28801
TEL: (704) 253-2834 or 253-2919
FAX: (704) 255-7953

Services: Provides technical assistance and small business loans to women, minorities, and low-income people.

North Dakota

Lake Agassiz Regional Council

417 Main Avenue
Fargo, ND 58103
Services: Statewide microloan program

Ohio

Appalachian Center for Economic Networks

94 North Columbus Road
Athens, Ohio 45701
TEL: (614) 592-3854
FAX: (614) 593-5451
Mission/Services: Revitalization of southeastern Ohio. Provides technical assistance and training to low-income populations, including women, people of color, and people with disabilities.

✔ Business Opportunity Success System (Project BO$$)

Ohio Rehabilitation Services Commission
400 E. Campus View Blvd.
Columbus, Ohio 43235-4604
TEL: (614) 438-1228
FAX: (614) 438-1289
Mission/Services: Project BO$$ was initiated by the Ohio Rehabilitation Services Commission to provide people with disabilities with a systematic approach to starting their own business. The project provides four components of services: market identification, management education, capital access, and technical assistance. A twelve hour introductory course is offered which provides a realistic view of business ownership.

Oklahoma - See Microloan Programs (Appendix D)

Oregon

Cascades West Financial Services, Inc.

408 Southwest Monroe
Corvallis, Oregon 97333
TEL: (541) 967-8551
FAX: (541) 967-4651
Mission: To make business capital available to low-income, minority, and women-owned businesses.

Pennsylvania

✔ **The Business Enterprise Venture**

Pittsburg Blind Association
300 South Craid Street
Pittsburg,PA 15213
TEL: (412) 237-2762
FAX: (412) 682-8104

Services: The program provides training, research, and technical assistance for business owners with disabilities. Guidance on how to obtain funding through state agencies is provided. Information on business possibilities and franchises is also available.

Ben Franklin Technology Center of South Eastern Pennsylvania

3624 Market Street
Philadelphia, Pennsylvania 19104
TEL: (215) 382-0380
FAX: (215) 387-6050

Mission: To make business capital available to low-income, minority, and women-owned businesses in Philadelphia and the surrounding area.

Bloomburg University College of Business

243 Sutliff Hall
Bloomsburg, Pennsylvania 17815
TEL: (717) 389-4591
FAX: (717) 389-3892

Mission: To create opportunities for self-employed persons through technical assistance and individual lending. Services to rural microentrepreneurs who are low- income, unemployed, or AFDC recipients.

Mennonite Economic Development Associates

430 East King Street
Lancaster, Pennsylvania 17601
TEL: (717) 393-6089
FAX: (717) 560-6549

Services: Provides technical assistance and small business loans to low-income persons in Lancaster.

Micro Enterprise Assistance Program

100 Red Oak Lane
Munhall, Pennsylvania 15120
TEL: (412) 462-5328
FAX: (412) 464-4417

Services: Provides technical assistance and small business loans to low income persons in the Pittsburg area.

South Carolina
Good Work
P.O. Box 25250
Durham, North Caroline 27702
TEL: (919) 682-8473
FAX: (919) 688-3615
Services: Provides technical assistance and small business lending to low-income individuals in Durham, Chapel Hill, Raleigh and surrounding areas.

South Dakota
Northeast South Dakota Energy Conservation Corporation
414 Third Avenue
Sisseton, South Dakota 57262
TEL: (605) 698-7654
FAX: (605) 698-3038
Services: Provides technical assistance and micro-loans to low-income, disadvantaged persons in northeast South Dakota.

Tennessee
Matrix, Inc.
220 Carrick Street
Knoxville, Tennessee 37921
TEL: (615) 525-6310
FAX: (615) 637-3920
Services: Provides technical assistance and small business loans to low-income women and minorities in the Knoxville area.

Texas - See Microloan Programs (Appendix D)

Utah
Utah Technology Finance Corporation
177 East 100 South
Salt Lake City, UT 84111
TEL: (801) 364-4346
FAX: (801) 364-4361
Services: Statewide Micro-loan program.

Vermont
Central Vermont Community Action Council, Inc.
P.O. Box 747

Barre, Vermont 05641
TEL: (802) 479-1053
FAX: (802) 479-5353

Services: Technical assistance and lending to low-income persons residing in central Vermont.

Community & Economic Development Office

Room 32, City Hall
Burlington, Vermont 05461
TEL: (802) 865-7144
FAX: (802)865-7024

Services: Technical and financial assistance to low-moderate income people.

Virginia

✔ ### George Washington University and DIAD Entrepreneurial Training Program

1800 Robert Fulton Drive, Suite 115
Reston, VA 22091
TEL/TDD: (703) 715-0460
FAX: (703) 715-0462

Services: Provides practical entrepreneurial skills to people with disabilities.

Washington - See Microloan Programs (Appendix D)

West Virginia

✔ ### Potomac Highlands Support Services

P.O. Box 2028
Martinsburg, WV 25401
TEL: (304) 263-4062
FAX: (304) 267-6184

Services: Provides a variety of services related to employment for people with disabilities. Self-employment has been an employment outcome for some participants of the program. Clients are referred to other agencies for direct services.

Monroe County Community Services Council

P.O. Box 403
Union, West Virginia 24883
TEL: (304) 772-3381
FAX: (304) 772-4014

Services: Provides technical assistance and peer lending to low and moderate income microentrepreneurs.

Wisconsin

CAP Services, Inc.
5499 Highway 10 East
Stevens Point, Wisconsin 54481
TEL: (715) 345-5200
FAX: (715) 345-5206

Services: Technical assistance and loans to low-income individuals and families.

✔ ### Business Development Initiative (BDI) and the Self-Employment Program for People with Disabilities
Wisconsin Department of Development
838 W. National Avenue
Milwaukee, WI 53207
TEL: (414) 382-1750
FAX: (414) 382-1754

Mission/Services: The goal of these programs is to assist people with disabilities who wish to become self-employed. Services include; business feasibility evaluation, business planning and financial packaging assistance, grants of up to $15,000 for consultation, research, and training, and a Micro-Loan program which provides loans of up to $25,000 or 50% of the project.

State Vocational Rehabilitation Offices

Alaska Division of Vocational Rehabilitation
801 West 10th Street, Suite 200
Juneau, AK 99801-1894
Director: Duane French
(907) 465-6922

Alabama Department of Rehabilitation Services
P.O. Box 11586
2129 E. South Blvd.
Montgomery, AL 36111-0586
Commissioner: Lamona H. Lucas
(334) 281-8780

Arizona Rehabilitation Services Administration
Department of Economic Security
1789 W. Jefferson, 2nd Floor, N.W.
Phoenix, Arizona 85007
Administrator: Roger Hodges
(602) 542-3651

American Samoa Department of Human Resources
Division of Vocational Rehabilitation
P.O. Box 4561
Pago Pago, AS 96799-4561
Chief Administrator: Pete Galea'i
(684) 699-1371

Arkansas Division of Services for the Blind
Dept. of Human Services
P.O. Box 3237
Little Rock, AR 72203-3237

Director: James C. Hudson
(501) 682-5463

Arkansas Rehabilitation Services
Dept. of Education
P.O. Box 3781
Little Rock, AR 72203
Commissioner: Bobby C. Simpson
(501) 296-1600

California Department of Rehabilitation
830 K Street Mall
P.O. Box 944333
Sacramento, CA 95814
Director: Brenda Premo
(916) 445-3971

Colorado Division of Vocational Rehabilitation
Dept. of Human Services
110 16th Street, 2nd Floor
Denver, CO 80202
Director: Diana Huerta
(303) 620-4152

Connecticut Bureau of Rehabilitation Services
Dept. of Social Services
10 Griffin Road, North
Windsor, CT 06095
Director: John F. Halliday
(860) 298-2003

Connecticut Board of Education and Services for the Blind
170 Ridge Road

Wethersfield, CT 06109
Executive Director: Kenneth R. Tripp
(203) 566-5800

Commonwealth of N. Mariana Islands

Vocational Rehabilitation Division
P.O. Box 1521 - CK
Saipan, N. Mariana Islands 96950
Director: Maria Perrson
(670) 664-6448

Delaware Division of Vocational Rehabilitation

Dept. of Labor, P.O. Box 9969
4425 N. Market Street
Wilmington, DE 19809-0969
Director: Andrea Guest
(302) 761-8275

Delaware Division for the Visually Impaired

Biggs Building
Health and Social Services Campus
1901 N. DuPont Highway
New Castle, DE 19720
Director: Debra A. Wallace
(302) 577-4731

District of Columbia Rehabilitation Services Administration

Dept. of Human Services
800 9th Street, S.W., 4th Floor
Washington, DC 20024
Acting Administrator: Elizabeth Parker
(202) 645-5703

Florida Division of Vocational Rehabilitation

Dept. of Labor/Employment Security
Building A
2002 Old St. Austine Road
Tallahassee, FL 32399-0696
Director: Tamara Bibb Allen
(904) 488-0059

Florida Division of Blind Services

Dept. of Labor and Employment Security
2540 Executive Ctr. Circle, W.
Douglas Building
Tallahassee, FL 32301
Director: Randy Touchton
(904) 488 1330

Georgia Division of Vocational Rehabilitation

Dept. of Human Resources
2 Peachtree Street, N.W., 23rd Floor
Atlanta, GA 30303-3166
Director: Peggy Rosser
(404) 657-3000

Guam Department of Vocational Rehabilitation

Government of Guam
P.O. Box 2950
Agana, Guam 96910
Director: Joseph Artero-Cameron
(671) 475-4668

Hawaii Vocational Rehabilitation & Services for the Blind

Dept. of Human Services
Bishop Trust Building
1000 Bishop Street, Room 605
Honolulu, Hawaii 96813
Administrator: Neil Shim
(808) 586-5355

Idaho Division of Vocational Rehabilitation

Len B. Jordon Building, Room 150
650 West State, P.O. Box 83720
Boise, Idaho 83720-0096
Interim Administrator: F. Pat Young
(208) 334-3390

Illinois Office of Rehab. Services

Dept. of Human Services
623 E. Adams Street, P.O. Box 19429
Springfield, IL 62794-9429
Assoc. Director: Carl Suter
(217) 782-2093

Indiana Division of Disability, Aging, and Rehabilitation Services
P.O. Box 7083
402 W. Washington St., Room W341
Indianapolis, IN 46207-7083
   Director: Bobby Conner
   (317) 232-1147

Iowa Division of Vocational Rehabilitation Services
Dept. of Education
510 E. 12th Street
Des Moines, IA 50319
   Administrator: Margaret Knudsen
   (515) 281-6731

Iowa Department for the Blind
524 4th Street
Des Moines, IA 50309-2364
   Director: R. Creig Slayton
   (515) 381-1334

Kansas Office of Voc. Rehabilitation
300 Southwest Oakley Street
Biddle Building, 1st Floor
Topeka, KS 66606-1995
   Commissioner: Joyce Cussimanio
   (913) 296-3911

Kentucky Dept. of Voc. Rehabilitation
500 Mero Street
Frankfort, KY 40601
   Commissioner: Sam Serraglio
   (502) 564-4566

Kentucky Department for the Blind
209 St. Clair Street, P.O. Box 757
Frankfort, KY 40602-0757
   Commissioner: Denise Placido
   (502) 564-4754

Louisiana Rehabilitation Services
Dept. of Social Services
8225 Florida Blvd.
Baton Rouge, LA 70806-4834
   Director: May Nelson
   (504) 925-4131

Maine Division of Vocational Rehabilitation Services
Dept. of Labor
35 Anthony Avenue, Station 150
Augusta, ME 04333-0150
   Acting Director; Arthur Jacobson
   (207) 624-5300

Maine Division for the Blind and Visually Impaired
Dept. of Labor
35 Anthony Avenue, Station 150
Augusta ME 04333-0150
   Director: Harold Lewis
   (207) 624-5323

Maryland Division of Rehab. Services
2301 Argonne Drive
Baltimore, MD 21218-1696
   Robert A. Burns
   (410) 554-9385

Massachusetts Rehabilitation Commission
Fort Point Place
27-43 Wormwood Street
Boston, MA 02210-1606
   Commissioner: Elmer C. Bartels
   (617) 727-2172

Massachusetts Commission for the Blind
88 Kingston Street
Boston, MA 02111-2227
   Commissioner: Charles Crawford
   (617) 727-5550 Ext. 4503

Michigan Jobs Commission-Rehabilitation Services
P.O. Box 30010
Lansing, MI 48909
   Director: Joseph A Skiba
   (517) 373-4026

Michigan Commission for the Blind
Family Independence Agency

201 N. Washington
Lansing, MI 48909
   Acting Director: James Buscetta
   (517) 373-2062

Minnesota Department of Economic Security

State Service f/t Blind & Visually
Handicapped
2200 University Ave. West, Suite 240
St. Paul, MN 55101
   Asst. Commissioner: Richard Davis
   (612) 642-0508

Minnesota Division of Rehabilitation Services

Dept. of Economic Security
390 N. Robert Street, 5th Floor
St. Paul, MN 55101
   Asst. Commissioner: Michael
      Coleman
   (612) 296-1822

Mississippi Department of Rehabilitation Services

P.O. Box 1798
Jackson, MS 39215-1698
   Executive Director: Butch McMillan
   (601) 853-5100

Missouri Department of Education

Div. of Vocational Rehabilitation
3024 W. Truman Blvd.
Jefferson City, MO 65109-0525
   Asst. Commissioner: Ronald W.
      Vessell
   (314) 751-3251

Missouri Rehabilitation Services for the Blind

Division of Family Services
P.O. Box 88
Jefferson City, MO 65103-0088
   Deputy Director: Sally Howard
   (573) 751 4249

Montana Division of Disability Services

Dept. of Public Health & Human Services
P.O. Box 4210, 111 Sanders
Helena, MT 59604
   Administrator: Joe A. Mathews
   (406) 444-2590

Nebraska Services for the Visually Impaired

Dept. of Public Institutions
4600 Valley Road
Lincoln, NE 68510-4844
   Director: James S. Nyman, Ph.D.
   (402) 471-2891

Nebraska Division of Rehabilitation Services

State Dept. of Education
301 Centennial Mall South, 6th Floor
Lincoln, NE 68509-4987
   Director: Frank C. Lloyd
   (402) 471-3645

Nevada Department of Employment, Training and Rehabilitation

505 East King Street, 5th Floor
Carson City, NV 89710
   Administrator: Elizabeth Breshears
   (702) 687-4440

New Hampshire Division of Vocational Rehabilitation

State Dept. of Education
70 Regional Drive, Building #2
Concord, NH 03301-9686
   Director: Paul Leather
   (603) 271-3471

New Jersey Division of Vocational Rehabilitation Services

New Jersey Dept. of Labor
CN 398, 135 East State Street
Trenton, NJ 08625-0398
   Director: Thomas Jennings
   (609) 292-5987

New Jersey Commission for the Blind & Visually Impaired

New Jersey Dept. of Human Services
153 Halsey Street, 6th Floor
P.O. Box 47017
Newark, NJ 07101
Executive Director: Jamie Hilton
(201) 648-2324

New Mexico Division of Rehabilitation

State Dept. of Education
435 St. Michael's Drive, Bldg. D
Sante Fe, NM 87505
Director: Terry Brigance
(505) 827-3511

New Mexico Commission for the Blind

PERA Building, Room 553
Sante Fe, NM 87503
Executive Director: Gary Haug
(505) 827-4479

New York Voc. Educational Services for Individuals with Disabilities

Room 1606 OCP
New York State Education Department
Albany, NY 12234
Director: Lawrence Gloeckler
(518) 474-2714

New York Commission for the Blind and Vocational Rehabilitation

State Dept. of Social Services
10 Eyck Office Building
40 N Pearl Street, 16th Floor
Albany, NY 12243-0001
Asst. Commissioner: Thomas A.
Robertson
(518) 473-1801

North Carolina Division of Vocational Rehabilitation Services

Dept. of Human Resources
805 Ruggles Drive, P.O. Box 26053
Raleigh. NC 27611
Director: Bob Philbeck
(919) 733-3364

North Carolina Division of Services for the Blind

Dept. of Human Resources
309 Ashe Avenue
Raleigh, NC 27606
Director: John B. DeLuca
(919) 733-9822

North Dakota Disability Services Division

Dept. of Human Services
Administrative Office
400 E, Broadway Avenue, Suite 303
Bismark, ND 58501-4038
Director: Gene Hysjulien
(701) 328-8950

Ohio Rehabilitation Services Commission

400 E. Campus View Blvd.
Columbus, OH 43235-4604
Administrator: Robert L. Rabe
(614) 438-1210

Oklahoma Department of Rehabilitation Services

3535 N.W. 58th Street, Suite 500
Oklahoma City, OK 73112-4815
Director: Linda S. Parker
(405) 951-3400

Oregon Vocational Rehabilitation Division

Dept. of Human Resources
500 Summer Street, N.E.
Salem, OR 97310-1018
Administrator: Joil Southwell
(503) 945-6201

Oregon Commission for the Blind

535 S.E. 12th Avenue

Portland, OR 97214
    Administrator: Charles Young
    (503) 731-3221

Pennsylvania Office of Vocational Rehabilitation
Dept. of Labor and Industry
1300 Labor & Industry Building
7th and Forster Streets
Harrisburg, PA 17120
    Executive Director: Gil Selders
    (717) 787-5344

Pennsylvania Bureau of Blindness & Visual Services
Dept. of Public Welfare
P.O. Box 2675
Harrisburg, PA 17105-2675
    Acting Director: Holly Strizzi
    (717) 787-6176

Puerto Rico Administration for Vocational Rehabilitation
Dept. of the Family
P.O. Box 1118
Hato Rey, Puerto Rico, 00919
    Administrator:
        Jose R. Santana, Ed.D.
    (787) 728-6550

Rhode Island Office of Rehabilitation Services
Dept. of Human Services
40 Fountain Street
Providence, RI 02903
    Acting Administrator:
        Raymond A. Carroll
    (401) 421-7005

South Carolina Commission for the Blind
1430 Confederate Avenue
Columbia, SC 29201
    Commissioner: Donald Gist
    (803) 734-7520

South Carolina Vocational Rehabilitation Department
P.O. Box 15
1410 Boston Avenue
West Columbia, SC 29171-0015
    Commissioner:
        P. Charles LeRosa, Jr.
    (803) 896-6504

South Dakota Division of Rehabilitation Services
East Highway 34
c/o 500 East Capitol
Pierre, SD 57501-5070
    Director: David Miller
    (605) 773- 3195

South Dakota Division of Service to the Blind and Visually Impaired
East Highway 34
c/o 500 East Capitol
Pierre, ND 57501-5070
    Director: Grady Kickul
    (605) 733-4644

Tennessee Division of Rehabilitation Services
Dept. of Human Services
Citizen Plaza Building, 15th Floor
400 Deaderick Street
Nashville, TN 37248
    Asst. Commissioner: Jack Van Hooser
    (615) 313-4891

Texas Rehabilitation Commission
4900 N. Lamar, Room 7100
Austin, TX 78751-2399
    Commissioner: Vernon M. Arrell
    (512) 424-4000

Texas Commission for the Blind
Administrative Building, Suite 320
4800 North Lamar
Austin, TX 78756
    Executive Director: Pat D. Westbrook
    (512) 459-2500

Republic of Palau Vocational Rehabilitation Services
Bureau of Education
P.O. Box 109
Koror, Palau 96940
Acting Coordinator: Bob Rengchol
(680) 488-2476

Utah State Office of Rehabilitation
250 E. 500 South
Salt Lake City. UT 84111
Executive Director:
R. Blaine Petersen, Ed.D.
(801) 538-7530

Vermont Division for the Blind and Visually Impaired
Agency of Human Services
Osgood Building, Waterbury Complex
103 S. Main Street
Waterbury, VT 05676
Director: Steven R. Stone
(802) 241-2211

Vermont Vocational Rehabilitation Division
Osgood Building, Waterbury Complex
103 S. Main Street
Waterbury, VT 05676
Director: Diane Dalmasse
(802) 241-2186

Virginia Department of Rehabilitative Services
8004 Franklin Farms Drive
P.O. Box K-300
Richmond, VA 23288-0300
Commissioner: John R. Vaughn
(804) 662-7010

Virginia Department for the Visually Handicapped
397 Azalea Avenue
Richmond, VA 23227-3697
Commissioner:

Roy Grizzard, Jr., Ph.D.
(804) 371-3145

Virgin Islands Division for Disabilities & Rehabilitation Services
Knud Hansen Complex, Building A
1303 Hospital Ground
St. Thomas, Virgin Islands 00802
Administrator: Beverly Plaskett
(809) 774-0930 Ext. 4190

Washington Division of Vocational Rehabilitation
Dept of Social and Health Services
P.O. Box 45340
Olympia, WA 98504-5340
Director: Jeanne Monro
(360) 438-8008

Washington Department of Services for the Blind
1400 South Evergreen Park Drive, S.W.
Suite 100, P.O. Box 40933
Olympia, WA 98504-0933
Director: Shirley Smith
(360) 586-6981

West Virginia Department of Rehabilitation Services
Dept. of Education and the Arts
State Capitol Complex
Charleston, WV 25305
Interim Director: William L. Tanzey
(304) 766-4601

Wisconsin Division of Vocational Rehabilitation
2917 International Lane
P.O. 7852
Madison, WI 53707-7852
Administrator:
Judy Norman-Nunnery, Ph.D.
(608) 243-5600

**Wyoming Division of
Vocational Rehabilitation**
Dept. of Employment
1100 Herschler Building
Cheyenne, WY 82002
       Administrator: Gary W. Child
       (307) 777-7389

Small Business Development Center
State Offices

Alabama SBDC
1717 11th Avenue S., Suite 419
Birmingham, AL 35294-4410
    John Sandefur, State Director
    (205) 934-7260

Alaska SBDC
430 W. 7th Avenue, Suite 110
Anchorage, AK 99501—3550
    Jan Fredericks, State Director
    (907) 274-7232

Arizona SBDC
Maricopa Community College
2411 West 14th Street, Suite 132
Tempe, AZ 85281
    Michael York, State Director
    (602) 731-8722

Arkansas SBDC
Univ. of Arkansas at Little Rock
100 South Main, Suite 401
Little Rock, AR 72201
    Janet Nye, State Director
    (501) 324-9043

California SBDC
Office of Small Business
CA Trade & Comm. Agency
801 K Street, Suite 1700
Sacramento, CA 95814-3520
    Kim Neri, State Director
    (916) 324-5068

Colorado SBDC
Office of Business Development

1625 Broadway, Suite 1710
Denver, CO 80202
    Joseph Bell, State Director
    (303) 892-3809

Connecticut SBDC
University of Connecticut
2 Bourn Place, U-94
Storrs, CT 06269-5094
    John O'Connor, State Director
    (860) 486-4135

Delaware SBDC
University of Delaware
005 Purnell Hall
Newark, DE 19716-2711
    Clinton Tymes, State Director
    (302) 831-1555

District of Columbia SBDC
Howard University
2600 6th Street, N.W. Room 125
Washington, DC 20059
    Woodrow McCutchen,
        Exec.Director
    (202) 806-1550

Florida SBDC
19 West Garden Street, Suite 300
Pensacola, FL 32501
    Jerry Cartwright, State Director
    (904) 444-2060

Georgia SBDC
The University of Georgia

Chicopee Complex
1180 East Broad Street
Athens, GA 30602-5412
Henry Logan, Jr., State Director
(706) 542-6762

Guam/Pacific Islands SBDC
University of Guam
College of Business & Public Admin.
303 University Dr., UOG Station
Mangilao, Guam 96923
Dr. Stephen L. Marder, Director
011 (671) 735-2590

Hawaii SBDC
University of Hawaii at Hilo
200 West Kiwili
Hilo, HI 96720-4091
Darryl Mieynek, State Director
(808) 974-7515

Idaho SBDC
Boise State University
1910 University Drive
Boise, Idaho 83725
James Hogge, State director
(208) 385-1640

Illinois SBDC
Dept. of Commerce & Community Affairs
620 East Adams St., 3rd Floor
Springfield, IL 62701-1615
Jeff Mitchell, State Director
(217) 524-5856

Indiana SBDC
One North Capitol, Suite 420
Indianapolis, IN 46204
Stephen Thrash, Exec. Director
(317) 264-6871

Iowa SBDC
Iowa State University Admin. Office
137 Lynn Avenue
Ames, IA 50014
Ronald Manning, State Director
(515) 292-6351

Kansas SBDC
214 S.W. 6th Street, Suite 205
Topeka, KS 66603
Debbie Bishop, State Director
(913) 296-6514

Kentucky SBDC
Center for Entrepreneurship
225 Gatton
College of Business and Economics
University of Kentucky
Lexington, KY 40506-0034
Janet Holloway, State Director
(606) 257-7668

Louisiana SBDC
Northeast Louisiana University
College of Business Administration
Rm. 2-57
Monroe, LA 71209
Dr. John Baker. State Director
(318) 342-5506

Maine SBDC
University of Southern Maine
96 Falmouth St., P.O. Box 9300
Portland, ME 04104
Charles Davis, State Director
(207) 780-4420

Maryland SBDC
7100 Baltimore Avenue, Suite 401
College Park, MD 20740-3627
James Graham, State Director
(301) 403-8300

Massachusetts SBDC
University of Massachusetts-Amherst
205 School of Management
Amherst, MA 03003-4935
John Ciccarelli, State Director
(413) 545-6301

Michigan SBDC
Wayne State University
2727 Second Avenue, Suite 107

Detroit, MI 48201
    Ronald Hall, State Director
    (313) 964-1798

Minnesota SBDC
Dept. of Trade and Economic
Development
500 Metro Square
121 7th Place East
St. Paul, MN 55101-2146
    Mary Kruger, State Director
    (612) 297-5770

Mississippi SBDC
Old Chemistry Building, Suite 216
University, MS 38677
    Raleigh Byars, State Director
    (601) 232-5001

Missouri SBDC
University of Missouri
300 University Place
Columbia, MO 65211
    Max Summers, State Director
    (573) 882-0344

Montana SBDC
Department of Commerce
1424 9th Avenue
Helena, MT 59620
    David Elenbaas, State Director
    (406) 444-4780

Nebraska SBDC
University of Nebraska at Omaha
60th & Dodge Streets, CBA Rm. 407
Omaha, NE 68182
    Robert Bernier, State Director
    (402) 554-2521

Nevada SBDC
University of Nevada - Reno
College of Bus. Administration -032,
Rm 411
Reno, NV 89557-0100
    Sam Males, State Director
    (702) 784-1717

New Hampshire SBDC
University of New Hampshire
108 McConnell Hall
Durham, NH 03824
    Elizabeth Lamoureaux, State Director
    (603) 862-2200

New Jersey SBDC
Rutgers Graduate School of Management
University Heights, 180 University Avenue
Newark, NJ 07102
    Brenda Hopper, State Director
    (201) 648-5950

New Mexico SBDC
Sante Fe Community College
6401 Richards Avenue
Sante Fe, NM 87505
    J. Roy Miller, State Director
    (505) 438-1362

New York SBDC
State University of New York
State University Plaza, S-523
Albany, NY 12246
    James King, State Director
    (518) 443-5398

North Carolina SBDC
NC Small Business & Technical Center
333 Fayetteville St. Mall, #1150
Raleigh, NC 27601
    Scott Daugherty, State Director
    (919) 715-7272

North Dakota SBDC
University of North Dakota
118 Gamble Hall
University Station Box 7308
Grand Forks, ND 58202
    Walter Kearns, State Director
    (701) 777-3700

Ohio SBDC
Ohio Department of Development
77 South High Street, 28th Floor
Columbus, OH 43215

Holly Schick, State Director
(614) 466-2711

Oklahoma SBDC
Southeastern Oklahoma State
517 University
Durant, OK 74701
    Grady Pennington, State Director
    800-522-6154

Oregon SBDC
Lane Community College
44 W. Broadway, Suite 501
Eugene, OR 97401
    Edward Cutler. State Director
    (541) 726-2250

Pennsylvnia SBDC
The Wharton School of the
University of Pennsylvania
423 Vance Hall
3733 Spruce Street
Philadelphia, PA 19104-6374
    Gregory Higgins, State Director
    (219) 898-1219

Puerto Rico SBDC
Inter American University of Puerto Rico
Edificio Union Plaza, Suite 701
Avenida Ponce de Leon, #416
Hato Ray, PR 00918
    Carmen Marti, State Director
    (787) 763-6811

Rhode Island SBDC
Bryant College
1150 Douglas Pike
Smithfield, RI 02917
    Douglas Jobling, State Director
    (401) 232-6111

South Carolina SBDC
University of South Carolina
College of Bus. Administration
Columbia, SC 29208

John Lenti, State Director
(803) 777-4907

South Dakota SBDC
University of South Dakota
414 E. Clark Street
Vermillion, SD 57069-2390
    Robert Ashley, Jr., State Director
    (605) 677-5498

Tennessee SBDC
The University of Memphis
Building 1, South Campus
Getwell Road
Memphis, TN 38152-0001
    Dr. Kenneth Burns, State Director
    (901) 678-2500

Texas-Dallas SBDC
Bill J. Priest Institute for Economic
Development
1402 Corinth Street
Dallas, TX 75215
    Elizabeth Kimback, Reg. Director
    (214) 860-5835

Texas-Houston SBDC
University of Houston
1100 Louisiana, Suite 500
Houston, TX 77002
    J.E. Cadou, Reg. Director
    (713) 752-8444

Texas-Lubbock SBDC
Texas Tech University
2579 S. Loop 289, Suite 210
Lubbock, TX 79423
    Craig Bean, Reg. Director
    (806) 745-3973

Texas-San Antonio SBDC
1222 North Main Street, Suite 450
San Antonia, TX 78212
    Robert McKinley, Reg. Director
    (210) 458-2450

Utah SBDC
Salt Lake Community College
1623 South State Street
Salt Lake City, UT 84115
    Mike Finnerty, State Director
    (801) 957-3480

Vermont SBDC
P.O. Box 422
Randolph, VT 05060
    Donald Kelpinski, State Director
    (802) 728-9101

Virgin Islands SBDC
University of the Virgin Islands
Sunshine Mall No. 1
Frederiksted, VI 00840
    Chester Williams, State Director
    (809) 692-5270

Virginia SBDC
901 East Byrd Street, Suite 1400
P.O. Box 446
Richmond, VA 22319
    Robert Wilburn, State Director
    (804) 371-8253

Washington SBDC
Washington State University
P.O. Box 644851
Pullman, WA 99164
    Carol Reisenberg, State Director
    (509) 339-1576

West Virginia SBDC
950 Kanawha Blvd. East
Charlston, WV 25301
    Hazel Kroesser-Palmer, State Director
    (304) 558-2960

Wisconsin SBDC
University of Wisconsin
432 North Lake Street, Room 423
Madison, WI 53706
    Erica McIntire, State Director
    (608) 263-7794

Wyoming SBDC
P.O. Box 3922
Laramie, WY 82071
    Diane Wolverton, State Director
    (307) 766-3505

SBA Micro-Loan Programs

Participating Intermediary Lenders and Non-Lending Technical Assistance Providers

1. **Alabama**   **Elmore Community Action Committee, Inc.**
   1011 W. Tallassee/P.O.Dr. H, Wetumpka, AL 36092
   Contact: Marion D. Dunlap
   Telephone: (334) 567-4361   *Fax:* (334) 567-0755
   Service Area: Autauga, Elmore and Montgomery counties

2. **Arizona**   **Chicanos Por La Causa, Inc.**
   1112 E. Buckeye Road, Phoenix, AZ 85034-4043
   Contact: Pete Garcia
   Telephone: (602) 257-0700   *Fax:* (602) 256-2740
   Service Area: Urban Maricopa and Pima counties, Graham and Gila counties
   (including Point of Pines Reservation and the Southwestern area of Fort Apache
   Reservation), Coconino and Mohave counties (including the Kaibab, Havasupai,
   and Hualapai Reservations and western portions of the Navajo and Hopi
   Reservations), Yavapai and La Paz counties

3. **Arizona**   **PPEP Housing Dev. Co/Micro Ind. Credit Rural Org.**
   802 East 46th Street, Tucson, AZ 85713
   Contact: John D. Arnold
   Telephone: (602) 622-3553   *Fax:* (602) 622-1480
   Service Area: Cochise, Santa Cruz, Pinal, Yuma, rural Pima, and rural Maricopa
   counties including the Fort Mcdowell, Gila River, Maricopa, Papago, Salt River,
   and San Xavier Indian reservations

4. **Arkansas**   **Arkansas Enterprise Group**
   605 Main Street, Ste 203, Arkadelphia, AR 71923
   Contact: Brian Kelley
   Telephone: (501) 246-9739   *Fax:* (501) 246-2182
   Service Area: Southern and extreme northeast areas of the State including
   Arkansas, Ashley, Bradley, Calhoun, Chicot, Clark, Clay, Cleveland, Columbia,
   Craighead, Dallas, Desha, Drew, Garland, Grant, Greene, Hempstead, Hot

Spring, Howard, Jefferson Lafayette, Lawrence, Lincoln, Little River, Lonoke, Miller, Mississippi, Montgomery, Nevada, Ouachita, Phillips, Pike, Poinsett, Polk, Prairie, Pulaski, Randolph, Saline, Sevier, and Union counties

5. **Arkansas**   **Delta Community Development Corporation**
335 Broadway/ P.O.B. 852, Forrest City, AR 72335
Contact: Fred Lee
Telephone: (501) 633-9113   *Fax:* (501) 633-9191

6. **Arkansas**   **White River Planning and Dev. District, Inc.**
1652 White Dr/ P.O.B. 2396, Batesville, AR 72503
Contact: Van C. Thomas
Telephone: (501) 793-5233   *Fax:* (501) 793-4035
Service Area: Cleburne, Fulton, Independence, Izard, Jackson, Sharp, Stone, Van Buren, White, and Woodruff counties

7. **California**   **Arcata Economic Development Corporation**
100 Ericson Court, Suite 100, Arcata, CA 95521
Contact: Kathleen E. Moxon
Telephone: (707) 822-4616   *Fax:* (707) 822-8982
Service Area: Del Norte, Humboldt, Mendocino, Siskiyou, and Trinity counties

8. **California**   **Center for Southeast Asian Refugee Resettlement**
875 O'Farrell Street, San Francisco, CA 94109
Contact: Vu-Duc Vuong
Telephone: (415) 885-2743   *Fax:* (415) 885-3253
Service Area: Alameda, Contra Costa, Marin, Merced, Sacramento, San Francisco, San Joaquin, San Mateo, Santa Clara, and Stanislaus counties

9. **California**   **Valley Rural Development Corporation**
3417 W. Shaw, Suite 100, Fresno, CA 93711
Contact: Michael E. Foley
Telephone: (209) 271-9030   *Fax:* (209) 271-9078
Service Area: Fresno, Kings, Kern, Stanislaus, Madera, Mariposa, Merced, Tuolumne, and Tulare counties

10. **Colorado**   **Colorado Enterprise Fund**
1881 Sherman St, Suite 530
P.O.B. 2135, Denver, CO 80201-2135
Contact: Cecilia H. Prinster
Telephone: (303) 860-0242   *Fax:* (303) 860-0409
Service Area: City of Denver, and Adams, Arapahoe Boulder, Denver, and Jefferson counties

11. **Colorado**   **Region 10 LEAP, Inc.**
P.O. Box 849, Montrose, CO 81402
300 North Cascade Street, Suite 1
Montrose, CO 81401
Telephone: (970) 249-2436   *Fax:* (970) 249-2488
Contact: Bob Bolt
Service Area: West Central area including Delta, Gunnison, Hinsdale,
Montrose, Ouray and San Miguel counties

12.   **Connecticut**   **New Haven Community Investment Corporation**
809 Chapel St, 2nd Floor, New Haven, CT 06510
Contact: Salvatore J. Brancati, Jr.
Telephone: (203) 776-6172   *Fax:* (203) 776-6837
Service Area: Statewide

13.   **Delaware**   **Wilmington Economic Development Corporaton**
605-A Market Street Mall, Wilmington, DE 19801
Contact: Edwin H. Nutter, Jr.
Telephone: (302) 571-9088   *Fax:* (302) 652-5679
Service Area: New Castle county, in the cities of Wilmington, Newark, New
Castle, Middletown, Odessa, and Townsend

14.   **Dist. of Columbia   ARCH Development Corporation**
1227 Good Hope Road, SE, Washington, DC 20020
Contact: Duane Gautier
Telephone: (202) 889-5023   *Fax:* (202) 889-5035
Service Area: Portions of the District of Columbia commonly referred to as
Adams Morgan, Mount Pleasant and Anacostia, Congress Heights, Columbia
Heights, and 14th Street Corridor

15.   **Dist. of Columbia   H Street Development Corporation**
501 H Street, NE, Washington, DC 20002
Contact: Yulonda Queen
Telephone: (202) 544-8353   *Fax:* (202) 544-3051
Service Area: West-the Anacostia River; East-7th Street, N.W.; North-Benning
Road to K Street; and South-the Southeast/Southwest Freeway: Servicing Capitol
Hill, H Street-N.E., Lincoln Park, Mt. Vernon Square, Judiciary Square, Benning
Road-West of the Anacostia River, Union Station, Stadium Armory, and Lower
North Capitol. Eastern border of North Capitol to Rhode Island to 7th Street,
N.W.; West-Anacostia River; North-Eastern Avenue to North Capitol; and
Southeast/Southwest Freeway: Servicing Eckington, Catholic University,
Michigan Park, Edgewood, Brookland, Ft. Lincoln, New York Avenue, Florida
Avenue, Brentwood-D.C., Woodridge, Trinidad, and N.E. Rhode Island Avenue

16. **Florida**　　**Community Equity Investments Inc.**
302 North Barcelona Street, Pensacola, FL 32501
Contact:　　Daniel R. Horvath
Telephone:　　(904) 444-2234　*Fax:* (904) 444-2264
Service Area:　　Florida Panhandle including Bay, Calhoun, Escambia, Gadsden, Gulf, Jackson, Holmes, Liberty, Leon, Franklin, Wakulla, Walton, Washington, Okaloosa, and Santa Rosa counties

17. **Florida**　　**United Gainesville Community Development Corporation, Inc.**
505 NW 2nd Avenue
P.O.B. 2518, Gainesville, FL 32602
Contact:　　Vian C. Guinyard
Telephone:　　(904) 376-8891　*Fax:* (904) 377-0288
Service Area:　　North Central section including Alachua, Bradford, Columbia, Dixie, Gichrist, Hamilton, Jefferson, LaFayette, Levy, Madison, Marion, Putman, Suwanee, Taylor, and Union counties

18. **Georgia**　　**Fulton County Development Corp/GRASP Enterprises**
55 Marietta St, NW, Ste 2000, Atlanta, GA 30303
Contact:　　Maurice S. Coakley
Telephone:　　(404) 659-5955　*Fax:* (404) 880-9561
Service Area:　　Fulton, Dekalb, Cobb, Gwinnett, Fayette, Clayton, Henry, Douglas, and Rockdale counties

19. **Georgia**　　**Small Business Assistance Corporation**
31 W. Congress St., Ste 100, Savannah, GA 31401
Contact: Tony O'Reily
Telephone:　　(912) 232-4700　*Fax:* (912) 232-0385
Service Area:　　Chatham, Effingham, Bryan, Bulloch, and Liberty counties

20. **Hawaii**　　**The Immigrant Center**
720 North King Street, Honolulu, HI 96817
Contact: Patrician Brandt
Telephone:　　(808) 845-3918　*Fax:* (808) 842-1962
Service Area:　　Island of O'ahu within the City and county of Honolulu

21. **Idaho**　　**Panhandle Area Council**
11100 Airport Drive, Hayden, ID 83835-9743
Contact:　　Jim Deffenbaugh
Telephone:　　(208) 772-0584　*Fax:* (208) 772-6196
Service Area:　　Northern Panhandle including Benewah, Bonner, Boundary, Kotenai, and Shoshone counties

22. **Illinois**   **Greater Sterling Development Corporation**
1741 Industrial Drive, Sterling, IL 61081
Contact: Reid Nolte
Telephone: (815) 625-5255   *Fax:* (815) 625-5094
Service Area: City of Sterling, Whiteside and Lee counties

23. **Illinois**   **Illinois Development Finance Authority**
233 S. Wacker Drive, Suite 5310 Chicago, IL 60606
Contact: Bobby J. Wilkerson
Telephone: (312) 793-5586   *Fax:* (312) 793-6347
Service Area: Statewide with the exceptions of Peoria, Tazwell, Woodford, Whiteside and Lee counties, the City of Sterling, and those portions of Chicago currently served by WSEP

24. **Illinois**   **The Economic Development Council for the Peoria Area**
124 SW Adams Street, Suite 300, Peoria, IL 61602
Contact: Michael Kuhns
Telephone: (309) 676-7500   *Fax:* (309) 676-7534
Service Area: Peoria, Tazwell and Woodford counties

25. **Illinois**   **Neighborhood Inst./Women's Self Employment Project**
20 N. Clark Street, Suite 400, Chicago, IL 60602
Contact: Connie Evans, President
Telephone: (312) 606-8255   *Fax:* (312) 606-9215
Service Area: Portions of the City of Chicago

26. **Indiana**   **Eastside Community Investments Inc.**
26 North Arsenal Avenue, Indianapolis, IN 46201
Contact: Dennis J. West
Telephone: (317) 637-7300   *Fax:* (317) 637-7581
Service Area: City of Indianapolis

27. **Indiana**   **Metro Small Business Assistance Corporation**
306 Civic Center Complex
1 NW Martin Luther King, Jr. Blvd.
Evansville, IN 47708-1869
Contact: Debra A. Lutz
Telephone: (812) 426-5857   *Fax:* (812) 426-5384
Service Area: Vanderburgh, Posey, Gibson, and Warrick counties

28. **Iowa**   **Siouxland Economic Development Corporation**
400 Orpheum Electric Building
P.O. Box 447, Sioux City, IA 51102
Contact: Kenneth A. Beekley
Telephone: (712) 279-6286   *Fax:* (712) 279-6920

Service Area:　Cherokee, Ida, Monoma, Plymouth, Sioux, and Woodbury counties

29.　Kansas　South Central Kansas Economic Development District, Inc.
151 North Volutsia, Wichita, KS 67214
Contact:　Jack E. Alumbaugh
Telephone:　(316) 683-4422　*Fax:* (316) 683-7326
Service Areas:　Butler, Chautauqua, Cowley, Elk, Greenwood, Harper, Harvey, Kingman, Marion, McPherson, Reno, Rice, Sedgwick and Sumner counties

Kansas　Center for Business Innovations, Inc.
4747 Troost Avenue, Kansas City, MO 64110
Contact:　Robert J. Sherwood
Telephone:　(816) 561-8567　*Fax:* (816) 756-1530
Service Areas:　Wyandotte, Johnson, Kansas City, and Leavenworth countics

30.　Kentucky　Community Ventures Corporation
1450 North Broadway, Lexington, KY 40505
Contact:　Kevin R. Smith
Telephone:　(606) 231-0054　*Fax:* (606) 231-0261
Service Area:　Anderson, Bourbon, Clark, Fayette, Harrison, Jessamine, Nicholas, Scott, and Woodford counties

31.　Kentucky　Kentucky Highlands Investment Corporation
P.O. Box 1738, London, KY 40743
Contact:　Jerry A. Rickett
Telephone:　(606) 864-5175　*Fax:* (606) 864-5194
Service Area:　Bell Clay, Clinton, Harlan, Jackson, Knox, Laurel, McCreary, Pulaski, Rockcastle, Wayne, and Whitley counties

32.　Kentucky　Louisville Central Development Corporation
1015 West Chestnut Street
Louisville, KY 40203
Contact:　Sam Watkins, Jr.
Telephone:　(502) 583-8821　*Fax:* (502) 583-8824
Service Area:　Russell neighborhood of Louisville

33.　Kentucky　Purchase Area Development District
1002 Medical Drive
P.O. Box 588, Mayfield, KY 42066
Contact:　Henry A. Hodges
Telephone:　(502) 247-7171　*Fax:* (502) 247-9000
Service Area:　Ballard, Calloway, Carlisle, Fulton, Graves, Hickman, McCracken and Marshall counties

34.　Louisiana　Greater Jennings Chamber of Commerce
414 Cary Ave./P.O. Box 1209, Jennings, LA　70546

		Contact:	Executive Director

           Contact: Executive Director
           Telephone: (318) 824-0933   *Fax:* (318) 824-0934
  Service Area: Jeff Davis Parish

35.   Maine   Coastal Enterprises, Inc
                 P.O. Box 268/ Water Street, Wiscasset, ME 04578
                 Contact: Ronald L. Phillips
                 Telephone: (207) 882-7552   *Fax:* (207) 882-7308
       Service Area: Statewide excluding Aroostock, Piscataquis, Washington, Oxford, Penobscot and Hancock counties

36.   Maine   Northern Maine Development Commission
                 2 South Main St./ P.O.B. 779, Caribou, ME 04736
                 Contact: Robert P. Clark
                 Telephone: (207) 498-8736   *Fax:* (207) 493-3108
       Service Area: Aroostook, Piscataquis, Washington, Penobscot and Hancock counties

37.   Maine   Community Concepts, Inc.
                 35 Market Sq./P.O.B. 278, South Parris, ME 04281
                 Contact: Charleen M. Chase
                 Telephone: (207) 743-7716   *Fax:* (207) 743-6513
       Service Area: Oxford county

38.   Maryland   Council for Economic Business Opportunity, Inc.
                 The Park Plaza
                 800 N. Charles St., Ste 300, Baltimore, MD 21201
                 Contact: Larry J. Smith
                 Telephone: (410) 576-2326   *Fax:* (410) 576-2498
       Service Area: City of Baltimore and Ann Arundel, Baltimore, Carroll, Harford, and Howard counties

39.   Massachusetts Economic Develvopment Industrial Corporation of Lynn
                 37 Central Square, 3rd Floor, Lynn, MA 01901
                 Contact: Peter M. DeVeau
                 Telephone: (617) 592-2361   *Fax:* (617) 581-9731
       Service Area: City of Lynn

40.   Massachusetts Jewish Vocational Service, Inc.
                 105 Chauncy St., 6th Floor, Boston, MA 02111
                 Contact: Barbara S. Rosenbaum
                 Telephone: (617) 451-8147   *Fax:* (617) 451-9973
       Service Area: (One Stop Capital Shop) Greater Boston with particular emphasis on the Mattapan (Boston), North Dorchester (Boston), and Central Square (Cambridge) neighborhoods

41. **Massachusetts Jobs for Fall River, Inc.**
   One Government Center, Fall River, MA 02722
   Contact: Stephen Pari
   Telephone: (508) 324-2620   *Fax* (508) 6787-2840
   Service Area: City of Fall River

42. **Massachusetts Springfield Business Development Fund**
   36 Court Street, Room 206, Springfield, MA 01103
   Contact: James Asselin
   Telephone: (413) 787-6050   *Fax:* (413) 787-6027
   Service Area: City of Springfield

43. **Massachusetts Western Massachusetts Enterprise Fund**
   308 Main Street, Suite 2B, Greenfield, MA 01301
   Contact: Christopher Sikes
   Telephone: (413) 774-4033   *Fax:* (413) 773-3562
   Service Area: Berkshire, Franklin counties, the towns of Chester & Chicopes
within Hampden county, the towns of Athol, Petersham, Phillipston &
Royalston within Worcester county and the following towns within Hampshire
county: Amherst, Chesterfield, Cummington, Easthampton, Goshen, Hadley,
Huntington, Middlefield, Northampton, Plainfield, Westhampton, Williamsburg
and Worthington

44. **Michigan**   **Ann Arbor Community Development Corp**
   2008 Hogback Road, Suite 2A, Ann Arbor, MI 48105
   Contact: Michelle Richards Vasquez
   Telephone: (734) 677-1400   *Fax:* (734) 677-1465
   Service Area: Washtenaw county

45. **Michigan**   **Detroit Economic Growth Corporation**
   150 W. Jefferson, Suite 1000, Detroit, MI 48226
   Contact: Nate Davis
   Telephone: (313) 963-2940   *Fax:* (313) 963-8839
   Service Area: City of Detroit

46. **Michigan**   **Community Capital and Development Corp**
   The Walter Reuther Center
   711 N. Saginaw St., Suite 123, Flint, MI 48503
   Contact: Bobby J. Wells
   Telephone: (810) 239-5847   *Fax:* (810) 239-5575
   Service Area: Genesee county

47. **Michigan**   **Northern Economic Initiatives Corp**
   228 West Washington Street, Marquette, MI 49855

Contact: Richard Anderson
Telephone: (906) 228-5571 Fax: (906) 228-5572
Service Area: Upper Peninsula including Alger, Baraga, Chippewa, Delta, Dickinson, Gogebic, Houghton, Iron, Keewenaw, Luce, Macinac, Marquette, Menonimee, Ontonagon, and Schoolcraft counties

48. **Minnesota**   **Northeast Entrepreneur Fund, Inc.**
Olcott Plaza, Suite 140
820 Ninth Street North, Virginia, MN 55792
Contact: Mary Mathews
Telephone: (218) 749-4191 Fax: (218) 741-4249
Service Area: Koochiching, Itasca, St.Louis, Aitkin, Carlton, Cook and Lake counties

49. **Minnesota**   **Women Venture**
2324 University Ave., St. Paul, MN 55114
Contact: Cynthia Paulson
Telephone: (612) 646-3808 Fax: (612) 291-2597
Service Area: Cities of Minneapolis and St. Paul and, Andra, Carver, Chisago, Dakota, Hennepin, Isanti, Ramsey, Scott, Washington, and Wright counties

50. **Minnesota**   **Minneapolis Consortium of Community Developers**
1808 Riverside Ave., Suite 206, Minneapolis, MN 55454-1035
Contact: Karen Reid
Telephone: (612) 371-9986 Fax: (612) 673-0379
Service Area: Portions of the City of Minneapolis

51. **Minnesota**   **Northwest Minnesota Initiative Fund**
722 Paul Bunyan Drive, NW, Bemidji, MN 56601
Contact: Tim Wang
Telephone: (218) 759-2057 Fax: (218) 759-2328
Service Area: Beltrami, Clearwater, Hubbard, Kittsson, Lake of the Woods, Mahnomen, Marshall, Norman, Pennington, Polk, Red Lake, and Rousseau counties

52. **Mississippi** **Delta Foundation**
819 Main Street, Greenville, MS 38701
Contact: Harry J. Bowie
Telephone: (601) 335-5291 Fax: (601) 335-5295
Service Area: Statewide excluding Issaquena, Sharkey, Humphreys, Madison, Leake, Kemper, Copiah, Hinds, Rankin, Newton, Smith, Jasper, Clarke, Jones, Wayne, and Greene counties

53. **Mississippi**   **Friends of Children of Mississippi, Inc.**
4880 McWillie Circle, Jackson, MS 39206
Contact: Marvin Hogan
Telephone: (601) 362-1541   *Fax:* (601) 362-1613
Service Area: Issaquena, Sharkey, Humphreys, Madison, Leake, Kemper,
Copiah, Hinds, Rankin, Newton, Smith, Jasper, Clarke, Jones, Wayne, and
Greene counties

54. **Missouri**   **Center for Business Innovations, Inc.**
4747 Troost Avenue, Kansas City, MO 64110
Contact: Robert J. Sherwood
Telephone: (816) 561-8567   *Fax:* (816) 756-1530
Service Area: Statewide

55. **Montana**   **Capital Opportunities/District IX HRDC, Inc.**
321 East Main St., Suite 300, Bozeman, MT 59715
Contact: Charlie Hill
Telephone: (406) 587-4486   *Fax:* (406) 585-3538
Service Area: Gallatin, Park and Meagher counties

56. **Montana**   **Montana Western Region Economic Development Group**
127 N. Higgins Avenue, Missoula, MT 59802
Contact: Catherine Brown
Telephone: (406) 543-3550   *Fax:* (406) 721-4584
Service Area: Lake, Mineral, Missoula, Ravalli, and Sanders counties

57. **Nebraska**   **Rural Enterprise Assistance Project**
101 South Tallman Street
P.O.Box 406, Walthill, NE 68067
Contact: Don Ralston
Telephone: (402) 846-5428   *Fax:* (402) 846-5420
Service Area: Antelope, Banner, Blaine, Boone, Box Butte, Boyd, Brown, Burt,
Cass, Cedar, Cherry, Cheyenne, Colfax, Custer, Dawes, Deuel, Dixon, Gage,
Garden, Garfield, Greeley, Holt, Jefferson, Johnson, Keya Paha, Kimball, Knox,
Lancaster, Loup, McPherson, Morrill, Nance, Nemaha, Otoe, Pawnee, Pierce,
Platte, Richardson, Rock, Saline, Saunders, Seward, Sheridan, Sioux, Scottsbluff,
Thurston, Wayne, and Wheeler counties

58. **Nebraska**   **West Central Nebraska Development District, Inc.**
201 East 2nd Street, Suite C
P.O. Box 599, Ogailala, NE 69153
Contact: Ronald J. Radil
Telephone: (308) 284-6077   *Fax:* (308) 284-6070
Service Area: Arthur, Chase, Dawson, Dundy, Frontier, Furnas, Gosper, Grant,

Hayes, Hitchcock, Hooker, Keith, Lincoln, Logan, Perkins, Red Willow and Thomas counties

59. **Nevada**   **NWF/Nevada Self Employment Trust**
                         560 Mill Street, Suite 260, Reno, Nevada 89502
                         Contact: Janice Barbour
                         Telephone: (702) 786-2335   *Fax:* (702) 786-8152
     Service Area: Statewide

60. **New Hampshire   Institute for Cooperative Community Development, Inc.**
                         2500 North River Road, Manchester, NH 03106
                         Contact: Don Mason
                         Telephone: (603) 644-3103   *Fax:* (603) 644-3130
     Service Area: Statewide excluding Grafton, Carol and Coos counties

                         Northern Community Investment Corporation
                         c/o 20 Main Street, St. Johnsbury, VT 05819
                         Contact: Carl J. Garbelotti
                         Telephone: (802) 748-5101   *Fax:* (802) 748-1884
     Service Area: Grafton, Carol and Coos counties

61. **New Jersey**   **Trenton Business Assistance Corporation**
                         Division of Economic Development
                         319 East State Street, Trenton, NJ 08608-1866
                         Contact: Elizabeth Janota
                         Telephone: (609) 989-3509   *Fax:* (609) 989-4243
     Service Area: Portions of the City of Trenton and Mercer county

62. **New Jersey**   **Greater Newark Business Development Consortium**
                         One Newark Center, 22nd Flr, Newark, NJ 07102-5265
                         Contact: David Means
                         Telephone: (201) 242-6237   *Fax:* (201) 824-6587
     Service Area: Bergen, Essex, Hudson, Middlesex, Monmouth, Morris, Passaic,
     and Somerset counties with the exception of the city of Jersey City

63. **New Jersey**   **Union County Economic Development Corporation**
                         Liberty Hall Corporate Center
                         1085 Morris Avenue, Suite 531, Union, NJ 07083
                         Contact: Maureen Tinen
                         Telephone: (908) 527-1166   *Fax:* (908) 527-1207
     Service Area: Union county

64. **New Jersey**   **Jersey City Economic Development Corporation**
                         601 Pavonia Avenue, Jersey City, NJ 07306

		Contact:	John Rogers

Contact: John Rogers
Telephone: (201) 420-7755   *Fax:* (201) 420-0306
Service Area: City of Jersey City

65.   **New Mexico**   **Women's Economic Self Sufficiency Team**
414 Silver SW, Albuquerque, NM 87102-3239
Contact: Agnes Noonan
Telephone: (505) 848-4760   *Fax:* (505) 241-2368
Service Area: Statewide

66.   **New York**   **Adirondack Economic Development Corporation**
Trudeau Road, P.O.B. 747, Saranac Lake, NY 12983
Contact: Ernest Hohmeyer
Telephone: (518) 891-5523   *Fax:* (518) 891-9820
Service Area: Clinton, Essex, Franklin, Fulton, Hamilton, Herkimer, Jefferson, Lewis, Oneida, Oswego, St. Lawrence, Saratoga, Warren and Washington counties

67.   **New York**   **Columbia Hudson Partnership**
444 Warren Street, Hudson, NY 12534-2415
Contact: Jayme B. Lahut
Telephone: (518) 828-4718   *Fax:* (518) 828-0901
Service Area: Columbia county

68.   **New York**   **Manhattan Borough Development Corporation**
15 Park Row, Suite 510, New York, NY 10038
Contact: Jeff Deasey
Telephone: (212) 791-3660   *Fax:* (212) 571-0873
Service Area: The borough of Manhattan

69.   **New York**   **Rural Opportunities, Inc.**
339 East Avenue, Suite 401, Rochester, NY 14604
Contact: Joan A. Dallis
Telephone: (716) 546-7180   *Fax:* (716) 546-7337
Service Area: Allegheny, Cattaraugua, Cayuga, Chatauqua, Erie, Genessee, Livingston, Niagara, Ontario, Orleans, Senece, Steuben, Wayne, Wyoming, and Yates counties

70.   **No. Carolina**   **Self-Help Ventures Fund**
301 W. Main Street, P.O. Box 3619
Durham, NC 27702-3619
Contact: Robert Schall
Telephone: (919) 956-8526   *Fax:* (919) 688-3615
Service Area: Statewide

71. **No. Carolina**   **W.A.M.Y. Community Action**
P.O. Box 552, Boone, North Carolina 28607
Contact: Jerry R. Fee
Telephone: (704) 264-2421   *Fax:* (704) 264-0952
Service Area: Watauga, Avery, Mitchell, and Yancey counties

72. **No. Dakota**   **Lake Agassiz Regional Council**
417 Main Avenue, Fargo, ND 58103
Contact: Irvin D. Rustad
Telephone: (701) 239-5373   *Fax:* (701) 235-6706
Service Area: Statewide

73. **Ohio**   **Enterprise Development Corporation**
900 East State Street, Athens, OH 45701
Contact: Karen A. Patton
Telephone: (614) 592-1188   *Fax:* (614) 593-8283
Service Area: Adams, Ashland, Athens, Belmont, Brown, Carrol, Columbiana, Coshocton, Gallia, Guernsey, Harrison, Highland, Holmes, Jackson, Jefferson, Knox, Lawrence, Meigs, Monroe, Morgan, Muskingum, Nocking, Noble, Perry, Pike, Ross, Scioto, Tuscarawas, Vinton and Washington counties

74. **Ohio**   **Columbus Countywide Development Corporation**
941 Chatham Lane, Suite 207, Columbus, OH 43221
Contact: Brad Shimp
Telephone: (614) 645-6171   *Fax:* (614) 645-8588
Service Area: City of Columbus, Franklin county

75. **Ohio**   **Hamilton County Development Company, Inc.**
1776 Mentor Avenue, Cincinnati, OH 45212
Contact: David K Main
Telephone: (513) 632-8292   *Fax:* (513) 631-4887
Service Area: City of Cincinnati, Adams, Brown, Butler, Clermont, Clinton, Highland, and Warren counties

76. **Ohio**   **Women's Entrepreneurial Growth Organization**
526 S. Main Street, Suite 235
P.O. Box 1848, Akron, OH 44325-1848
Contact: Holly Riggs
Telephone: (330) 379-9280   *Fax:* (330) 379-9283
Service Area: Ashtabula, Cuyahoga, Geauga, Lake, Lorain, Mahoning, Medina, Portage, Stark, Summit, Trumbull, Wayne counties

77. **Oklahoma**   **Rural Enterprises, Inc.**
422 Cessna Street, Durant, OK 74701

Contact:	Sherry Harlin	
Telephone:	(405) 924-5094	*Fax:* (405) 920-2745
Service Area:	Statewide	

78. Oklahoma Tulsa Economic Development Corporation
907 S. Detroit Ave., Suite 1001, Tulsa, OK 74120
Contact: Frank F. McCrady III
Telephone: (918) 585-8332   *Fax:* (918) 585-2473
Service Area: Adair, Canadian, Cherokee, Cleveland, Craig, Creek, Delaware, Haskell, Hayes, Hughes, Kay, Latimer, Leflore, Lincoln, Logan, McIntosh, Muskogee, Noble, Nowata, Okfuskee, Oklahoma, Okmulgee, Osage, Ottawa, Pawnee, Payne, Pittsburg, Pottawatomie, Rogers, Seminole, Sequoyah, Wagoner, Washington, and Wayne counties including the city of Tulsa

79. Oregon Cascades West Financial Services, Inc.
P.O. Box 686, Albany, OR 97321
Contact: Robert Wisniewski
Telephone: (541) 967-8551   *Fax:* (541) 967-4651
Service Area: Benton, Clackamas, Hood River, Jefferson, Lane, Lincoln, Linn, Marion, Multnomah, Polk, Tillamook, Wasco, Washington, Yamhill counties

80. Pennsylvania The Ben Franklin Technical Center of SE Pennsylvania
3625 Market Street, Philadelphia, PA 19104-2615
Contact: Barry Stein
Telephone: (215) 382-0380   *Fax:* (215) 382-6050
Service Area: Bucks, Chester, Delaware, Montgomery and Philadelphia counties

81. Pennsylvania The Washington County Council on Economic Development
703 Courthouse Square, Washington, PA 15301
Contact: Malcolm L. Morgan
Telephone: (412) 228-6816   *Fax:* (412) 250-6502
Service Area: Southwestern area of Pennsylvania including Greene, Fayette and Washington counties

82. Pennsylvania York County Industrial Development Corporation
One Market Way East, York, PA 17401
Contact: David B. Carver
Telephone: (717) 846-8879   *Fax:* (717) 843-8837
Service Area: York county

83. Puerto Rico Corporation for the Economic Development of the City of San Juan
Ave. Munos Rivera, #1127, Rio Piedras, PR 00926
Contact: Jesus M. Rivera Viera
Telephone: (787) 756-5080   *Fax:* (787) 753-8960
Service Area: Territory wide

84. **So.Carolina**   **Charleston Citywide Local Development Corporation**
75 Calhoun St., 3rd Floor, Charleston, SC 29403
Contact: Sharon Brennan
Telephone: (803) 724-3796   *Fax:* (803) 724-7354
Service Area: City of Charleston

85. **So.Carolina**   **Santee Lynches Regional Development Corporation**
Post Office Drawer 1837, Sumter, SC 29151
Contact: Linda Shippley
Telephone: (803) 775-7381   *Fax:* (803) 773-9903
Service Area: Clarendon, Kershaw, Lee and Sumter counties

86. **So. Dakota**   **Lakota Fund**
P.O.Box 340, Kyle, South Dakota 57752
Contact: Dani Not Help Him
Telephone: (605) 455-2500   *Fax:* (605) 455-2385
Service Area: Bennett County, Pine Ridge Indian Reservation, and areas of
Shannon and Jackson counties which are surrounded by Indian Lands, and exclusive of northern Jackson county

87. **So. Dakota**   **NE South Dakota Energy Conservation Corporation**
414 Third Avenue, East, Sisseton, SD 57262
Contact: Arnold Petersen
Telephone: (605) 698-7654   *Fax:* (605) 698-3038
Service Area: Beadle, Brown, Buffalo, Campbell, Clark, Codington, Day,
Edmunds, Faulk, Grant, Hand, Hyde, Jerauld, Kingsbury, McPherson, Marshall,
Miner, Potter, Roberts, Sanborn, Spink, and Walworth counties

88. **Tennessee**   **South Central Tennessee Development District**
815 S. Main St., P.O.B. 1346, Columbia, TN 38402
Contact: Joe Max Williams
Telephone: (615) 381-2040   *Fax:* (615) 381-2053
Service Area: Bedford, Coffee, Franklin, Giles, Hickman, Lawrence, Lewis,
Lincoln, Marshall, Maury, Moore, Perry, and Wayne counties

89. **Texas**   **Business Resource Center Incubator**
4601 N. 19th, Waco, TX 76708
Contact: Lu Billings
Telephone: (817) 754-8898   *Fax* (817) 756-0776
Service Area: Bell, Bosque, Coryell, Falls, Hill, and McLennan counties

90. **Texas**   **San Antonio Local Development Corporation**
100 Military Plaza,
4th Floor City Hall, San Antonio, TX 78205
Contact: Oscar Perez

> *Telephone:* (210) 207-8152
> *Service Area:* Atascosa, Bandera, Bexar, Comal, Frio, Gillespie, Guadalupe, Karnes, Kendall, Kerr, Medina, and Wilson counties

91. **Texas**

Southern Dallas Development Corporation
1402 Corinth, Suite 1150, Dallas, TX 75215
Contact: Jim Reid
Telephone: (214) 428-7332   *Fax:* (214) 426-6847
Service Area: Portions of the City of Dallas

92. **Utah**

Utah Technology Finance Corporation
177 East 100 South, Salt Lake City, UT 84111
Contact: Don Welty
Telephone: (801) 364-4346   *Fax:* (801) 364-4361
Service Area: Statewide

93. **Vermont**

Economic Development Council of Northern Vermont, Inc.
155 Lake Street, St. Albans, VT 05478
Contact: Connie Stanley-Little
Telephone: (802) 524-4546   *Fax:* (802) 527-1081
Service Area: Chittenden, Franklin, Grand Isle, Lamoille, and Washington counties

94. **Vermont**

Northern Community Investments Corporation
20 Main St., P.O. Box 904, St. Johnsbury, VT 05819
Contact: Carl J. Garbelotti
Telephone: (802) 748-5101   *Fax:* (802) 748-1884
Service Area: Caledonia, Essex, and Orleans counties

95. **Virginia**

Ethiopian Community Development Council, Inc.
1038 S. Highland Street, Arlington, VA 22204
Contact: Tsehaye Teferra
Telephone: (703) 685-0510   *Fax:* (703) 685-0529
Service Area: Prince William, Arlington and Fairfax counties and the cities of Alexandria and Falls Church

96. **Virginia**

Business Development Centre, Inc.
147 Mill Ridge Road, Lynchburg, VA 24502
Contact: Rich Stallings
Telephone: (804) 582-6100   *Fax:* (804) 582-6106
Service Area: Amherst, Appomattox, Bedford, Campell counties, the cities of Lynchburg and Bedford, and the Town of Amherst

97. **Virginia**

People Incorporated of Southwest Virginia
1173 West Main Street, Abingdon, Virginia 24210

Contact: Robert G. Goldsmith
Telephone: (540) 623-9000 *Fax:* (504) 628-9000
Service Area: Buchanan, Dickenson, Lee, Russell, Scott, Washington, Wise counties and the cities of Bristol and Norton

98. **Washington** **Snohomish County Private Industry Council**
917 134th St. SW, Suite A-10, Everett, WA 98204
Contact: Emily Duncan
Telephone: (206) 743-9669 *Fax:* (206) 745-1177
Service Area: Adams, Chelan, Douglas, Grant, King, Kittitas, Klickitat, Okanogan, Pierce, Skagit, Snohomish, Whatcom, and Yakima counties

99. **Washington** **Tri-Cities Enterprise Association**
2000 Logston Boulevard, Richland, WA 99352
Contact: Dallas E. Breamer
Telephone: (509) 375-3268 *Fax:* (509) 375-4838
Service Area: Benton and Franklin counties

100. **W. Virginia** **Ohio Valley Industrial and Business Development Corporation**
12th and Chapline Streets, Wheeling, WV 26003
Contact: Terry Burkhart
Telephone: (304) 232-7722
Service Area: Marshall, Ohio, Wetzel, Brooke, Hancock, and Tyler counties

W. Virginia **The Washington County Council on Economic Development**
703 Courthouse Square, Washington PA 15301
Contact: Malcolm L. Morgan
Telephone: (412) 228-6816 *Fax:* (412) 250-6502
Service Area: Preston and Monongalia counties

101. **Wisconsin** **Advocap, Inc.**
19 W 1st Street, POB 1108, Fond du Lac, WI 54936
Contact: Morton Gazerwitz
Telephone: (414) 922-7760 *Fax"* (414) 922-7214
Service Area: Fond du Lac, Green Lake, and Winnebago counties

102. **Wisconsin** **Impact Seven, Inc.**
651 Garfield Street S, Alema, WI 54805-7031
Contact: William Bay
Telephone: (715) 263-2532
Service Area: Statewide with the exceptions of Fond du Lac, Green Lake, Kenosha, Milwaukee, Oasukee, Racine, Walworth, Waukesha, Washington, and Winnebago counties and, inner city Milwaukee

103. Wisconsin   **Women's Business Initiative Corporation**
1915 N. Martin Luther King, Milwaukee, WI 53212
Contact: Wendy Werkmeister
Telephone: (414) 372-2070   *Fax:* (414) 372-2083
Service Area: Kenosha, Milwaukee, Oazukee, Racine, Walworth, Washington, and Waukesha counties

TECHNICAL ASSISTANCE GRANT RECIPIENTS

1. Alaska   **Southeast Alaska Small Business Development Center**
400 Willoughby, Suite 211, Juneau, AK 99801-1724
Contact: Charles M. Northrip
Telephone: (907) 463-3789   *Fax:* (907) 463-3929
Service Area: Through SBDCs, the Alaska Panhandle

2. California   **Women's Initiative for Self-Employment**
450 Mission, Suite 402, San Francisco, CA 94105
Contact: Sophia Raday
Telephone: (415) 247-9473   *Fax:* (415) 247-9471
Service Area: Defined sectors of San Francisco Bay Area

3. Connecticut   **American Woman's Economic Development Corporation**
Plaza West Office Centers
200 West Main St., Suite 140, Stamford, CT 06902
Contact: Fran Polak
Telephone: (203) 326-7914
Service Area: SW corner including Ansonia, Beacon Falls, Bethel, Bridgeport, Bridgewater, Brookfield, Danbury, Darien, Derby, Easton, Fairfield, Greenwich, Milford, Monroe, New Canaan, New Fairfield, New Milford, Newtown, Norwalk, Oxford, Redding, Ridgefield, Seymour, Shelton, Sherman, Stamford, Stratford, Trumbull, Weston, Westport, and Wilton counties

4. Florida   **Lee County Employment & Economic Development Corporation**
2121 West 1st St., Suite One
P.O. Box 2285, Fort Myers, FL 33902-2285
Contact: Roy H. Kennix
Telephone: (941) 337-2300   *Fax:* (941) 337-4558
Service Area: Community Redevelopment Areas of Lee County including Charleston Park, Dunbar, Harlem Heights, No. Fort Myers, and State Road 80

5. **Illinois** **Women's Business Development Center**
8 South Michigan Ave., Ste 400, Chicago, IL 60603
Contact: Joyce Wade
Telephone: (312) 853-3477 *Fax:* (312) 853-0145
Service Area: Boone, Cook, DeKalb, DuPage, Kane, Kankakee, Kendall, Lake, McHenry, Will, and Winnebago counties

6. **Indiana** **Hoosier Valley Economic Development Corporation**
1613 E 8th, POB 843, Jeffersonville, IN 47131
Contact: Jerry L. Stephenson
Telephone: (812) 288-6451 *Fax:* (812) 284-8314
Service Area: Clark, Crawford, Floyd, Harrison, Orange, Scott, and Washington counties

7. **Iowa** **Institute for Social and Economic Development**
1901 Broadway, Suite 313, Iowa City, IA 52240
Contact: John F. Else
Telephone: (319) 338-2331 *Fax:* (319) 338-5824
Service Area: Statewide

8. **Kansas** **Great Plains Development, Inc.**
100 Military Plaza, Suite 128
P.O. Box 1116, Dodge City, KS 67801
Contact: Carlyle Kienne
Telephone: (316) 227-6406 *Fax:* (315-225-6051
Service Area: Statewide

9. **Michigan** **Cornerstone Alliance**
185 East Main, Benton Harbor, MI 49022-4440
Contact: D. Jeffrey Noel
Telephone: (616) 925-6100 *Fax:* (616) 925-4471
Service Area: Berrien County and Benton Harbor

10. **Minnesota** **Neighborhood Development Center, Inc.**
651 1/2 University Avenue, St. Paul, MN 55104
Contact: Mihailo Temali
Telephone: (612) 291-2480 *Fax:* (612) 291-2597
Service Area: Districts 3,5,6,8,9, and 16 of the City of St. Paul

11. **Missouri** **Community Development Corporation of Kansas City**
2420 East Linwood Blvd, Suite 400
Kansas City, MO 64109
Contact: Donald Maxwell
Telephone: (816) 924-5800 *Fax:* (816) 921-3350
Service Area: Cass, Clay, Platte, Ray and Jackson counties

12. **Montana** **Montana Department of Commerce - SBDC Division**
1424 9th Ave., POB 200501, Helena, MT 59620-0501
Contact:　　Gene Marcille
Telephone:　(406) 444-4780　*Fax:* (406) 444-1872
Service Area:　Through SBDCs, Cascade, Chouteau, Fergus, Glacier, Golden Valley, Judity Basin, Musselshell, Petroleum, Pondera, Teton, Toole and Wheatland counties, and the Blackfeet, Flathead, and Fort Peck Reservations, and the Crow, Fort Belknap, Northern Cheyenne and Rocky Boys Reservations and their Trust Lands

13. **Nebraska** **Omaha Small Business Network, Inc.**
2505 North 24th Street, Omaha, NE 68110
Contact:　　Kelvin Cingman
Telephone:　(402) 346-8262　*Fax:* (402) 451-2876
Service Area:　Areas of the City of Omaha known as the North Omaha and South Omaha Target Areas

14. **New Jersey** **New Jersey Small Business Development Center**
180 University Avenue, Newark, NJ 07102-1895
Contact:　　Andrew B. Rudczynski
Telephone:　(201) 648-5950
Service Area:　Through SBDCs, statewide

15. **New Mexico** **New Mexico Community Development Loan Fund**
P.O. Box 705, Albuquerque, NM 87103-0705
Contact:　　Vangie Gabaldon
Telephone:　(505) 243-3196　*Fax:* (201) 648-1110
Service Area:　Statewide

16. **New York** **Brooklyn Economic Development Corporation**
30 Flatbush Ave, Ste 420, Brooklyn, NY 11217-1197
Contact:　　Joan Bartolomeo
Telephone:　(718) 522-4600　*Fax:* (505) 243-8803
Service Area:　The five boroughs of New York City

17. **No.Carolina** **North Carolina Rural Economic Development Center, Inc.**
1300 St. Mary's St, Suite 500, Raliegh, NC 27601
Contact:　　Billy Ray Hall
Telephone:　(919) 715-2725　*Fax:* (919) 715-2731
Service Area:　Statewide

18. **Ohio** **Women Entrepreneurs, Inc.**
36 E 4th Street, Suite 925, Cincinnati, OH 45202
Contact:　　Sandy Evers

Telephone: (513) 684-0700   *Fax:* (513) 665-2452

Service Area: Brown, Butler, Clermont, Hamilton, and Warren counties

19. **Pennsylvania**   **Philadelphia Commercial Development Corporation**
1315 Walnut St., Ste 600, Philadelphia, PA 19107
Contact: Linda Karl
Telephone: (215) 790-2200   *Fax:* (215) 790-2222
Service Area: Bucks, Montgomery, Philadelphia, Chester, and Delaware counties

20. **Texas**   **Greater Corpus Christi Business Alliance**
1201 N Shoreline, P.O.Box 640
Corpus Christi, TX 78403
Contact: Kenneth Arnold
Telephone: (512) 881-1843   *Fax:* (512) 882-4256
Service Area: Nueces and San Patricio counties

21. **Vermont**   **Champlain Valley Office of Economic Opportunity, Inc.**
191 North Street, Burlington, VT 05401
P.O. Box 1603, Burlington, VT 05402
Contact: Robert Kiss
Telephone: (802) 862-2771   *Fax:* (802) 660-3454
Service Area: Statewide

22. **Virginia**   **The Commonwealth of VA Department of Economic Development**
901 E. Byrd St., 19th Floor, Richmond, VA 23219
P.O. Box 798, Richmond, VA 23218
Contact: Robert R. Blackmore
Telephone: (804) 371-8253   *Fax:* (804) 225-3384
Service Area: Through SBDCs, statewide

Glossary of Financial Terms

Accounts Payable:
Obligations owed by the business for goods or services received but not yet paid for.

Accounts Receivable:
Monies earned, but not yet received from customers.

Accumulated Depreciation:
The total depreciation which has accrued over a period of time on capital equipment.

Amortization:
The process of gradually paying off a liability over a period of time.

Assets:
Tangible or intangible resources or properties owned by the business.

Balance Sheet:
A statement of the financial position of a company at a particular point in time.

Break-even Point:
The point of activity when total revenue equals expenses.

Capital:
The funds necessary to start or expand a business.

Collateral:
An asset (s) pledged to secure a loan.

Contribution Margin:
The difference between the selling price and the cost of an item.

Cost of Goods Sold:
The direct cost of those items which will be sold to the customer. Cost of goods sold includes inventory to be sold, or materials used to make products.

Current Assets:
Valuable business resources that will be turned into cash within a year.

Current Liabilities:
Amounts owed by a business which are due within one year.

Debt:
Borrowed money.

Depreciation:
A business expense which addresses the wear and tear on business equipment and long-term assets.

Direct Costs:
Costs directly associated with the manufacture of a product or a delivery of a service. Examples include contract labor and inventory or costs of goods sold.

Equity:
Is an investment into a business. The owner's equity is their investment or share of the ownership.

Fixed Costs:
Costs which always remain the same. These costs do not vary in relation to sales.

Gross Profit:
Profit after the costs of goods sold have been deducted from sales, but prior to deducting operating costs.

Income Statement:
A useful financial statement which compares revenues to expenses.

Indirect Costs:
Operational costs that are indirect to the manufacture of a product or delivery of a service such as rent, advertising or insurances.

Inventory:
Material owned by a business used in production, resale, or as an office expense.

Long-term Liabilities:
Liabilities that will not come due within a year.

Net Worth:
Otherwise referred to as Owner's Equity. It is the value of a business in financial terms. Determined by subtracting liabilities from assets.

Net Profit:
Profit after all costs, including taxes, have been accounted for. The net performance of the business to be disbursed to owners or retained in the business.

Operating Costs:
Generally referred to as those costs which are necessary to operate a business on an ongoing basis. Not one-time costs.

Overhead:
A term used to describe general and administrative costs incurred by the business. These costs are directly related to the production of a product or delivery of a service.

Proforma:
A projection of the future activities of a business.

Profit:
The excess in sales over expenses.

Revenues:
Total sales generated in a stated period.

Variable Costs:
Costs which fluctuate proportionately to sales.

Financial Forms

Form 1: Personal/Family Budget

Monthly Non-Business Income
  Spouse's Salary   _____
  Investment Income   _____
  Social Security   _____
  Other Income   _____
  Retirement Benefits   _____
  Less Taxes   _____
  Net Monthly Income   _____
  Total Monthly Income   _____

Monthly Non-Business Expenses
  Rent/Mortgage   _____
  Utilities   _____
  Homeowner's Insurance   _____
  Property Taxes   _____
  Home Repairs   _____
  Groceries   _____
  Telephone   _____
  Tuition
  Transportation   _____
  Child Care   _____
  Medical Expenses   _____
  Clothing   _____
  Insurance Premiums:
      Life, Disability, Auto, Medical   _____
  Miscellaneous:
      Entertainment, Vacation,
      Gifts, Dues, Fees, etc.   _____
      Auto Loans   _____
      Consumer Debt   _____
  Total Monthly Expenses   _____

  Monthly Surplus/Deficit:
  (Income-Expenses)   _____

Form 2: Personal Financial Statement

Assets

    Cash   _____

    Stocks, Bonds, Other Securities   _____

    Accounts/Notes Receivable   _____

    Life Insurance Cash Value   _____

    Rebates/Refunds   _____

    Autos/Vehicles   _____

    Real Estate   _____

    Vested Pension/Retirement Accounts _____

    Other Assets   _____

    Total Assets   _____

Liabilities:

    Real Estate Loans   _____

    Auto Loan Balance   _____

    Notes Payable   _____

    Taxes   _____

    Other Liabilities   _____

    Total Liabilities   _____

Net Worth

    (Total Assets-Total Liabilities)   _____

Form 3: Projected Balance Sheet

BUSINESS NAME:

	YR	YR	YR	YR

ASSETS
Current Assets
    Cash
    Marketable Securities
    Accounts Receivable
    Inventory
    Prepaid Expenses
    Other
    Total Current Assets

Fixed (Long Term) Assets
    Building & Equipment
    Less Accumulated Depreciation
    Net Buildings & Equipment
    Land
    Other
    Total Fixed Assets
    Goodwill

    Total Assets

LIABILITIES
Short-Term Assets
    Accounts Payable
Long-Term Assets
    Notes Payable
    Other
    Total Liabilities

OWNER'S EQUITY
    Common Stock
    Retained Earnings
    Total Equity

LIABILITIES & OWNER'S EQUITY

Form 4: Projected Income Statement

BUSINESS NAME	Mo.1	Mo.2	Mo.3	Mo.4	Mo.5	Mo.6	Mo.7	Mo.8	Mo.9	Mo.10	Mo.11	Mo.12	TOTAL	RATIO
Revenues														
Sales														
Less Discounts & Allowances														
Net Sales														
Cost of Goods Sold														
Materials														
Labor														
Other														
Gross Profit														
Operating Expenses														
Acctg & Legal Fees														
Advertising														
Salaries/Wages														
Bad Debt														
Depreciation														
Entertainment														
Insurance														
Loan Payment														
Office Supplies														
Postage														
Printing														
Repairs and Maint.														
Rent														
Telephone														
Travel														
Miscellaneous														
Other														
Total Expenses														
Before Tax Profit														
Less Estimated Tax														

Form 5: Monthly Cash Flow Projections

BUSINESS NAME	Mo. 1	Mo. 2	Mo. 3	Mo. 4	Mo. 5	Mo. 6	Mo. 7	Mo. 8	Mo. 9	Mo. 10	Mo. 11	Mo. 12
Beg. Cash Bal.												
Cash Receipts												
Sales												
Collections from												
Credit Accounts												
Loan/Invested Capital												
Total Cash Receipts												
Total Cash Available												
Cash Paid Out												
Materials												
Labor												
Acctg & Legal Fees												
Telephone												
Advertising												
Bad Debt												
Dues & Subscriptions												
Entertainment												
Insurance												
Loan Payment												
Office Supplies												
Owner's Draw												
Postage												
Printing												
Repairs and Maint.												
Rent												
Supplies												
Taxes												
Utilities												
Total Cash Paid Out												
Ending Cash Balance												

Sample Business Plan - Manufacturing Business: Phoenix International

PHOENIX WORLDWIDE, INC.

Business Plan

GARY SMITH, OWNER
2323 Bristol Road
Burton, MN 12345
(555) 743-8370

Table of Contents

Executive Summary

Gary Smith, owner of Titan Manufacturing, Inc., a successful re-manufacturer of forklifts is establishing another corporation which will manufacture newly designed forklifts, parts, and components.

The new company, Phoenix Worldwide, Inc., will be successful because of the owner's extensive experience in this industry, the tremendous market demand for the products, and the limited number of competitors currently in the market. The manufacturing rights to Phoenix's products has already been purchased by the owner and considerable interest has ensued from potential customers since this transaction.

Titan Manufacturing is a proven company with an excellent financial track record. Gary Smith established the business nine years ago, and since then the company has expanded to be a major player in the market.

Gary Smith has researched this new business venture for some time, and when the timing was right he bought out Phoenix Lift & Equipment, Inc. and is now ready to pursue expedient entry into the market.

In the wake of Titan's success, Gary Smith intends to build his new company. Phoenix Worldwide, Inc. has unlimited growth potential and all of the ingredients for success:

- **Market Demand**
- **Management Experience**
- **Limited Competition**
- **Financial Strength of Titan Manufacturing and its owner**

Statement of Purpose

Phoenix Worldwide, Inc. is seeking a loan for approximately $800,000 in order to build a facility, purchase materials, and pay overhead costs. Gary Smith will personally invest an additional $100,000. The monies will be used in the following manner:

Land and Building	$500,000
Initial Inventory of Drive Axcels	150,000
Working Capital	250,000
Total	**$900,000**

Gary Smith is negotiating with the county to obtain the best possible deal for commercial property. Smith will finance the property as the owner and lease it back to the company.

The company is planning to begin manufacturing operations immediately after construction of the facility is completed. The target date is March 1, 1995.

The loan will be repaid with profits. The financial projections reveal that the company will earn sufficient profits and maintain adequate cash balances to repay the loan.

Description

Phoenix Worldwide, Inc. is a new business to be established as a Corporation in the state of Minnesota. The company will manufacture a line of forklifts from the product designs formerly owned by Phoenix Lift & Equipment, Inc. of Dallas, Texas. Phoenix Lift and Equipment was established over 20 years ago by Bob Jones. The company was one of the three major forklift manufacturers with annual sales averaging $23.2 million per year for the last five years in business.

Gary Smith purchased Phoenix's manufacturing rights, prints, drawings, and patents for $125,000. No fixed assets were purchased. Jones sold the business to pursue other business ventures. Phoenix's products are well known in the industry for their quality and progressive design. The company's forklifts, for example, can haul up to 140,000 pounds. The closest competitor can haul only 110,000 pounds.

Phoenix lift trucks are used in the steel and automotive industries. They can be found in factories, ship yards, and steel mills, and are used for heavy hauling. The average lift truck takes approximately two months to manufacture and prices range between $125,000 and $400,000.

Market Analysis

Target Market

Phoenix's target markets include aircraft manufacturers, automotive manufacturers, steel companies, steel mills, ship yards, and any industry which needs to haul heavy equipment.

Many of Titan's current customers are also potential customers of Phoenix. These customers include Hughes Aircraft, General Motors, Ford Motor, and Rockwell International.

The economic resurgence of the last five years has created many opportunities for the aircraft, automotive and other related industries. This economic growth is expected to continue and with this growth comes opportunities for expansion. Phoenix understands its customers' needs and will stand ready to provide high quality products and services.

Competition

There are two primary manufacturers of fork lifts and fork lift accessories:

- Bison Manufacturing, Mississippi - builds basically the same products as Phoenix. In business since the 50's. A family owned business. Builds an excellent product but the owners are too complacent about customer service. Sales estimated at $130 million annually.

- Reder Manufacturing, Kansas - Also sells a good product. Estimated annual sales - $70 million.

Both of these companies market their products through dealerships located throughout the world.

4

Competitive Advantage

Capacity

Phoenix Worldwide can offer customers greater capacity for hauling materials. Phoenix's forklifts haul up to 140,000 pounds. The closest competitor's products will haul up to only 110,000 pounds!

Having greater capacity for hauling will increase the productivity of Phoenix's customers and as a result, increase their profits!

Increased Availability

The typical waiting period for forklifts is 12 months. Phoenix intends to cut the waiting period in half, and increase the availability of these products for its customers.

Individualized Componentry

Phoenix will allow customers to request products with components made by their company. For example, Ford Motor can procure a product made with Ford components.

No other forklift manufacturer offers this feature. And it does not result in any additional manufacturing costs.

Marketing Plan

Products

Phoenix Worldwide, Inc. offers 10 products, which are used for different applications and purposes.

Pricing

Phoenix's prices will be comparable to those of its competitors. Sales prices will range between $125,000 and $400,000 depending upon capacity and features of the product sold. Customers must make a 10% deposit when ordering and the balance due will be expected upon delivery.

Credit may be offered to some customers, but only in very special cases. The company will not carry excessive receivables on its books.

Promotional Strategy

Phoenix Worldwide will sell its products through dealers. Dealers are required to purchase at least one unit in order to qualify as a dealer. The company will sponsor seminars on product features for dealers.

The company will also heavily advertise its products in national trade publications such as "Network News," a material handling publication widely read by purchasing agents all over the world.

Advertising in the Special Carriers and Rigging Association's publication will also create interest for the Phoenix product line.

Full-color brochures will be developed and mailed to prospective customers.

Promotional Budget - First Year

Advertising	$ 30,000
Brochures - Printing	10,000
Postage	5,000
Training Program	15,000
Total	$ 60,000

The vast majority of the marketing budget will be spent during the first quarter. The company plans to aggressively market the business during its first few months of operation.

Location

The company will be located on 17 acres of county-owned, commercially zoned land on I-29. The location is approximately 15 miles from Titan Manufacturing's current facility.

A 20,000 square foot facility will be constructed to house the company's operations. Construction costs are estimated at approximately $500,000.

The owner has negotiated with county representatives who agree to sell the property for $1 in exchange for starting the business in the county and creating jobs. The property has an appraised value of approximately $10,000 per acre.

The owner plans to keep ownership of the property and the building in his name, and lease it back to the company.

Management

Gary Smith will manage the day-to-day operations of the company. He has hired a General Manager to oversee Titan Manufacturing which will free up his time to pursue his new venture. Mr. Smith plans to spend 90% of his time with the new company, ensuring its growth and stability. Gary Smith is well qualified to manage Phoenix Worldwide. He has operated a highly successful company for the past nine years. The owner will not take a draw from the new business until the company is well on its way to profitability.

Personnel

Phoenix Worldwide, Inc. will immediately hire 25 employees. The following is a listing of job titles, job descriptions and pay rates:

Receptionist
Answer the telephone, filing, typing, opening and receiving mail and issuing purchase orders to vendors. Pay Rate - $18,000/year.

Accounts Payable/Receivable/Payroll Clerk
Bill customers, pay monthly bills, do weekly payroll and make necessary tax deposits. This individual will be responsible for federal and state taxes.
Pay Rate - $27,500/year.

Burners/Welders
All burner/welders must pass a welding test to work for Phoenix Worldwide. They will be certified under the rules and regulations of the American Welding Society. The burner/welders will burn out all steel parts; frame, mast, counterweight, and all other steel components needed. This work will be supervised by the welder foreman. Pay Rate - $9 - $12/hour.

Welders/Fabricators
The welder/fabricator's job is much like that of the burner/welder. In many cases they may do the same job. They must also pass a test to be certified. Duties of this job include welding all parts cut by the burner and completing the frame assembly. Pay Rate - $12/hour.

Machine Assemblers
Machine assemblers assemble the components including; the front drive axle, rear steer axle tires, fuel tank, hydraulic tank, dash, gauges, cylinders, valves, and mast. Pay Rate - $8 - 9 per hour.

Final Assembly Workers
The final assembly workers will complete the assembly of the unit.
Pay Rate - $10 - $12 per hour.

Inspection/Quality Control/ Testing
This individual will completely inspect the unit and perform load tests. All machines must meet or exceed OSHA and ANSI 56.1 safety standards. They will be supervised by the assembly foreman. Pay Rate - $8 - $9 per hour.

Painters
After inspection and testing, the forklift will be primed, painted, and shipped to

the customer with all safety decals installed. Pay Rate - $8 -$10 per hour.

Laborers
These workers will be responsible for keeping the factory clean, including rest rooms and yard areas. Pay Rate - $6 - $7 per hour.

Welding and Assembly Foreman
Will be working foreman. Pay Rate - $14 per hour.

Machinist
Machine all necessary pins, bushings, shafts, etc. needed to build units. Pay Rate - $15 per hour.

Proposed Personnel and Pay Roll Schedule

Direct Labor- Year One

Job Title	Pay Rate	No. of Workers	$ Paid ea.	Total
Burners/Weld	$11/hr	5	$22,880	$114,400
Welders/Fab.	$12/hr	5	$24,960	$124,800
Mach. Assem.	$9/hr	5	$18,720	$ 93,600
Final Assem.	$11/hr	3	$22,880	$ 68,640
Inspec/Q.C.	$9/hr	2	$18,720	$ 37,440
Painters	$9/hr	2	$18,720	$ 37,440
Laborers	$7/hr	2	$14,560	$ 29,120
Machinist	$15/hr	1	$31,200	$ 31,200
Weld Foreman	$14/hr	1	$29,120	$ 29,120
Assem. Foreman	$13/hr	1	$27,040	$ 27,040
Receptionist		1		$ 18,000
Totals		27		$592,800

Summary of Operations

The manufacturing process begins when the steel is delivered to the facility. The burners/welders cut the steel to size. Next, the welders/fabricators will assemble and weld the frame and mast assembly. The assemblers will assemble the drive train and accessories. Next, the final assembly workers will complete the forklift, add fluids, start the engine, and complete a quick inspection.

The Inspection/Quality Control unit will make all the necessary inspections and perform a load test. The painter will then clean, prime and paint the forklift. When dry, the name and safety decals will be affixed to the unit.

After all production and testing has been completed, the forklift will be prepared for delivery to the customer.

Phoenix Worldwide Profit & Loss Projections - Year 1

	MO.1	MO.2	MO.3	MO.4	MO.5	MO.6	MO.7	MO.8	MO.9	MO.10	MO.11	MO.12	TOTAL	RATIO
REVENUES														
Sales	0	0	0	200,000	200,000	200,000	400,000	400,000	400,000	600,000	600,000	600,000	3,600,000	100.00%
Other	0	0	0	0	0	0	0	0	0	0	0	0	0	0.00%
TOTAL REVENUES	0	0	0	200,000	200,000	200,000	400,000	400,000	400,000	600,000	600,000	600,000	3,600,000	100.00%
Direct Costs														
Materials	0	0	0	80,000	80,000	80,000	160,000	160,000	160,000	240,000	240,000	240,000	1,440,000	40.00%
Labor	49,400	49,400	49,400	49,400	49,400	49,400	49,400	49,400	49,400	49,400	49,400	49,400	592,800	16.47%
Labor Costs	7,410	7,410	7,410	7,410	7,410	7,410	7,410	7,410	7,410	7,410	7,410	7,410	88,920	0.02
TOT. DIR. COSTS	56,810	56,810	56,810	136,810	136,810	136,810	216,810	216,810	216,810	296,810	296,810	296,810	2,121,720	58.94%
GROSS MARGIN	-56,810	-56,810	-56,810	63,190	63,190	63,190	183,190	183,190	183,190	303,190	303,190	303,190	1,478,280	41.06%
INDIRECT COSTS														
Telephone	800	800	800	800	800	1,000	1,000	1,000	1,000	1,000	1,000	1,000	11,000	0.31%
Salaries/Wages	7,100	7,100	7,100	7,100	7,100	7,100	7,100	7,100	7,100	7,100	7,100	7,100	85,200	2.37%
Acctg/Professional Fees	500	500	500	500	500	500	500	500	500	500	500	500	6,000	0.17%
Payroll Expense	1,065	1,065	1,065	1,065	1,065	1,065	1,065	1,065	1,065	1,065	1,065	1,065	12,780	0.36%
Car, Delivery, Travel	1,000	1,000	1,000	1,000	1,000	1,000	1,000	1,000	1,000	1,000	1,000	1,000	12,000	0.33%
Advertising/Promotion	10,000	5,000	5,000	5,000	3,125	3,125	3,125	3,125	3,125	3,125	3,125	3,125	50,000	1.39%
Entertainment	2,000	2,000	2,000	2,000	2,000	2,000	2,000	2,000	2,000	2,000	2,000	2,000	24,000	0.67%
Repairs and Maint.	500	500	500	500	500	500	500	500	500	500	500	500	6,000	0.17%
Supplies	1,000	1,000	1,000	1,000	1,000	1,000	1,000	1,000	1,000	1,000	1,000	1,000	12,000	0.33%
Rent	5,000	5,000	5,000	5,000	5,000	5,000	5,000	5,000	5,000	5,000	5,000	5,000	60,000	1.67%
Insurance	3,000	3,000	3,000	3,000	3,000	3,000	3,000	3,000	3,000	3,000	3,000	3,000	36,000	1.00%
Utilities	3,000	3,000	3,000	3,000	3,000	3,000	3,000	3,000	3,000	3,000	3,000	3,000	36,000	1.00%
Miscellaneous	5,000	5,000	5,000	5,000	5,000	5,000	5,000	5,000	5,000	5,000	5,000	5,000	60,000	1.67%
Taxes, Real Estate	500	500	500	500	500	500	500	500	500	500	500	500	6,000	0.17%
Loan Interest Expense	2,750	2,750	2,750	2,750	2,750	2,750	2,750	2,750	2,750	2,750	2,750	2,750	33,000	0.92%
Depreciation	1,355	1,355	1,355	1,355	1,355	1,355	1,355	1,355	1,355	1,355	1,355	1,355	16,260	0.45%
TOTAL INDIRECT COSTS	43,215	38,215	38,215	38,215	36,340	36,540	36,540	36,540	36,540	36,540	36,540	36,540	449,980	12.50%
NET INCOME BEFORE TAXES	-100,025	-95,025	-95,025	24,975	26,850	26,650	146,650	146,650	146,650	266,650	266,650	266,650	1,028,300	28.56%
Less Estimated Tax													349,622	9.71%
NET PROFIT													678,678	0.18

11

Phoenix Worldwide Profit & Loss Projections - Year 2

	MO 1	MO 2	MO 3	MO 4	MO 5	MO 6	MO 7	MO 8	MO 9	MO 10	MO 11	MO 12	TOTAL	RATIO
REVENUES														
Sales	600000	600000	600000	600,000	600,000	600,000	600,000	600,000	600,000	600,000	600,000	600,000	7,200,000	100.00%
Other	0	0	0	0	0	0	0	0	0	0	0	0	0	0.00%
TOTAL REVENUES	600,000	600,000	600,000	600,000	600,000	600,000	600,000	600,000	600,000	600,000	600,000	600,000	7,200,000	100.00%
DIRECT COSTS														
Materials	240,000	240,000	240,000	240,000	240,000	240,000	240,000	240,000	240,000	240,000	240,000	240,000	2,880,000	40.00%
Labor	90,000	90,000	90,000	90,000	90,000	90,000	90,000	90,000	90,000	90,000	90,000	90,000	1,080,000	15.00%
Labor Costs	13,500	13,500	13,500	13,500	13,500	13,500	13,500	13,500	13,500	13,500	13,500	13,500	162,000	0.0225
TOTAL DIRECT COSTS	343,500	343,500	343,500	343,500	343,500	343,500	343,500	343,500	343,500	343,500	343,500	343,500	4,122,000	57.25%
GROSS MARGIN	256,500	256,500	256,500	256,500	256,500	256,500	256,500	256,500	256,500	256,500	256,500	256,500	3,078,000	42.75%
INDIRECT COSTS														
Telephone	1,400	1,400	1,400	1,400	1,400	1,400	1,400	1,400	1,400	1,400	1,400	1,400	16,800	0.23%
Salaries/Wages	10,153	10,153	10,153	10,153	10,153	10,153	10,153	10,153	10,153	10,153	10,153	10,153	12 ,836	1.69%
Acctg/Professional Fees	1,000	1,000	1,000	1,000	1,000	1,000	1,000	1,000	1,000	1,000	1,000	1,000	12,000	0.17%
Payroll Expense	1,522	1,522	1,522	1,522	1,522	1,522	1,522	1,522	1,522	1,522	1,522	1,522	18,275	0.25%
Car, Delivery, Travel	2,000	2,000	2,000	2,000	2,000	2,000	2,000	2,000	2,000	2,000	2,000	2,000	24,000	0.33%
Advertising/Promotion	5,000	5,000	5,000	5,000	3,125	3,125	3,125	3,125	3,125	3,125	3,125	3,125	45,000	0.62%
Entertainment	4,000	4,000	4,000	4,000	4,000	4,000	4,000	4,000	4,000	4,000	4,000	4,000	48,000	0.67%
Repairs and Maint.	1,000	1,000	1,000	1,000	1,000	1,000	1,000	1,000	1,000	1,000	1,000	1,000	12,000	0.17%
Supplies	2,000	2,000	2,000	2,000	2,000	2,000	2,000	2,000	2,000	2,000	2,000	2,000	24,000	0.33%
Rent	5,000	5,000	5,000	5,000	5,000	5,000	5,000	5,000	5,000	5,000	5,000	5,000	60,000	0.83%
Insurance	4,000	4,000	4,000	4,000	4,000	4,000	4,000	4,000	4,000	4,000	4,000	4,000	48,000	0.67%
Utilities	6,000	6,000	6,000	6,000	6,000	6,000	6,000	6,000	6,000	6,000	6,000	6,000	72,000	1.00%
Miscellaneous	10,000	10,000	10,000	10,000	10,000	10,000	10,000	10,000	10,000	10,000	10,000	10,000	120,000	1.67%
Taxes, Real Estate	500	500	500	500	500	500	500	500	500	500	500	500	6,000	0.08%
Interest Payment	2,750	2,750	2,750	2,750	2,750	2,750	2,750	2,750	2,750	2,750	2,750	2,750	33,000	0.46%
Depreciation	1,355	1,355	1,355	1,355	1,355	1,355	1,355	1,355	1,355	1,355	1,355	1,355	16,260	0.23%
Owner's Draw	5,000	5,000	5,000	5,000	5,000	5,000	5,000	5,000	5,000	5,000	5,000	5,000	60,000	0.83%
TOTAL INDIRECT COSTS	53,575	53,575	53,575	53,575	51,700	51,700	51,700	51,700	51,700	51,700	51,700	51,700	627,911	8.72%
NET INCOME BEFORE TAXES	202,924	202,924	202,924	202,924	204,799	204,799	204,799	204,799	204,799	204,799	204,799	204,799	2,450,088	0.34
Less Estimated Tax													833,030	0.11
NET PROFIT													1,617,058	0.22

12

PHOENIX WORLDWIDE CASH FLOW PROFORMA - YR 1

	START-UP	MO 1	MO 2	MO 3	MO 4	MO 5	MO 6	MO 7	MO 8	MO 9	MO 10	MO 11	MO 12
BEG. CASH BAL.	0	250,085	148,705	52,325	-44,055	-20,435	5,060	30,355	175,650	320,945	466,240	731,535	996,830
Sales	0	0	0	0	200,000	200,000	200,000	400,000	400,000	400,000	600,000	600,000	600,000
Invested Capital	100,000	0	0	0	0	0	0	0	0	0	0	0	0
Loan Proceeds	800,000	0	0	0	0	0	0	0	0	0	0	0	0
TOTAL CASH AVAILABLE	900,000	250,085	148,705	52,325	155,945	179,565	205,060	430,355	575,650	720,945	1,066,240	1,331,535	1,596,830
CASH EXPENDITURES													
Materials	100,000	0	0	0	80,000	80,000	80,000	160,000	160,000	160,000	240,000	240,000	240,000
Labor	15,000	49,400	49,400	49,400	49,400	49,400	49,400	49,400	49,400	49,400	49,400	49,400	49,400
Labor Costs	2,250	7,410	7,410	7,410	7,410	7,410	7,410	7,410	7,410	7,410	7,410	7,410	7,410
Telephone	2,000	800	800	800	800	800	1,000	1,000	1,000	1,000	1,000	1,000	1,000
Salaries/Wages	7,100	7,100	7,100	7,100	7,100	7,100	7,100	7,100	7,100	7,100	7,100	7,100	7,100
Acctg/Professional Fees	2,000	500	500	500	500	500	500	500	500	500	500	500	500
Payroll Expense	1,065	1,065	1,065	1,065	1,065	1,065	1,065	1,065	1,065	1,065	1,065	1,065	1,065
Car, Delivery, Travel	1,000	1,000	1,000	1,000	1,000	1,000	1,000	1,000	1,000	1,000	1,000	1,000	1,000
Advertising/Promotion	10,000	10,000	5,000	5,000	5,000	3,125	3,125	3,125	3,125	3,125	3,125	3,125	3,125
Entertainment	2,000	2,000	2,000	2,000	2,000	2,000	2,000	2,000	2,000	2,000	2,000	2,000	2,000
Repairs and Maint.	0	500	500	500	500	500	500	500	500	500	500	500	500
Supplies	1,000	1,000	1,000	1,000	1,000	1,000	1,000	1,000	1,000	1,000	1,000	1,000	1,000
Rent	0	5,000	5,000	5,000	5,000	5,000	5,000	5,000	5,000	5,000	5,000	5,000	5,000
Insurance	0	3,000	3,000	3,000	3,000	3,000	3,000	3,000	3,000	3,000	3,000	3,000	3,000
Utilities	1,500	3,000	3,000	3,000	3,000	3,000	3,000	3,000	3,000	3,000	3,000	3,000	3,000
Miscellaneous	5,000	5,000	5,000	5,000	5,000	5,000	5,000	5,000	5,000	5,000	5,000	5,000	5,000
Taxes, Real Estate	0	500	500	500	500	500	500	500	500	500	500	500	500
Loan Interest Expense	0	2,750	2,750	2,750	2,750	2,750	2,750	2,750	2,750	2,750	2,750	2,750	2,750
Depreciation	0	1,355	1,355	1,355	1,355	1,355	1,355	1,355	1,355	1,355	1,355	1,355	1,355
TOTAL OPERATING EXPENSES	149,915	101,380	96,380	96,380	176,380	174,505	174,705	254,705	254,705	254,705	334,705	334,705	334,705
CAPITAL EXPENDITURES													
Land and Building	500,000	0	0	0	0	0	0	0	0	0	0	0	0
Other	0	0	0	0	0	0	0	0	0	0	0	0	0
TOTAL CASH EXPENDITURES	649,915	101,380	96,380	96,380	176,380	174,505	174,705	254,705	254,705	254,705	334,705	334,705	334,705
ENDING CASH BAL.	250,085	148,705	52,325	-44,055	-20,435	5,060	30,355	175,650	320,945	466,240	731,535	996,830	1,262,125

13

PHOENIX WORLDWIDE CASH FLOW PROFORMA - YR 2

	MO 1	MO 2	MO 3	MO 4	MO 5	MO 6	MO 7	MO 8	MO 9	MO 10	MO 11	MO 12
BEG. CASH BALANCE	690,000	607,819	558,510	528,925	511,174	502,398	497,133	493,973	492,078	490,941	490,258	489,849
Sales	600,000	600,000	600,000	600,000	600,000	600,000	600,000	600,000	600,000	600,000	600,000	600,000
Invested Capital	0	0	0	0	0	0	0	0	0	0	0	0
TOTAL CASH AVAILABLE	1,290,000	1,207,819	1,158,510	1,128,925	1,111,174	1,102,398	1,097,133	1,093,973	1,092,078	1,090,941	1,090,258	1,089,849
CASH EXPENDITURES												
Materials	516,000	483,127	463,404	451,570	444,469	440,959	438,853	437,589	436,831	436,376	436,103	435,939
Labor	90,000	90,000	90,000	90,000	90,000	90,000	90,000	90,000	90,000	90,000	90,000	90,000
Labor Costs	13,500	13,500	13,500	13,500	13,500	13,500	13,500	13,500	13,500	13,500	13,500	13,500
Telephone	1,400	1,400	1,400	1,400	1,400	1,400	1,400	1,400	1,400	1,400	1,400	1,400
Salaries/Wages	10,153	10,153	10,153	10,153	10,153	10,153	10,153	10,153	10,153	10,153	10,153	10,153
Acctg/Professional Fees	1,000	1,000	1,000	1,000	1,000	1,000	1,000	1,000	1,000	1,000	1,000	1,000
Payroll Expense	1,522	1,522	1,522	1,522	1,522	1,522	1,522	1,522	1,522	1,522	1,522.95	1,522.95
Car, Delivery, Travel	2,000	2,000	2,000	2,000	2,000	2,000	2,000	2,000	2,000	2,000	2,000	2,000
Advertising/Promotion	5,000	5,000	5,000	5,000	3,125	3,125	3,125	3,125	3,125	3,125	3,125	3,125
Entertainment	4,000	4,000	4,000	4,000	4,000	4,000	4,000	4,000	4,000	4,000	4,000	4,000
Repairs and Maint.	1,000	1,000	1,000	1,000	1,000	1,000	1,000	1,000	1,000	1,000	1,000	1,000
Supplies	2,000	2,000	2,000	2,000	2,000	2,000	2,000	2,000	2,000	2,000	2,000	2,000
Rent	5,000	5,000	5,000	5,000	5,000	5,000	5,000	5,000	5,000	5,000	5,000	5,000
Insurance	4,000	4,000	4,000	4,000	4,000	4,000	4,000	4,000	4,000	4,000	4,000	4,000
Utilities	6,000	5,000	6,000	6,000	6,000	6,000	6,000	6,000	6,000	6,000	6,000	6,000
Miscellaneous	10,000	10,000	10,000	10,000	10,000	10,000	10,000	10,000	10,000	10,000	10,000	10,000
Taxes, Real Estate	500	500	500	500	500	500	500	500	500	500	500	500
Interest Payment	2,750	2,750	2,750	2,750	2,750	2,750	2,750	2,750	2,750	2,750	2,750	2,750
Depreciation	1,355	1,355	1,355	1,355	1,355	1,355	1,355	1,355	1,355	1,355	1,355	1,355
Owner's Draw	5,000	5,000	5,000	5,000	5,000	5,000	5,000	5,000	5,000	5,000	5,000	5,000
TOTAL CASH EXPENDITURES	682,180	649,308	629,585	617,751	608,775	605,265	603,159	601,895	601,137	600,682	600,409	600,245
ENDING CASH BALANCE	607,819	558,510	528,925	511,174	502,398	497,133	493,973	492,078	490,941	490,258	489,849	489,603

14

Phoenix Worldwide Projected Balance Sheet ·3 Yr. Projections

	Yr 1/Starting Bal.	Yr. 2	Yr. 3
Assets			
Cash/Invested Cash	100,000	494,000	670,000
Accounts Receivable	0	180,000	200,000
Inventory	100,000	42,000	84,000
Other Current Assets	0	0	0
Total Current Assets	**200,000**	**716,000**	**954,000**
Fixed Assets			
Machinery & Equipment	25,000	25,000	25,000
Furniture & Fixtures	2,000	2,000	2,000
Land	170,000	170,000	170,000
Building	500,000	500,000	500,000
Total Fixed Assets	**697,000**	**697,000**	**697,000**
Accumulated Depreciation	0	16,260	32,520
Net Fixed Assets	697,000	680,740	664,480
Other Assets			
Goodwill	0	50,000	100,000
Manufacturing Rights	125,000	125,000	125,000
Capitalized R & D	0	0	0
Miscellaneous	0	0	0
Total Other Assets	**125,000**	**175,000**	**225,000**
Total Assets	**1,022,000**	**1,571,740**	**1,843,480**
Liabilities			
Accounts Payable	0	50,000	50,000
Taxes Payable	0	0	0
Short-term Note Payable	300,000	150,000	0
Current Portion L.T. Debt	0	0	0
Long-Term Debt	500,000	434,264	368,528
Total Liabilities	**800,000**	**634,264**	**418,528**
Equity			
Preferred Stock	0	0	0
Common Stock	222,000	222,000	222,000
Retained Earnings	0	715,476	1,202,952
Total Equity	**222,000**	**937,476**	**1,424,952**
Total Liabilities & Equity	**1,022,000**	**1,571,740**	**1,843,480**

15

Assumptions to Financial Projections

1. Production of forklifts begins in month two. The final product of the first unit is sold in month four to allow for 6-8 weeks for completion of product.

2. The average unit sales price is $200,000. Therefore, an estimated 18 units will be sold in the first year, 36 in the second, and 41 in the third.

3. Cost of goods sold includes the cost of materials and direct labor. The cost of materials is estimated at 40%.

4. In year one, direct labor costs are estimated at 16.47% of sales. In year two these costs are estimated at 15% of sales. See page 9 for a schedule of payroll for the first year.

5. Payroll expense is estimated at 15% of payroll and salary costs.

6. Rent of $5000 to be paid to owner for use of land and building.

7. Loan interest expense is based on a $300,000 line of credit at 11% interest.

8. The initial cash reflected on balance sheet is the owner's initial investment.

9. Land is valued at $10,000 per acre for 17 acres.

10. There are no final quotes for constructions costs. $500,000 is an approximated amount.

11. The business is expected to pay down the line of credit within two years. All payables are paid within the 30 days due.

12. Long-term debt, annual principal, and interest is estimated using a 10% interest rate for a 15 year period. Annual payments estimated at $65,736.

13. Depreciation is calculated as follows:

Machinery & Equipment	7 years	$ 25,000	=	$ 3,600
Building	39.5 years	$500,000	=	$12,660
Total Depreciation				$16,260

14. Cash flow projections do not include deductions for taxes and loan payments.

PHOENIX WORLDWIDE, INC. PRODUCT INFORMATION

MODEL	CAPACITY	LOAD CENTER
15,000 - 20,000 LB. Low Rider Cushion Tire		
AC 150ALR	15,000 LB	24"
AC200 ABT	20,OOO LB	24"
15,000 - 80,000 LB Cushion Tire		
AC 150 AHT	15,000 LB	24"
AC 200 AHT	20,000 LB	24"
AC 250 AHT	25,000 LB	24"
AC 300 AHT	30,000 LB	24"
AC 350 AHT	35,000 LB	24"
AC 400 AHT	40,000 LB	36"
AC 520 BHT	52,000 LB	36"
AC 620 BHT	62,000 LB	36"
AC 700 BHT	70,000 LB	36"
AC 800 BHT	80,000 LB	36"
15,000 - 52,000 LB Cushion Tire Electric		
AC 150 AHTE	15,000 LB	24"
AC 200 AHTE	20,000 LB	24"
AC 250 AHTE	25,000 LB	24"
AC 300 AHTE	30,000 LB	24"
AC 400 AHTE	40,000 LB	24"
AC 450 AHTE	45,000 LB	24"
20,000 - 140,000 LB Pneumatic Tire		
AP 200 A	20,000 LB	24"
AP 250 A	25,000 LB	24"
AP 300 A	30,000 LB	24"
AP 300 B	30,000 LB	36"
AP 360 B	36,000 LB	36"
AP 400 B	40,000 LB	48"
AP 400 C	40,000 LB	48"

AP 450 C	45,000 LB	48"
AP 520 B	52,000 LB	36"
AP 520 C	52,000 LB	48"

20,000 - 140,000 LB Pneumatic Tire - Continued:

AP 620 C	62,000 LB	48"
AP 800 C	80,000 LB	48"
AP 950 C	95,000 LB	48"
AP 1000 C	100,000 LB	48"
AP 1400 C	140,000 LB	48"

TITAN INC. - COMPANY & PRODUCT INFORMATION

Thank you for this opportunity to introduce you to our company.

Titan Manufacturing, Inc. has been a leader in industrial equipment manufacturing, repairs, and modifications for over 10 years. We sell and lease new and used equipment as well as parts and components.

Our area of expertise is in the manufacturing of masts and carriages for forklifts and the repair and modifying of masts for specific uses. Much of our work comes from forklift manufacturing companies and rental companies.

Most of our customers come to us through word of mouth, but in our increasing effort to expand we have found it necessary to seek out potential customers and present our products and services.

Our list of customers includes General Motors, Ford, and Detroit Diesel, in addition to a number of other large companies.

Our Products and Services Include:

> Rigging and Remanufacturing Forklifts and Masts
> Forklifts and rigging trucks available from 2500 lbs. to 80,000 lbs,
>   solid or pneumatic tires
> Propane - 2500 lbs. to 22,000 lbs.
> Gas - 2500 lbs. To 40,000 lbs.
> Diesel - 15,000 lbs. to 80,000 lbs.
> Forklift options include rotators, sideshifters, fork positioners, cabs
> Bulldozers available with winches and rubber grouser bars for in-plant use
> Manlifts, scissorlifts, aerial platform to any height
> Skid steers
> Tow tractors
> Sweepers (propane or gas)
> Teleporters up to 37 feet
> Rough terrain forklifts
> Carry deck cranes
> Electric or hand pallet trucks

Equipment available for purchase or lease. Rental contracts available by day, week or month.

Operators available upon request.

Our service trucks operate on a 24-hour basis. All trucks are equipped with welders, torches, and air compressors.

All modifications and welding services are state certified.

We believe our services can be of great use to you and help you cut costs of current repairs, rentals and equipment replacement.

Gary Smith, Sr.

1234 River Road
Burton, MN 12345

Education

| 1963-1967 | Burton High School |
| | General Education |

| 1968-1969 | Western Technical School |
| | Heavy Equipment Repair |

Occupational Skills/Abilities

Crane operator, truck driver, certified welder, and heavy equipment repair.

Work Experience

| 1986 - Present | Owner |
| | Titan Manufacturing, Burton MN |

| 1968 - 1986 | Engineer |
| | Babox Manufacturing |

References

| George Talbott | Union Official |
| | 555-222-3333 |

| Henry Zimmerman | Banker |
| | 555-888-9900 |

| Chip Lawrence | Supplier |
| | 555-333-4455 |

Other Interests

Member in good standing of Local #111 Operating Engineers, Fraternal Order of Police, Masonic Lodge, Elks Club

ROY ROBERTS ARCHERY CENTER

Business Plan

Owners

Roy Roberts
Bob Bailey

Table of Contents

Statement of Purpose

Roy Roberts and Bob Bailey are expanding Roy Roberts Archery to include an indoor and outdoor archery range and a snack shop. Presently the business sells archery supplies and accessories, and services and repairs archery equipment. Expansion will allow the owners to capitalize on the increasing popularity for archery and hunting-related services. By adding new services the archery center will attract more customers as well as expand sales from existing customers.

The owners are seeking financing of $258,000 to establish the archery center, range and snack shop. These funds, in addition to a $50,000 investment by the owners, will be used to purchase the property, build and furnish the structure, and purchase inventory. Funds will also be used as working capital.

The owners intend to use the land, building, and fixtures as collateral, as well as their current stock of inventory worth $50,000.

Roy Roberts and Bob Bailey are confident that sales generated from the business will be more than adequate to repay the loan.

Business Description

Roy Roberts Archery is located at 12345 McNichols, in the Township of Acme, Minnesota. The business is located behind the home of the owner, Roy Roberts. The business is currently registered as an S-Corporation through the State of Minnesota and is 100% owned by Roy Roberts. When the expansion occurs, Bob Bailey will purchase 49% of the stock.

Roy Roberts Archery was established nine years ago by Roy Roberts. Since then, the business has grown steadily. Today, the business grosses an average of $67,000 annually and supports 1.5 employees. Roy Roberts has been involved in the archery business for 14 years. He has one of the finest reputations in the area because of his extensive knowledge and experience. Bob Bailey, a hunting enthusiast, has been working with Roy to learn more about archery and about how to run an archery business.

After the expansion, the business will continue to sell bows and arrows and other supplies and accessories, but will also offer a full-service archery range and a snack shop with a lounge area. The range will attract archery leagues and clubs and will sponsor tournaments throughout the year.

Roberts and Bailey are interested in purchasing a parcel of property located off Venice Road, 3.5 miles west of 1-23. Bailey and Roberts have submitted an offer to purchase the property for $35,000. The sale is contingent upon their ability to obtain financing for the entire project. They plan to build a 16,000 square foot facility. The center, when completed will be one of the largest, full-service archery centers in the state.

The archery range during peak periods should generate significant revenues, not only in range fees, but in equipment and snack sales as well. The range area will be rented as hall space during the off season— October, November, April through July. These months happen to be peak months for weddings, reunions, and other parties where hall space would be needed.

Planned Hours of Operation:

Peak Periods (August, September, December-March):
   10:00 A.M. to 9:00 P.M. Monday through Saturday
   10:00 A.M. to 3:00 P.M. Sundays

Off Peak Periods (October, November, April-July)
   10:00 A.M. to 8 A.M. Mondays through Thursdays for the range, store and snack shop.
   10:00 A.M. to 8:00 P.M. on Fridays - Store only (range will be available for hall rentals).
   Saturdays and Sundays - the range, store and snack bar will be closed due to hall rentals.

Marketing

Target Market

Roy Roberts Archery Center's target market is comprised of bow hunters, target archers, and 3-D target archers. Bow hunters comprise the largest percentage of this group, approximately 85%. However, the number of target archers is growing dramatically.

Hunting has attracted more women over recent years contributing to its rapid popularity over the last decade. According to the Department of Natural Resources, one out of every ten Minnesota residents hunt.

The business currently attracts customers within a 45 mile radius. With the range, Roy Roberts Archery Center (RRAC) should attract customers from all over southeast Minnesota and possibly throughout the midwest.

Roberts has 600 names on his mailing list of potential customers. This list will be continually expanded throughout the life span of the business.

Products and Services

The Store
The store will carry a wide assortment of archery equipment and supplies. The store will also carry sportswear on consignment. The supplier will provide sportswear and when an item is sold they receive 60% of the sale price. Roy Roberts Archery receives 40% on average of retail sales.

The store will continue to repair and service archery equipment. This service will be available any time the store is open and customers may wait for repairs in the snack shop or borrow one of the stores bows and check out the range.

The Range
The range will comprise 12,000 feet of the facility and will accommodate dozens of archers at a time. The center will offer a 3-D indoor range as well as an outdoor range. The range is expected to attract approximately 50 customers per night during peak periods. Open range times, leagues, and scheduled tournaments will be offered. Pop-up targets will also be provided for an additional fee.

The Snack Bar & Lounge
Customers will enjoy a comfortable place to take a break, relax, socialize, and enjoy something to eat or drink. The snack bar will offer a variety of beverages, snacks, and hot foods.

Food will be prepared off-site by a food service and delivered to the center daily. The snack bar will offer sandwiches, baked goods, soups, chili, and hot-dogs. The snack bar will not be a full kitchen facility. Customers will have available two microwaves to heat sandwiches and baked goods.

Pricing

RRAC's pricing will remain competitive for all of its products and services. Prices in the store may be slightly more than prices found at archery shops and sporting goods stores because the range and snack shop creates an added value and the perception of additional value should warrant slightly higher prices.

Prices established on products are determined by wholesale costs, product demand, and prices offered by competitors. The mark-up on archery supplies and accessories is between 30% and 100% depending on the item.

Fees for servicing archery equipment are based on the type of work needed and are generally determined by the time required to do the work. Typically, a fee of $25 per hour would be charged for repair work.

Prices for range fees will be based upon hours of usage. Yearly membership rates will be available. There will also be fees for tournaments and leagues.

Range Fees:

Open Range		Tournament Fees		3-D		League Fees
Hourly:	$3	Entry:	$10	Hourly:	$8	Per day: $6
Yearly Membership:	$125	Trophy fee: $25		Trophy Fee: $25		

Prices charged in the snack bar will be based on typical price levels and will be determined with input from food vendors.

4

Marketing Strategies

RRAC will use various types of advertising and marketing strategies to promote its products and services. Initially, the business will promote its Grand Opening heavily through local archery clubs, the media, and through mailers sent to customers. An emphasis will be placed on its indoor range and the fact that it has the largest facility in the state.

RRAC will also sponsor and promote target tournaments which are becoming increasingly popular and are very profitable. These tournaments should attract participants from all over the midwest. Tournaments will be promoted through advertisements in hunting magazines and individual mailers.

Radio advertising will also be used to promote RRAC's products and services. Radio will be effective for promoting the target range and any special events and discounts. Special attention will be paid to listener demographics, and radio spots will be geared to those stations and times that match RRAC's target market.

Customers will be surveyed on an ongoing basis to find out how they heard about RRAC. This will determine if current marketing strategies have been effective and how advertising costs may be better appropriated.

Promotional Budget

Direct Mail - Postage	$3,000
Radio Advertising	1,500
Magazine Advertising Minnesota Bow Hunters	300
Misc. Advertising	1,500
Printing - Brochures, Flyers	2,000
Total Annual Promotional Expense	$8,300

Competition

There are a number of competitors who offer archery-related products and services operating within RRAC's target area.

JJ's Sporting Goods,
Located in Waldo, Minnesota, 10 miles from RRAC
20 years in business. No archery range. Large, full-service archery store. Reputation for good service.

Twin Cities Archery and Camping,
Located in Northfield, 30 miles from RRAC
Approximately 11 years in business. No range. No snack bar. Good service.

Blare's
Located in Medford, 20 miles from RRAC
6-7 years in business. Gun and archery supplies. Good quality bows and sporting goods. A little over-priced. 20-yard indoor range - computerized shooting system. No snack bar.

Swartz Mountain
Located in Morriston, 2 miles from RRAC
Complete sporting goods store with good quality bows and archery accessories. New store - in business less than a year. No range.

Bob's Archery
In Montgomery, 45 miles from RRAC
Very limited supply of archery equipment and accessories. Offers no service. Indoor archery range. Capacity: 60 per night. No snack bar.

Brown's Sporting Goods
Located in Madison Lake, 35 miles from RRAC
Sporting goods store with good quality archery equipment. Limited service. Has indoor range that holds a capacity of 50-70 per night. No snack bar.

Hal's Sportings
Located in Lakeville, 40 miles from RRAC
18 yard indoor and outdoor archery ranges.

Ed's Archery
45 miles from RRAC in Tompsonville. 20 yard archery range. No snack bar.

Hicks
25 miles from RRAC, Indoor 20 yard computer range. Capacity 4-6 at a time. 40 per night. No snack bar.

Competitive Advantage

1. KNOWLEDGE OF SERVICE - Years of experience in the industry.

2. 3-D INDOOR RANGE - No other facility has an indoor 3-D range. The closest 3-D range is north of Minneapolis, over 70 miles away. And this facility is much smaller than RRAC's proposed archery center.

3. SIZE - Many of the small archery businesses do not stay in business. This is due mostly to poor management and to the fact that they do not attract a wide enough market area.

4. ENTERTAINMENT CENTER - No other business offers a complete entertainment center with a range, snack shop, lounge, and retail sales and service.

Location

RRAC's new facility will be located near I-23. The location will be easily accessed by people coming from all over the state of Minnesota, from Iowa, and from western Wisconsin. Tournaments and other special events may attract customers from other areas in the midwest.

The facility is 16,000 square feet with the majority of space (12,000 square feet) designated for the archery range. The other space will be used for the snack bar, the archery store, the service area, storage space, office space, and rest rooms.

The owner's have received a quote of $200,000 to construct the facility. This includes the costs for building construction, plumbing, electrical, and painting.

Management

The Roy Roberts Archery Center will be managed jointly by its two owners. Their respective duties and responsibilities are to be as follows:

Roy Roberts
Sales and service - managing sales, service, and snack bar staff. Scheduling, hiring, firing, and other personnel management issues. Customer relations and coordination of special events. Management of the range activities.

Bob Bailey
Inventory control, shipping, and receiving. Bookkeeping, cost control, and management of office staff. Marketing and advertising. Fletching bows and assisting with sales and service.

Salaries:

Bob Bailey will not take a salary until six months after the business opens, and then will be paid $300 per week. Roy Roberts will take a minimum salary of $300 per week in the first year.

In the second year, salaries will be increased to $600 per week. No benefits will be offered to owners or employees in the first two years.

Personnel

RRAC will hire four employees to fill the following positions:

Repair Technician and Sales Person
This employee will handle the service desk during all peak hours. During off-peak hours, they will assist with sales or in other areas as needed. This person will have experience and interest in repairing archery equipment. Some training will be provided if necessary. This full-time position will be compensated at $8.00 per hour.

Snack Bar Cashier
The cashier will be responsible for handling the cash register, stocking food, and keeping the snack bar clean and orderly. Two persons shall he hired as needed for approximately 25 hours each week per person. Each will be paid $5.00 per hour.

Office Manager
The office manager will be responsible for most clerical functions - answering the phone, filing, and typing. They will also handle record keeping and finances, including payroll, payment of payroll taxes, accounts payable, and banking. One person will be hired for this position for 25 hours per week at $6.50 per hour. This individual will also assist with sales or elsewhere when needed.

Start-Up Costs

Archery Center

Building	$200,000
Land	35,000
Furnishings/Office	3,000
Computer	2,500
Copy Machine	800
Fax Machine	200
Cash Register	350
Sign	600
Bow Press	450
Fletching Jigs (12)	640
Targets	1,450
Security Alarm	3,100
Miscellaneous	2,000
Subtotal	$250,090

Snack Bar/Hall Rental

Microwave Ovens	$ 400
Hot-dog Cooker	300
Crock pots	120
Food stock	710
Cash Register	250
Trays (50)	160
Paper products	200
Trash Cans	220
Cleaning products	50
Glass cooler (for sodas)	1,500
Food cases	1,200
Small freezer	400
Vacuum cleaner	350
Ice maker	1,725
Beer Cooler	1,650
Beer Pitchers (140)	240
Tables - 50 @ $65 each	3,250
Chairs - 350 @ $22 each	7,700
Miscellaneous	2,000
Subtotal	$ 22,425

Operating Costs - 3 months
Salaries/Wages		$ 13,000
Payroll Expense	1,965	
Utilities		1,050
Telephone		600
Insurance		900
Advertising		2,000
Professional Services		500
Office Expense		300
Loan Payments		10,880
Miscellaneous		<u>4,000</u>
Subtotal		$ 35,295
Total Start-up Costs		$307,810

Roy Roberts Archery Center Profit & Loss Projections - yr. 1

	JUNE	JULY	AUG.	SEPT.	OCT.	NOV.	DEC.	JAN.	FEB.	MARCH	APRIL	MAY	TOTAL	RATIO
REVENUES														
Range Fees	500	3500	4500	5000	1250	2000	5000	6000	7000	8000	1500	1500	45750	19.73%
Sales - Archery	5000	8500	16000	18500	9000	8000	7500	12500	12500	14500	10500	8500	131000	56.51%
Sales - Food	200	1000	1500	2500	500	1000	2000	2500	3000	3500	750	500	19150	8.26%
Service Fees	300	750	2000	2500	1500	1000	2000	3000	3500	4000	2500	1500	24550	10.59%
Hall Rental Fees	1750	1750	1750	0	875	0	875	0	0	0	1750	2625	11375	4.91%
TOTAL REVENUES	7750	15500	25750	28500	13125	12000	17375	24000	26000	30000	17000	14625	231825	100.00%
COST OF GOODS SOLD	2860	5225	9625	11550	5225	5060	4275	6750	6975	8100	5062.5	4050	74757.5	32.25%
GROSS MARGIN	4890	10275	16125	16950	7900	6940	13100	17250	19025	21300	11937.5	10575	157067.5	67.75%
OPERATING EXPENSES														
Telephone	200	200	200	200	200	200	200	200	200	200	200	200	2400	1.04%
Salaries/Wages	4365	4365	4355	4365	4365	4365	5665	5665	5665	5665	5665	5665	60180	25.96%
Accounting	400	0	0	800	0	0	200	0	0	200	0	0	1600	0.66%
Payroll Expense	654.75	654.75	654.75	654.75	654.75	654.75	849.75	849.75	849.75	849.75	849.75	849.75	9027	3.72%
Taxes-Sales	300	510	950	1110	540	480	450	750	750	870	630	510	7860	3.24%
Taxes-City	100	0	100	0	100	0	100	0	100	0	100	0	600	0.25%
Advertising	692	692	692	692	692	692	692	692	692	692	692	692	8304	3.42%
Supplies	100	100	100	100	100	100	100	100	100	100	100	100	1200	0.49%
Insurance	0	0	900	0	0	900	0	0	900	0	0	900	3600	1.48%
Utilities	300	300	300	300	300	300	300	300	300	300	300	300	3600	1.48%
Miscellaneous	200	200	200	200	200	200	200	200	200	200	200	200	2400	0.99%
Loan Payment	4670	4670	4670	4670	4670	4670	4670	4670	4670	4670	4670	4670	56040	23.10%
TOTAL OPERERATING EXPENSES	11981.75	11691.75	13141.75	13091.75	11821.75	12561.75	13426.75	13426.75	14426.75	13746.75	13406.75	14086.75	156811	64.64%
NET INCOME BEFORE TAXES	-7091.75	-373.75	2983.25	3858.25	-3921.75	-5621.75	-326.75	3823.25	4598.25	8153.25	-1469.25	-3511.75	256.5	0.11%

12

Roy Roberts Archery Center Profit & Loss Projections - yr. 2

	JUNE	JULY	AUG.	SEPT.	OCT.	NOV.	DEC.	JAN.	FEB.	MARCH	APRIL	MAY	TOTAL	RATIO
REVENUES														
Range Fees	1000	3500	5800	8500	1500	2500	7500	8500	9000	9500	2000	1500	60800	19.39%
Sales - Archery	7000	11500	20500	22250	16500	12500	12000	14500	15500	17000	12500	11000	172750	55.10%
Sales - Food	500	1500	2000	3500	750	1500	2500	3000	3000	3500	1000	1000	23750	7.58%
Service Fees	1200	2500	6000	6500	4000	3000	2500	3500	4000	5000	2500	1500	42200	13.46%
Hall Rental Fees	1750	2625	1750	875	875	0	875	0	0	0	2625	2625	14000	4.47%
TOTAL REVENUES	11450	21625	36050	41625	23625	19500	25375	29500	31500	35000	20625	17625	313500	100.00%
COST OF GOODS SOLD	4125	7150	12375	14162.5	9487.5	7700	6525	7875	8325	9225	6075	5400	98425	31.40%
GROSS MARGIN	7325	14475	23675	27462.5	14137.5	11800	18850	21625	23175	25775	14550	12225	215075	68.60%
OPERATING EXPENSES														
Telephone	250	250	250	250	250	250	250	250	250	250	250	250	3000	0.96%
Salaries/Wages	8265	8265	8265	8265	8265	8265	8265	8265	8265	8265	8265	8265	99180	31.64%
Accounting	500	0	500	0	500	0	500	0	0	200	0	0	2200	0.91%
Payroll Expense	1239.75	1239.75	1239.75	1239.75	1239.75	1239.75	1239.75	1239.75	1239.75	1239.75	1239.75	1239.75	14877	6.13%
Taxes-Sales	420	690	1230	1335	990	750	720	870	930	1020	750	660	10365	4.27%
Taxes-City	120	0	120	0	120	0	120	0	120	0	120	0	720	0.30%
Advertising	1000	1000	1000	1000	1000	1000	1000	1000	1000	1000	1000	1000	12000	4.95%
Supplies	150	150	150	150	200	200	200	200	200	200	200	200	2200	0.91%
Insurance	0	0	900	0	0	900	0	0	900	0	0	900	3600	1.48%
Utilities	400	400	500	500	500	500	500	500	300	300	300	300	5000	2.06%
Miscellaneous	300	300	300	300	300	300	400	400	400	400	400	400	4200	1.73%
Loan Payment	4670	4670	4670	4670	4670	4670	4670	4670	4670	4670	4670	4670	56040	23.10%
TOTAL OPERATING EXPENSES	17314.75	16964.75	19124.75	17709.75	18034.75	18074.75	17864.75	17394.75	18274.75	17544.75	17194.75	17884.75	213382	87.97%
NET INCOME BEFORE TAXES	-9989.75	-373.75	813.25	9752.75	-3897.25	-6274.75	985.25	4230.25	4900.25	8230.25	-2644.75	-5659.75	1693	0.70%

Roy Roberts Archery Center Proforma Cash Flow Projections - Yr 1

	START-UP	JUNE	JULY	AUG.	SEPT	OCT	NOV	DEC.	JAN.	FEB.	MARCH	APRIL	MAY	TOTAL
Beg. Cash Bal.	50000	26565	19473.25	18056.5	21039.75	36448	37751.25	37389.5	41337.75	51911	63484.25	79737.5	83330.75	83869
Range Fees	0	500	3500	4500	5000	1250	2000	5000	6000	7000	8000	1500	1500	45750
Sales - Archery	0	5000	8500	16000	18500	3000	8000	7500	12500	12500	14500	10500	8500	131000
Sales - Food	0	200	100	150	2500	500	1200	2000	2500	3000	3500	750	500	19150
Service Fees	0	300	750	2000	2500	1500	1000	2000	3000	3500	4000	2500	1500	24550
Hall Rental Fees	0	1750	1750	1750	0	875	0	875	0	0	0	1750	2625	11375
Total Revenues	50000	7750	1550	25750	28500	13125	12200	17375	24000	26000	30000	17000	14625	231825
Loan Proceeds	403000	0	0	0	0	0	0	0	0	0	0	0	0	0
TOTAL CASH AVAILABLE	453000	34315	34973.25	43806.5	49539.75	43573	49951.25	54764.5	65337.75	77911	93484.25	96737.5	97955.75	315694
CASH EXPENDITURES														
Purchases	710	2860	5225	9625	11550	5225	5060	5225	8250	8525	9900	6187.5	4950	82582.5
Telephone	100	200	200	200	200	200	200	200	200	200	200	200	200	2400
Salaries/Wages	0	4365	4365	4365	4365	4365	4365	5665	5665	5665	5665	5665	5665	60180
Accounting	0	400	0	0	800	0	0	200	0	0	200	0	0	1600
Payroll Expense	0	654.75	654.75	654.75	654.75	654.75	654.75	849.75	849.75	849.75	849.75	849.75	849.75	9027
Taxes-Sales	0	300	510	960	1110	540	480	450	750	750	870	630	510	7860
Taxes-City	0	100	0	100	0	100	100	100	100	100	0	100	0	600
Advertising	500	692	692	692	692	692	692	692	692	692	692	692	692	8304
Supplies	250	100	100	100	100	100	100	100	100	100	100	100	100	1200
Insurance	0	0	0	900	0	0	900	0	0	900	0	0	900	3600
Utilities	0	300	300	300	300	300	300	300	300	300	300	300	300	3600
Miscellaneous	3900	200	200	200	200	200	200	200	200	200	200	200	200	2400
Loan Payment	0	4670	4670	4670	4670	4670	4670	4670	4670	4670	4670	4670	4670	56040
TOTAL OPERATING EXPENSES	5460	14841.75	16916.75	22766.75	13091.75	11821.75	12561.75	13426.75	13426.75	14426.75	13746.75	13406.75	14086.75	156811
CAPITAL EXPENDITURES														
Land and Building	383460	0	0	0	0	0	0	0	0	0	0	0	0	0
Furnishings, Fixtures, Equipment	37515	0	0	0	0	0	0	0	0	0	0	0	0	0
TOTAL CASH EXPENDITURES	426435	14841.75	16916.75	22766.75	13091.75	11821.75	12561.75	13426.75	13426.75	14426.75	13746.75	13406.75	14086.75	156811
ENDING CASH BAL.	26565	19473.25	18056.5	21039.75	36448	37751.25	37389.5	41337.75	51911	63484.25	79737.5	83330.75	83869	158883

14

Roy Roberts Archery Center Projected Balance Sheet

Assets	Yr 1/Start. Bal.	Yr. 2	Yr. 3
Current Assets			
Cash	$36,000	$13,305	$10,000
Marketable Securities	0	100,000	100,000
Inventory	50,000	50,000	50,000
Fixed Assets			
Furniture & Fixtures	$25,000	$25,000	$25,000
Equipment	12,000	12,000	8,000
Less Depreciation	0	(4,000)	(4,000)
Net Equipment	12,000	8,000	4,000
Building	200,000	200,000	192,000
Less Accum. Depreciation-	0	(8,000)	(8,000)
Net Building	200,000	192,000	184,000
Land	35,000	35,000	35,000
Total Assets	**$358,000**	**$423,305**	**$408,000**
Liabilities			
Accounts Payable-	0	40,000	30,000
Note Payable - Bank	$258,000	242,092	227,002
Total Liabilities	**$258,000**	**282,092**	**257,002**
Owner's Equity			
Common Stock - RR	$ 50,000	50,000	50,000
Common Stock - BB	50,000	50,000	50,000
Retained Earnings -	0	41,213	50,998
Total Equity	**$100,000**	**141,213**	**150,998**
Liabilities and Owners Equity	**$358,000**	**$423,305**	**$408,000**

Assumptions to Proformas

1. Range fees based on the following projections:

    Year One:

    Open Range Fees
    25 shooters/day @6.00 ea. for 26 weeks(peak period) $27,300

    Memberships
    40 members/year @ $125 ea.   5,000

    League Fees
    Four leagues for 12 weeks ea.
    40 participants per league at $6 ea./wk   11,250

    Tournament Fees
    Two tournaments with 120 participants ea. @ $8   1,930

    Total Range Fees - Year One $45,750

    Year Two:

    Open Range Fees
    35 shooters per day $38,220

    Memberships
    50 memberships @ $125   6,250
    League Fees
    Four leagues @ 50 participants/league   14,400

    Tournament Fees
    No change   1,930

    Total Range Fees - Year Two $60,800

2. Archery sales, food sales, and service fees experience seasonal fluctuations.

3. Hall rental fees are included during off-season months based on two or three nights per month@ $875 per night. This is based on quotes of hall rentals obtained in the area.

4. Cost of goods sold based on 55% of archery and food sales.

5. Loan payment amount based upon a fixed loan of $258,000 at 11.5% for 10 years.

    Approx.   Capital Required for Start-up: $308,000
              Less: Owner's Cash Investment   (50,000)
              Loan Amount $258,000

6. Depreciation calculations based on straight-line method, 3 years for equipment and 25 years for the building.

Robert A. Bailey
5432 Lima Lane
Webberville, Minnesota 54321
323-555-6899

Education

Engineering Design Certificate. Lakeland Community College
Completed one year vocational certification program of study in mechanical drafting.
Training included:

Engineering Design	Machining
Descriptive Geometry	Technical Math
Computer Aided Design	

Truck Driver Diploma. Advanced Truck Driving School
State certified Driver

High School Diploma. Webberville High School, June 1980.

Employment

Sales Representative, Sears Auto Parts Dept., Webberville, Minnesota
    January 1989-Present

Truck Driver, LBS Trucking Company, Minneapolis, Minnesota
    January 1988-November 1988.

Security Guard,   Security Services Inc., Minneapolis
    May 1983- October 1987.

References available upon request.

Roy Roberts
12345 McNichols Road
Acme, Minnesota 54322
323-555-6677

Education

| 1/91 - 5/92 | Delta College, Tompsonville, Minnesota |
| | General Subjects |

1977   Waldo High School, Waldo, Minnesota

Personal Information

I am a responsible self-starter who enjoys a challenge or an opportunity to excel. I have owned and managed three businesses where my responsibilities included: maintaining inventory, shipping and receiving merchandise, supervision and training of employees, sales and customer relations.

Work Experience

6/86 - Present   Roy Roberts Archery
Acme, Minnesota
Owner: Responsible for maintaining inventory, purchasing,
      receiving. I supervise a staff of three in sales, customer relations,
      and bow mechanics.

1977 -1987   Nissa Motors
General Assembler: Performed various duties in interior assembly, brake
      assembly and steering column assembly

9/75 - 5/81   Roy's Woodcutting
Acme, Minnesota
Owner/Manager

Military

10/72 - 9/75   United States Marine Corp.
Obtained the rank of Corporal/E4

Served as VIP driver night motor pool with staff of three.

Proposed Menu Selections

Beverages	Snacks	Hot Food
Soda pop	Chips, pretzels, etc.	Hot dogs
Coffee	Candy bars	Chili
Tea	Popcorn	Soups
Iced Tea	Baked Goods -	Sandwiches
Juices	Cookies, brownies, danish, etc.	Salads
Milk		

All food items will be prepared off-site and delivered fresh daily. The snack shop will make coffee, soups, and chili only.

Sample Business Plan - Service Business:
Innovative Creations

INNOVATIVE CREATIONS

Business Plan

Susan Jones
23 Liberty Drive
Sinkorswim, USA 12345
(333) 444-5555

Statement of Purpose

Susan Jones, owner of Innovative Creations is establishing her business to meet an increasing demand for desk-top publishing services in the Sinkorswim area. Research has revealed that an unmet need exists in the market place for creative and responsive desk-top publishing specialists.

Susan Jones has 12 years of experience in the desk-top publishing field. She has already secured three contracts and is confident in her ability to attract additional customers. Susan Jones has lived in Sinkorswim for 20 years and knows many people in the community.

The business will be operated initially from the owner's home and will require minimal operating costs. To establish the business, the owner must acquire the funds needed to purchase equipment and pay initial operating expenses. This plan is being developed as an operating tool for the owner and as a mechanism for seeking the necessary start-up capital of $10,000.

Susan Jones plans to generate $20,000 in sales her first year in business, with a 20-25% increase in business over the next three years. Her goal is to have her loan paid off no later than the end of her second year in business. She carefully budgeted expenditures and conservatively estimated sales to ensure that her goal is realized.

Table of Contents

Description

Innovative Creations was established by Susan Jones as a sole-proprietorship. The business provides desk-top publishing services to businesses and individuals in Sinkorswim and the surrounding areas. Specific services include:

- designing brochures, logos, and trademarks
- layout and design for annual reports and technical documents
- resume design
- layout for directories, publications, and newsletters

Services also include handling printing and all other needs associated with publishing a written document. Innovative Creations plans to provide customers with the most comprehensive and reliable service available. The owner plans to be available to customers six days a week, from 8:00 a.m. to 6:00 p.m., Monday through Saturday. She will make her services convenient to customers by coming directly to their businesses or homes for meetings and presentations. Innovative Creations will also provide a free delivery service.

Market Analysis

Innovative Creations will target small or medium-sized businesses in Sinkorswim and the surrounding areas. Sinkorswim is a thriving community with a population of 8,950. According to the most recent census data, Sinkorswim's population increased 2% in 1995 and is expected to increase 10% by the year 2000.

According to a recent Chamber of Commerce report, there are approximately 750 businesses operating within a 30 mile radius of Sinkorswim. Most of these businesses, 570, have less than 5 employees.

The majority of businesses this size do not have in-house staff to perform desk-top publishing functions. Most do not have the necessary equipment or the time to perform desk-top publishing duties. Innovative Creation's owner recently surveyed 15 local businesses to assess their desk-top publishing needs. Five indicated that they would utilize an independent firm at least four times a year, eight indicated they would need these services twice a year, and only two businesses had no need for desk-top publishing services at all.

According to a recent article in Enterprise Magazine, "Desk-top publishing concerns are among the fastest growing businesses in the United States." The article further states that the growth in these services stems from the recent trend in corporate downsizing. Because desk-top publishing is generally not a key function of most businesses, these services are generally cheaper when contracted out.

The total market share for desk-top publishing services in Sinkorswim is an estimated $187,500. (Based on an average expenditure of $250 per company. Source: American Desk-top Publishers Association). Currently two businesses offer desk-top publishing services in the market area. If Innovative Creations captures 1/3 of the market, expected revenues will be $62,500.

While the owner understands that it is unlikely that 1/3 of the market will be captured in her first year, she does feel confident that with her experience and connections, this goal can be obtained by the end of her third year in business.

Competition

Only two businesses exist in the Sinkorswim market area that provide desk-top publishing services:

Grady's Printing:

Grady's is located in downtown Sinkorswim. The location is easily accessed by most local businesses. Grady's has been in business since 1980 and, although desk-top publishing is not its primary business, currently has the largest share of the market.

Printing services are the primary focus of Grady's and, as a result, the desk-top publishing services are often performed in a "cookie-cutter" fashion. The business employs two college graduates who work full-time performing desk-top pub-

2

lishing. They are both recent graduates and probably have no more than three years of combined experience.

Grady's charges between $45 and $60 per hour.

Quality Publishing & Design

Quality Publishing is located in a small office complex 5 miles from town off I-88. The business has been around for two years. The business offers high quality, creative services and seems to target larger businesses and professional corporations, such as law offices and consulting firms.

The owner, Bob Kramer, is dynamic and competitive. He has a number of years of experience and is well qualified and talented. The business employs two part-time desk-top publishers and a part-time office manager.

Fees average between $50-$70 per hour.

Competitive Advantage

Innovative Creations' target market is small and medium sized companies. Research completed by the owner indicates that these companies are price sensitive and may not always understand what value desk-top publishing can add to their business. They may not have had the capability or the time to handle desk-top publishing in-house.

In accordance with our research, Innovative Creations' competitive advantage is "a quality service at a reasonable price." Prices for services will range between $40 - $50 per hour. Our customers will be those that require more sophistication than can be obtained from Grady's, and who are looking for reasonable fees.

Innovative Creations will focus on the fact that it is a home-based business with minimal overhead, and as a result, able to keep fees lower than its competitors.

Marketing Strategies

The business will be marketed initially by submitting a press release to the local newspaper. The paper usually prints stories about new businesses in the area.

The owner plans to implement a direct sales strategy. First, the owner will send announcements to her contacts and former customers. Second, letters will be mailed to her list of prospects. Third, the owner plans to schedule appointments with business owners to discuss the services available through Innovative Creations. The sales plan will also include follow-up calls to those businesses who are not completely sold on the services.

An advertisement will appear in the local yellow pages. Innovative Creations will advertise through the Chamber of Commerce and the local newspaper. The owner will attend Chamber of Commerce meetings and will take every available opportunity to network with local business owners.

Marketing Budget

Yellow Pages Advertising	$500
Postage	200
Printing	400
Chamber Dues	125
Miscellaneous Advertising	600
Total Marketing Costs	$1825

Management

All functions of the business will be managed and performed by Susan Jones. She will be responsible for providing customers with quality work in a timely manner. She will also be responsible for keeping the necessary records for the business and for promoting the business.

Ms. Jones is uniquely qualified to operate a desk-top publishing business. She has years of experience in the desk-top publishing industry where she has worked on all aspects of document preparation and design. She has the capacity to assist a client with all aspects of creating promotional and instructional documents.

Personnel

It is not expected that employees will be hired within the first year of operations. Employees may be added as demand for services increases and when the business can support the increased financial responsibilities.

If, and when, employees are hired they will possess a minimum of two years of experience in the desk-top publishing industry. The owner is prepared to provide extensive training. Potential candidates should possess adequate design skills as demonstrated by previous work history and should have good written and verbal communication skills.

Financial Statements

INNOVATIVE CREATIONS

Projected Balance Sheet

Assets	Beg. Bal. 7/31/99	7/31/00
Short Term		
Cash on Hand	$2,000	12,000
Long Term		
Computer Equipment*	$8,600	8,600
Less Depreciation		(4,300)
Office Equipment & Furnishings	4,000	4,000
Total Assets	$14,600	20,300
Liabilities		
Accounts Payable	$ 200	1,000
Notes Payable - Bank	10,000	4,000
Total Liabilities	$ 10,200	5,000
Net Worth	$ 4,400	15,300

*Computer Equipment	
ILM Pentium II, Monitor	$2,000
HPD Laser Color Printer & Scanner	1,100
Power MC Classic	2,500
Software	3,000
Total	$8,600

INNOVATIVE CREATIONS

Projected Income Statement

	1999	2000	2001
Sales	$20,000	$25,000	$ 31,250
Expenses			
Accounting	200	200	200
Advertising	1,100	1,000	900
Dues	125	125	125
Entertainment	300	400	400
Insurance	200	200	200
Loan Repayment	6,000	4,000	0
Maintenance	100	200	200
Owner's Draw	10,000	12,000	15,000
Office Supplies	500	500	500
Printing	750	1,000	1,300
Postage	200	400	600
Telephone	1,200	1,500	1,800
Travel	1,000	1,450	1,600
Miscellaneous	500	1,000	1,500
Total Expenditures	$22,175	$23,975	$ 24,325
Before Tax Profit/Loss	($2,175)	$ 1,025	$ 7,800

Assumes a 25% annual increase in sales.

INNOVATIVE CREATIONS

Proposed Sources and Uses of Funds

Sources:

Susan Jones, Owner Investment	$ 4,600
XYZ Bank	10,000
Total Sources of Funds	$ 14,600

Uses:

Capital Equipment List

ILM Pentium II	$ 2,000
HPD Laser Color Printer & Scanner	1,100
Power MC Classic	2,500
Software	3,000
Office Equipment & Furnishings	4,000
Working Capital	$ 2,000
Total Uses of Funds	$14,600

<h1 align="center">Susan Jones</h1>
<h2 align="center">Personal Financial Statement</h2>

Assets

Bank Savings Account	$ 2,000
Mutual Funds:	
Retirement	12,000
Non-retirement	5,600
1990 ZZX Automobile	16,500
Furnishings	10,000
Total Assets	$46,100

Liabilities

Credit Card	
Amex	$ 500
Mastercard	2,200
Car loan - XYZ Bank	12,800
Total Liabilities	$15,500

Net Worth   **$30,600**

Susan Jones

Education:	**Sinkorswim Community College, 3.4 GPA,**	1976-1979
	Crenshaw College for the Arts, 3.1 GPA,	1979-1981

Employment: **Administrative Assistant to Art Director**
Crenshaw College for the Arts;   1981-1983

- Responsible for coordinating curriculum for art and design classes.
- Organized art shows and designed college brochures and promotional material.

Graphic Artist
Grady's Printing,   1983-1990
- Responsible for creating and designing logos and brochures for the business community.
- Provided services to over 600 satisfied customers.

Awards & Certifications:

Lang County Art Fellowship Award

President, Crenchaw College Alumni

Lang Business School - Small Business Certification Program

Hobbies & Interests:

Reading and creative writing, biking, water sports

Attachment

R&L Tool & Dye
333 Main Street
Sinkorswim, USA 12345
January 4, 1991

To Whom It May Concern:

I am pleased to write this letter of support for Susan Jones. As a business owner in Sinkorswim, I understand the importance of good customer service. Susan Jones has provided my business with graphic arts and desk-top publishing services for the past four years. She has provided high quality work in a timely manner.

We have been immensely pleased with her work and intend to continue a working relationship with her new business.

Sincerely,

Joe Brown
President

Free or Low Cost Government Services, Resources and Information

The federal government provides the owners of businesses and people starting businesses free or low cost information, services and resources. Any person, even those with limited financial resources, can gather a wealth of information on just about anything; you just have to know where to look and who to ask. The following pages provide an index of government agencies, the services they offer and their telephone numbers and addresses. These agencies are paid for by you, the taxpayer, and are there to provide business owners with answers to a variety of questions.

Small Business Information

Service Corp of Retired Executives (SCORE)
SCORE is an organization of retired executives who volunteer their time to counsel existing and potential business owners. This program is part of the U.S. Small Business Administration and the services are free of charge. Contact the SCORE information desk at 800-827-5722 to find the nearest SCORE office to you or write:

> SCORE
> 409 3rd St. S.W., 5th Floor
> Suite 5900
> Washington, DC 20023-3212

Small Business Development Centers (SBDC)
The Small Business Development Centers provide counseling, training and small business assistance to existing businesses and start-ups. There are centers located all over the country. They are usually associated with a university, college or chamber of commerce. For more information call (202) 205-6766 or contact the SBDC nearest you.

U.S. Small Business Administration (SBA)
The SBA offers many services including loans and government contracting assistance. The SBA also offers at a minimal charge hundreds of very useful pamphlets on a variety of issues pertaining to starting and managing a small business. For additional information contact the SBA Hotline: 800-827-5722 or 202-205-6600.

U.S. Government Printing Office

The U.S. Government Printing office is an excellent source of information on business management. For a nominal fee you can receive booklets on a variety of subjects. To obtain a listing of available booklets contact:

> Superintendent of Documents
> U.S. Government Printing Office
> Washington, DC 20402
> (202) 783-3238
> Fax (202) 512-2168

Department of Commerce: Minority/Womens Services

Provides counseling for small businesses and help finding financing.

> U.S. Department of Commerce
> Minority Business Development Agency
> Information Clearinghouse
> (202) 377-1936

Market Research/Data

U.S. Chamber of Commerce

The U.S. Chamber of commerce provides data on both large and small businesses throughout the United States. It is an excellent way to obtain information about your competitors.

> Chamber of Commerce
> 1615 H Street, N.C.
> Washington, DC., 20062
> (202) 463-5503

Library of Congress

The Library of congress routinely conducts searches free of charge for businesses looking to solve a problem or find information. The National Referral Service is a good starting point for most searches, call (202) 707-5522.

Research and Development

U.S. Small Business Administration: SBIR Program

(Small Business Innovation & Research). Obtain information about obtaining government grants for research, product development, and marketing new products. Contact: (202) 205-6450.

Government Contracting

SBA Office of Procurement and Technical Assistance
Maintains capability profiles on small businesses interested in federal procurement opportunities. Disseminates information on federal procurement guidelines.

> SBA Procurement Assistance
> 409 3rd. Street West
> Washington, D.C. 20416
> (202) 653-6938 or (202) 653-6586.

Doing Business with the Government
A how-to booklet on government contracting and marketing to federal agencies. Available for $2.50 from:

> Consumer Information Center
> Dept. 11-W
> Pueblo, CO 81008

Exporting

U.S. Small Business Administration
Offers one-to-one export counseling, export resource materials, matchmaker trade expeditions, international trade loan guarantees, publications and electronic bulletin board services. For more information contact the SBA at (212) 254-3454.

U.S. Department of Agriculture
Offers exporter market assistance, information on foreign markets, export promotion programs, and technical assistance. For more information contact the USDA at (212) 466-5620.

Financial Services

SSA/Plan for Achieving Self Support Information
Changes in Social Security Administration's policies and procedures for work incentive programs and other programs: SSAs Internet Site, Social Security Online, at http://www.ssa.gov, or call toll free 1-800-722-1213.

U.S. Small Business Administration (SBA)
The SBA offers many services including loans and government contracting assistance. The SBA also offers at a minimal charge hundreds of very useful pamphlets on a variety of issues pertaining to starting and managing a small business. For additional information contact the SBA Hotline: 800-827-5722 or 202-205-6600.

Advocacy

U.S. Chamber of Commerce Center for Small Business

The U.S. Chamber of Commerce is the largest volunteer business federation in the world. It is actively involved with representing small business before the government. The Small Business Program provides members with an information exchange in its newsletter, The Small Business Update, and other publications.

> U.S. Chamber of Commerce Center for Small Business
> 1615 H. Street, N.W.
> Washington, D.C. 20062
> (202) 463-5503

President's Committee on Employment of People with Disabilities

Provides advocacy services, information, and referral to people with disabilities.

> 1331 F. Street N.W.
> Washington, DC 20004-1107
> (202) 376-6200 Voice Mail
> (202) 376-6219 Fax
> (202) 376-6205 TDD

If you encounter problems or have any questions that are not likely to be answered by any of the agencies listed, contact The Business Assistance Program through the U.S. Business Liaison office at 202-377-3176 or write: Business Liaison Room 5898C, Department of Commerce, Washington, D.C., 20230.

Index

To Order Unlikely Entrepreneurs

Call 1-800-733-9712
or mail the convenient order form below to:

North Peak Publishing
P.O. Box 6832
Traverse City, MI 49696-6832

or Fax your order to
616-935-3104

Price $21.95
Michigan orders add 6% sales tax

Number of Books_____

Amount: _____

Tax: _____

Shipping & Handling: _____

Total: _____

Payable in U.S. funds (no cash orders accepted).
Shipping and handling $3.50 for one book, $1.00 for each additional book.

Payment Method:

❏ VISA   ❏ Master Card   ❏ Check or Money Order

Card #_____ Expiration date _____

Signature as on charge card _____

Daytime phone number _____

Name_____

Address_____ _____

City _____State_____Zip_____

Please allow six to eight weeks for delivery. Prices subject to change without notice. Source key Small Business, Self-Employment, Disability, Success in Business.